Given

Story and Art by **Natsuki Kizu**　　　　volume **2**

CONTENTS

SUBLIME
SuBLime Manga Edition

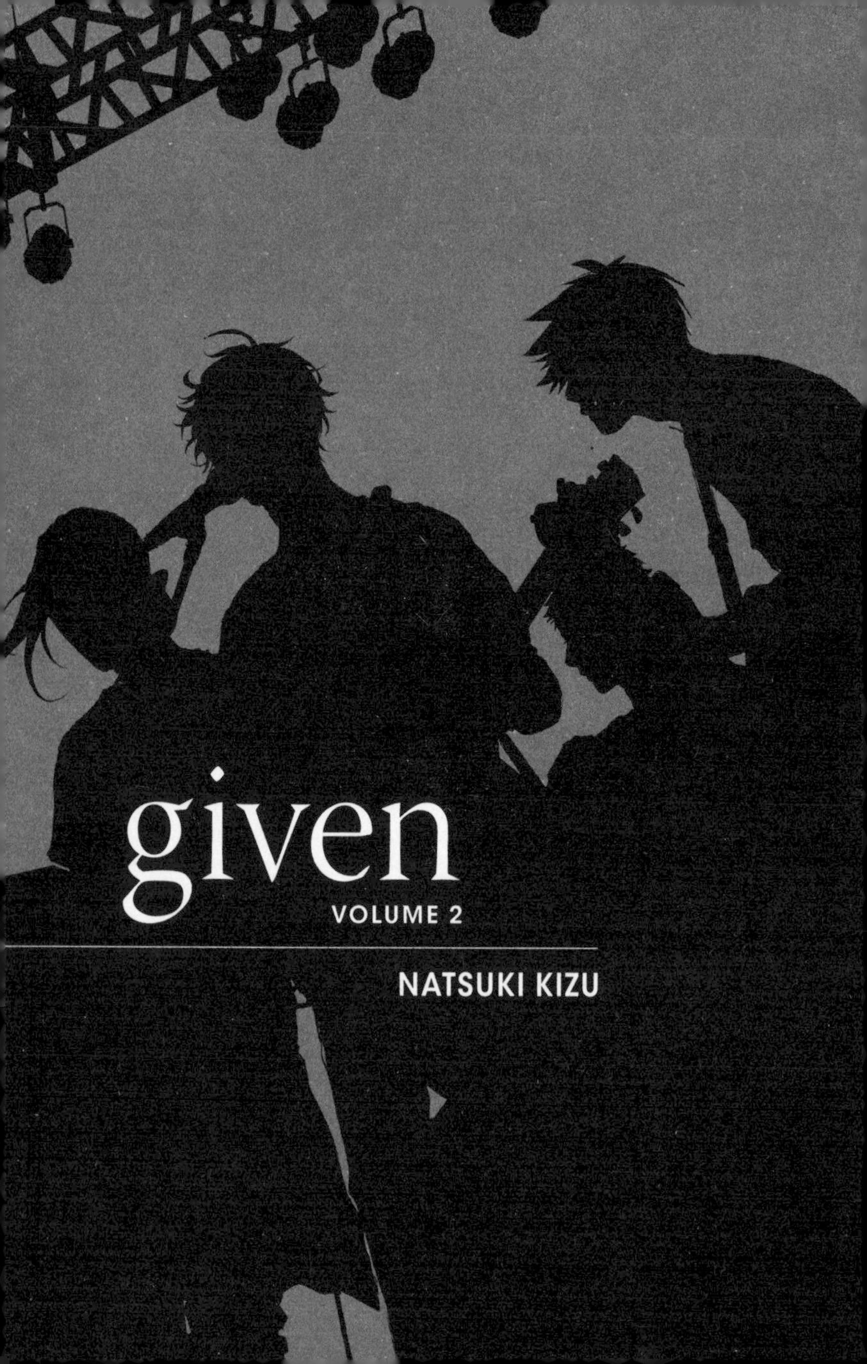
given
VOLUME 2
NATSUKI KIZU

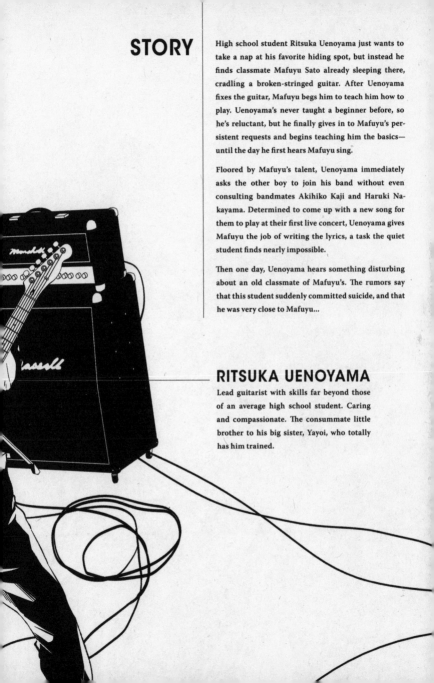

STORY

High school student Ritsuka Uenoyama just wants to take a nap at his favorite hiding spot, but instead he finds classmate Mafuyu Sato already sleeping there, cradling a broken-stringed guitar. After Uenoyama fixes the guitar, Mafuyu begs him to teach him how to play. Uenoyama's never taught a beginner before, so he's reluctant, but he finally gives in to Mafuyu's persistent requests and begins teaching him the basics—until the day he first hears Mafuyu sing.

Floored by Mafuyu's talent, Uenoyama immediately asks the other boy to join his band without even consulting bandmates Akihiko Kaji and Haruki Nakayama. Determined to come up with a new song for them to play at their first live concert, Uenoyama gives Mafuyu the job of writing the lyrics, a task the quiet student finds nearly impossible.

Then one day, Uenoyama hears something disturbing about an old classmate of Mafuyu's. The rumors say that this student suddenly committed suicide, and that he was very close to Mafuyu...

RITSUKA UENOYAMA

Lead guitarist with skills far beyond those of an average high school student. Caring and compassionate. The consummate little brother to his big sister, Yayoi, who totally has him trained.

MAFUY

High school classmate of Uenoyama's. Has an impressive singing voice. Attached to Uenoyama ever since he fixed Mafuyu's broken guitar.

HARUKI NAKAYAMA

Graduate student. The band's bassist. He's extremely good-natured and kind.

AKIHIKO KAJI

University student. The band's drummer. A bit of a playboy who's popular without ever trying.

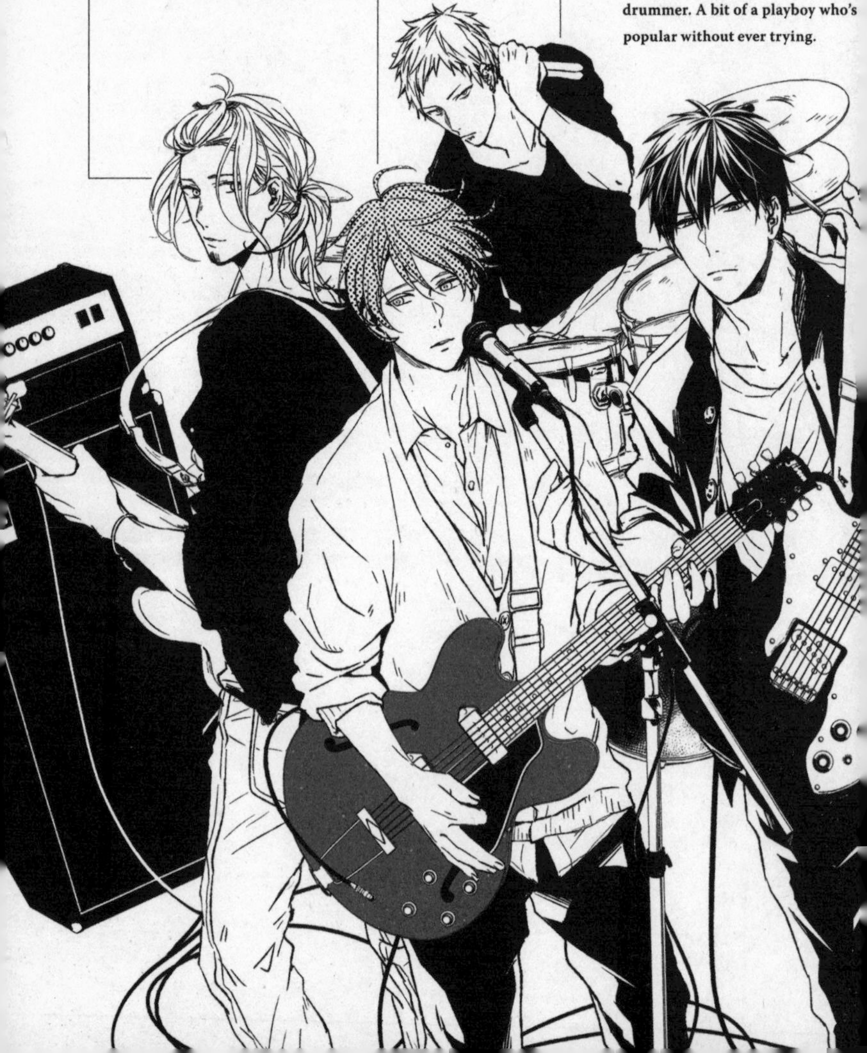

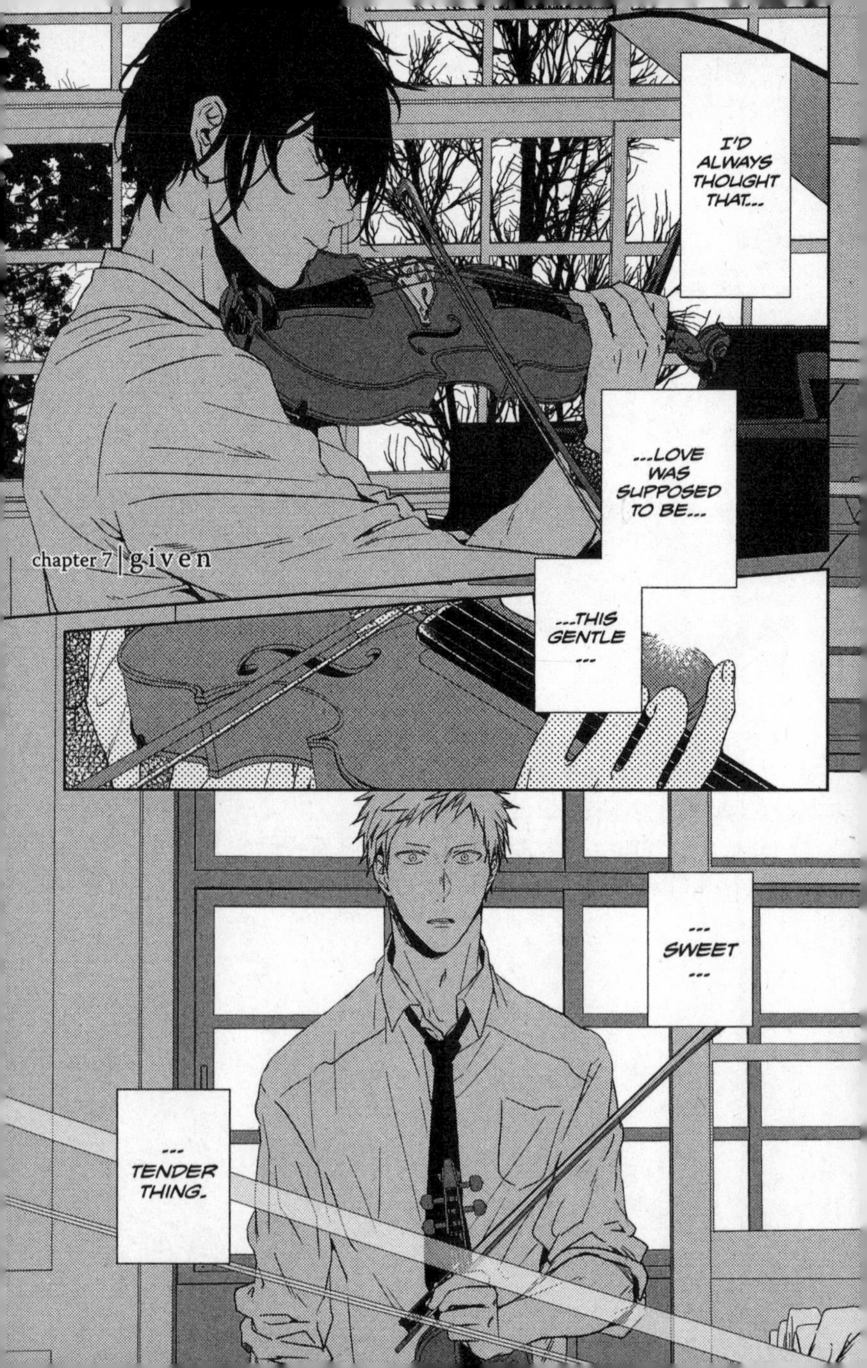
I'D ALWAYS THOUGHT THAT...
...LOVE WAS SUPPOSED TO BE...
chapter 7 | given
...THIS GENTLE ...
... SWEET ...
... TENDER THING.

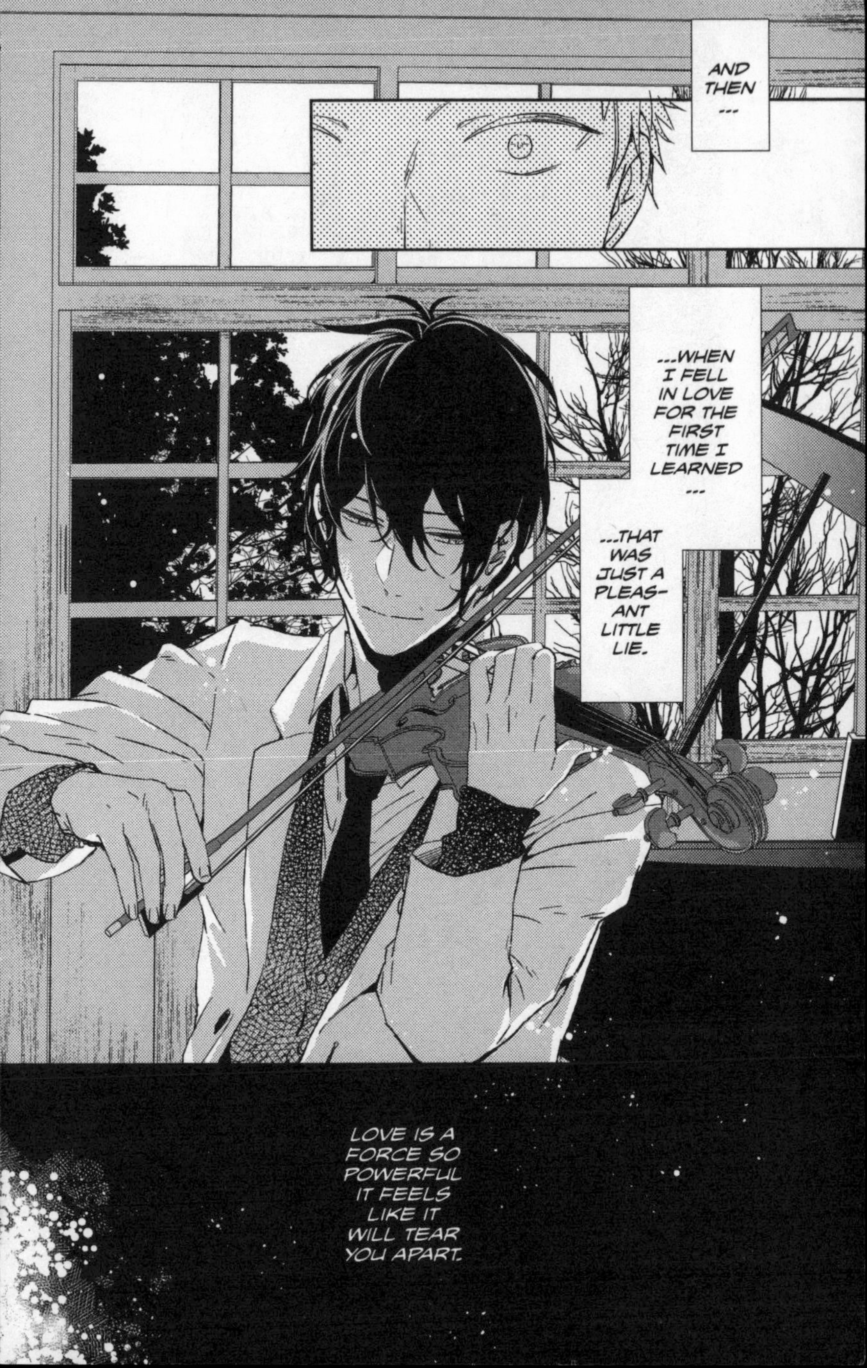
AND THEN ...
...WHEN I FELL IN LOVE FOR THE FIRST TIME I LEARNED ...
...THAT WAS JUST A PLEAS-ANT LITTLE LIE.
LOVE IS A FORCE SO POWERFUL IT FEELS LIKE IT WILL TEAR YOU APART.

given

chapter 7

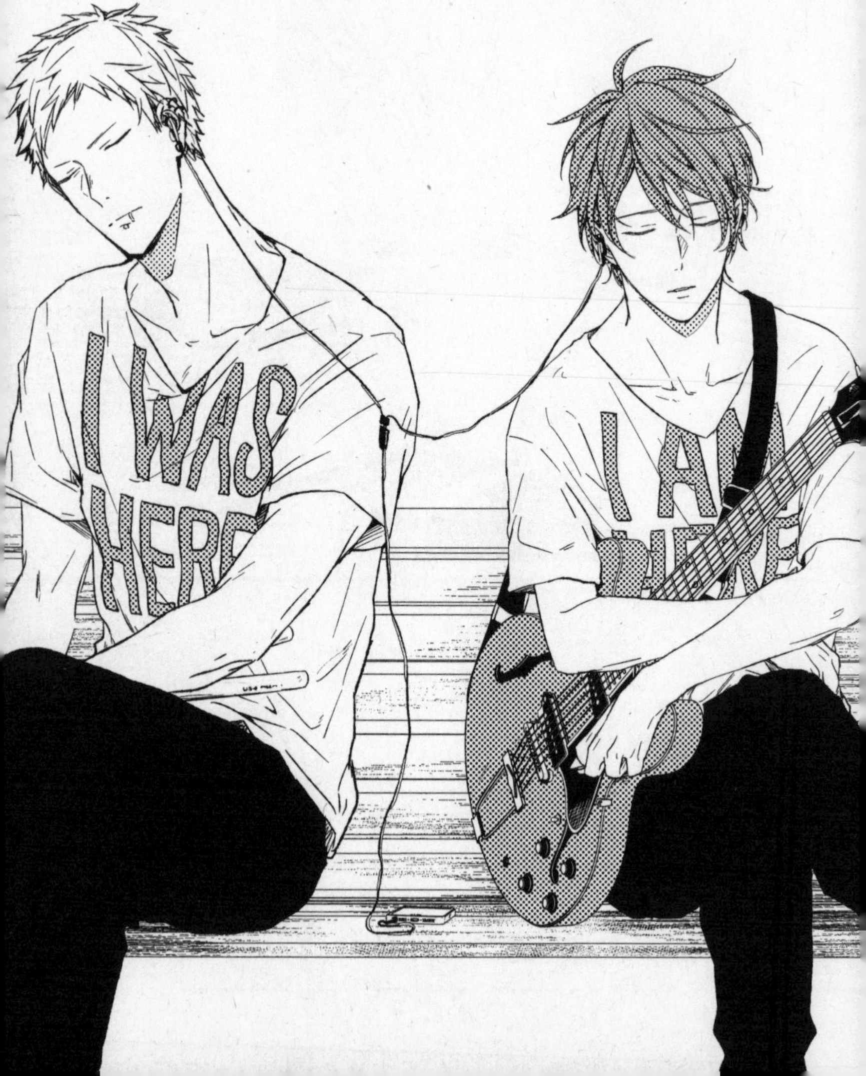
I WAS HERE

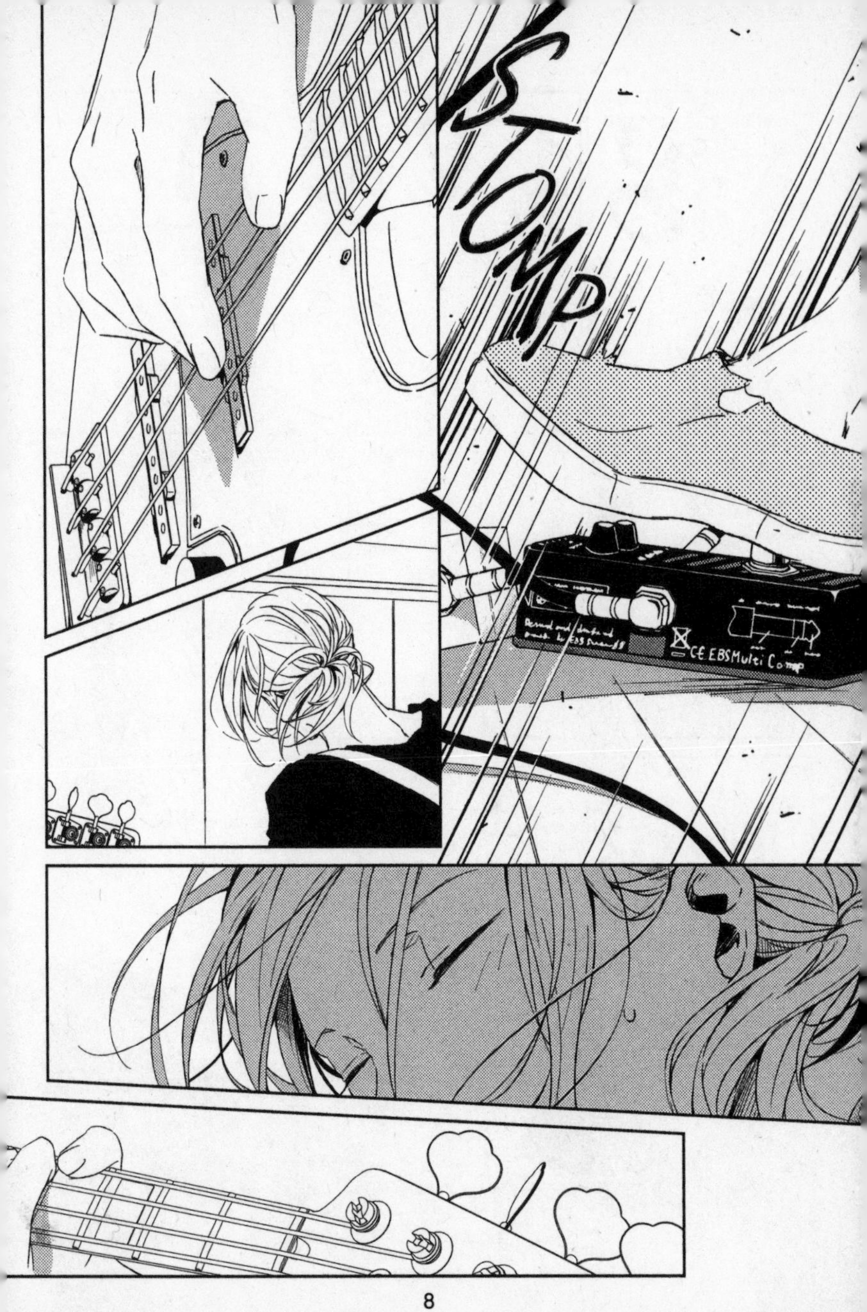
STOMP
CE EBSMulti Comp

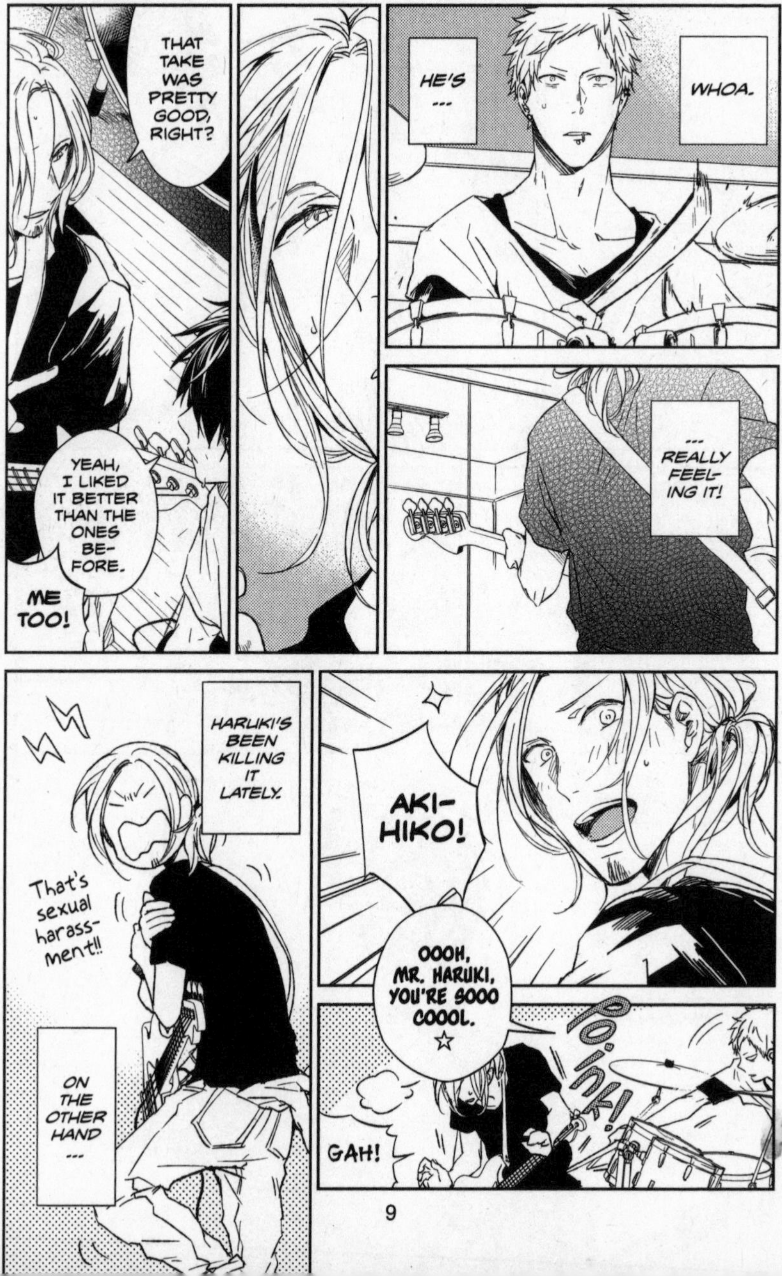
WHOA.
HE'S ---
--- REALLY FEEL- ING IT!
THAT TAKE WAS PRETTY GOOD, RIGHT?
YEAH, I LIKED IT BETTER THAN THE ONES BE- FORE.
ME TOO!
AKI- HIKO!
OOOH, MR. HARUKI, YOU'RE SOOO COOOL. ☆
POINK!
GAH!
HARUKI'S BEEN KILLING IT LATELY.
That's sexual harass- ment!!
ON THE OTHER HAND ---

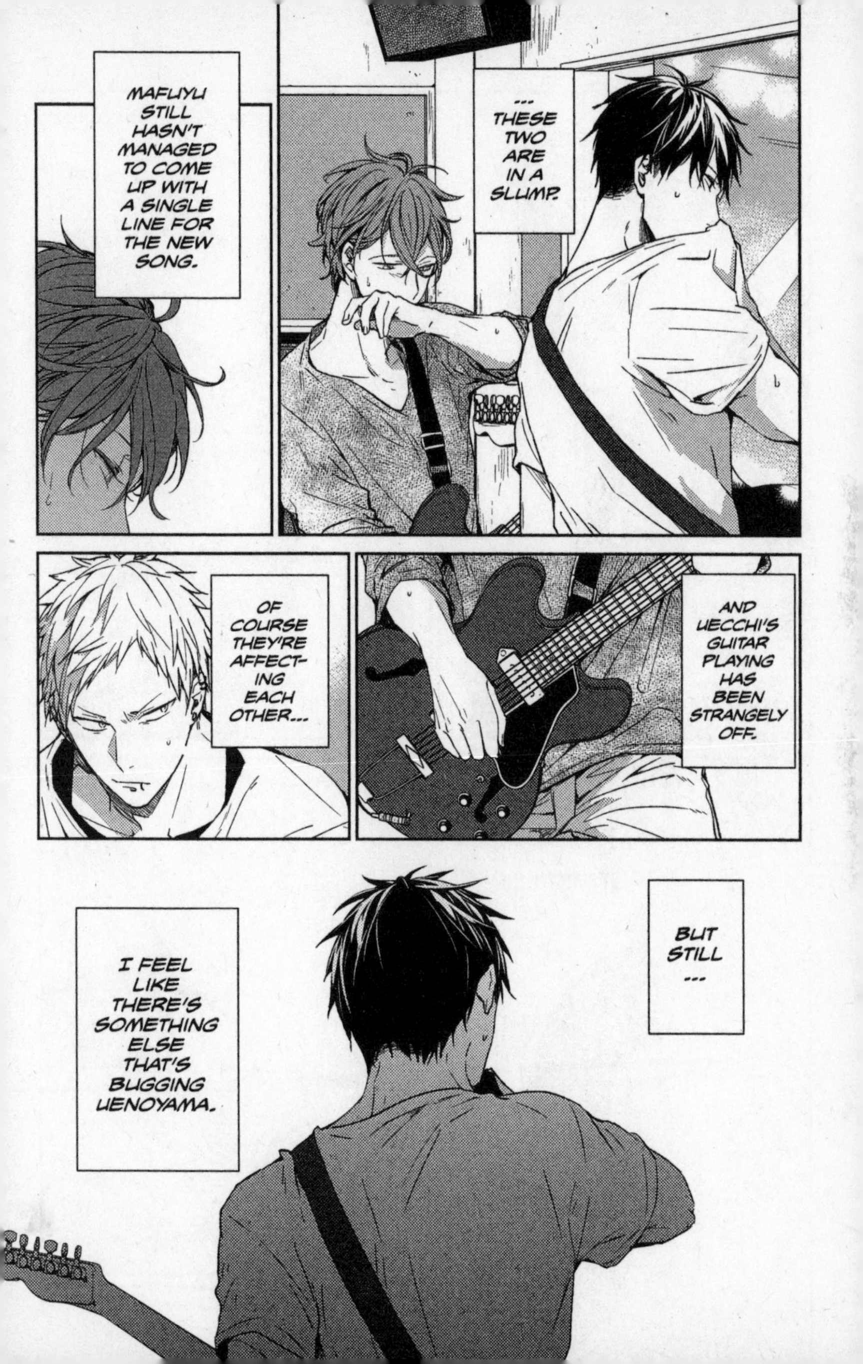
...THESE TWO ARE IN A SLUMP?
MAFUYU STILL HASN'T MANAGED TO COME UP WITH A SINGLE LINE FOR THE NEW SONG.
AND UECCHI'S GUITAR PLAYING HAS BEEN STRANGELY OFF.
OF COURSE THEY'RE AFFECTING EACH OTHER...
BUT STILL ...
I FEEL LIKE THERE'S SOMETHING ELSE THAT'S BUGGING UENOYAMA.

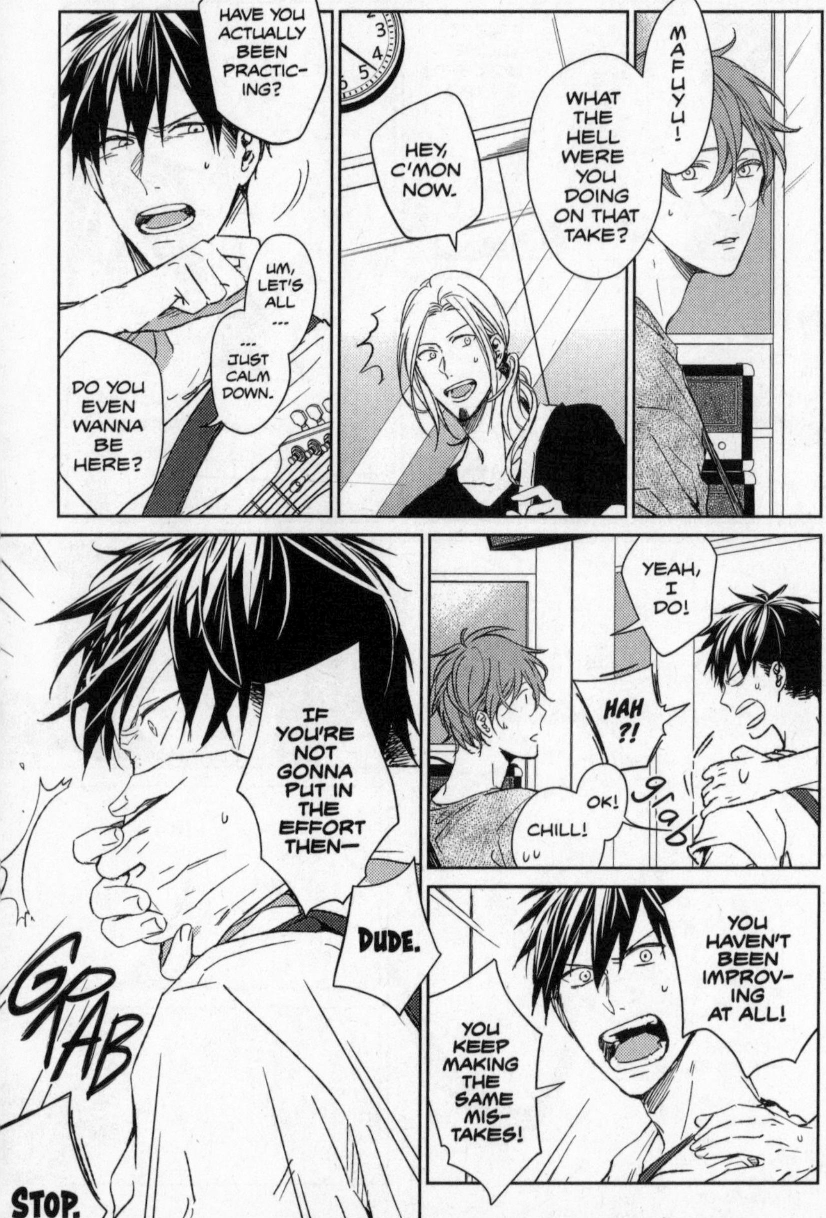
MAFUYU!
WHAT THE HELL WERE YOU DOING ON THAT TAKE?
HEY, C'MON NOW.
HAVE YOU ACTUALLY BEEN PRACTIC-ING?
UM, LET'S ALL ...
... JUST CALM DOWN.
DO YOU EVEN WANNA BE HERE?
YEAH, I DO!
HAH ?!
grab
OK!
CHILL!
YOU HAVEN'T BEEN IMPROV-ING AT ALL!
YOU KEEP MAKING THE SAME MIS-TAKES!
IF YOU'RE NOT GONNA PUT IN THE EFFORT THEN—
DUDE.
GRAB
STOP.

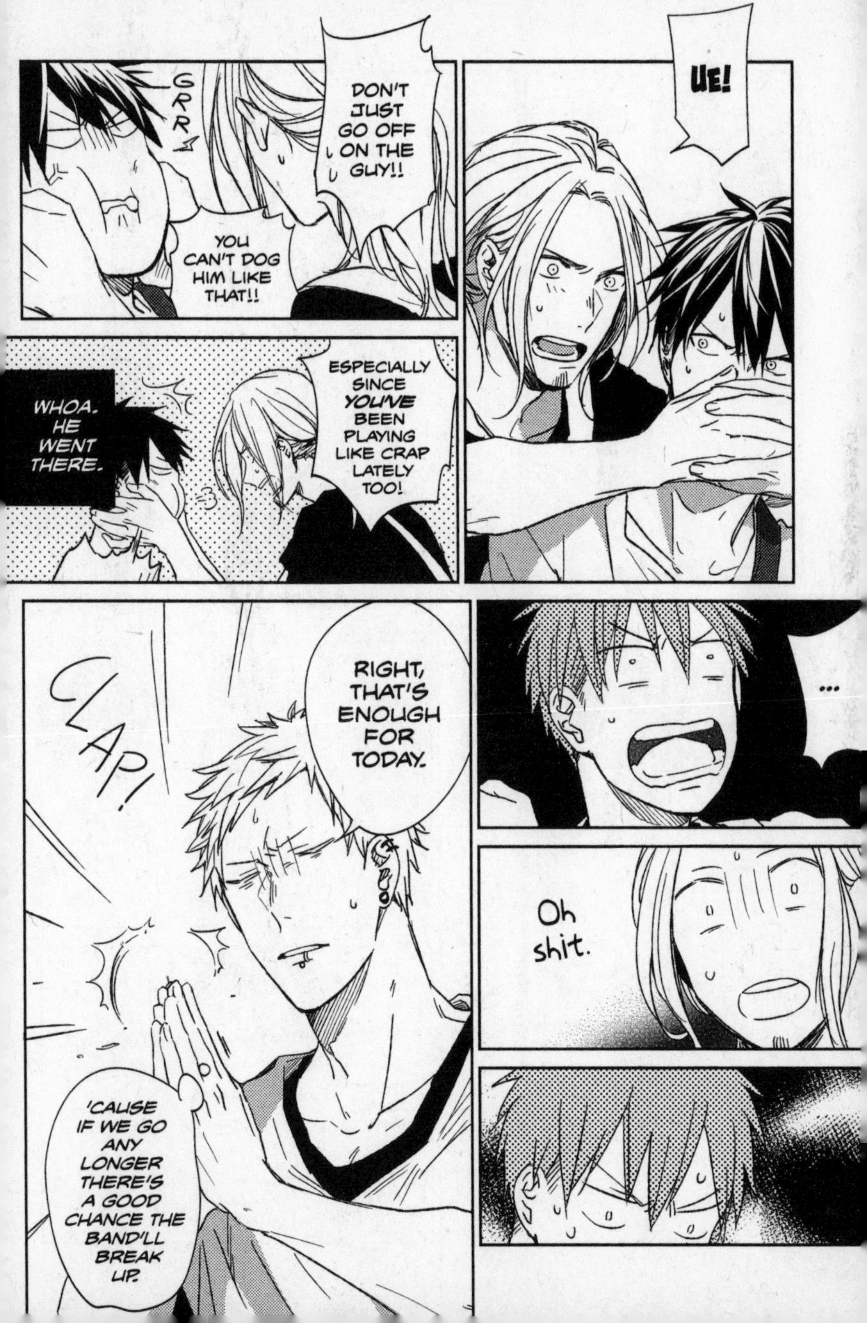
UE!
GRR
DON'T JUST GO OFF ON THE GUY!!
YOU CAN'T DOG HIM LIKE THAT!!
ESPECIALLY SINCE *YOU'VE* BEEN PLAYING LIKE CRAP LATELY TOO!
WHOA. HE WENT THERE.
...
Oh shit.
RIGHT, THAT'S ENOUGH FOR TODAY.
CLAP!
'CAUSE IF WE GO ANY LONGER THERE'S A GOOD CHANCE THE BAND'LL BREAK UP.

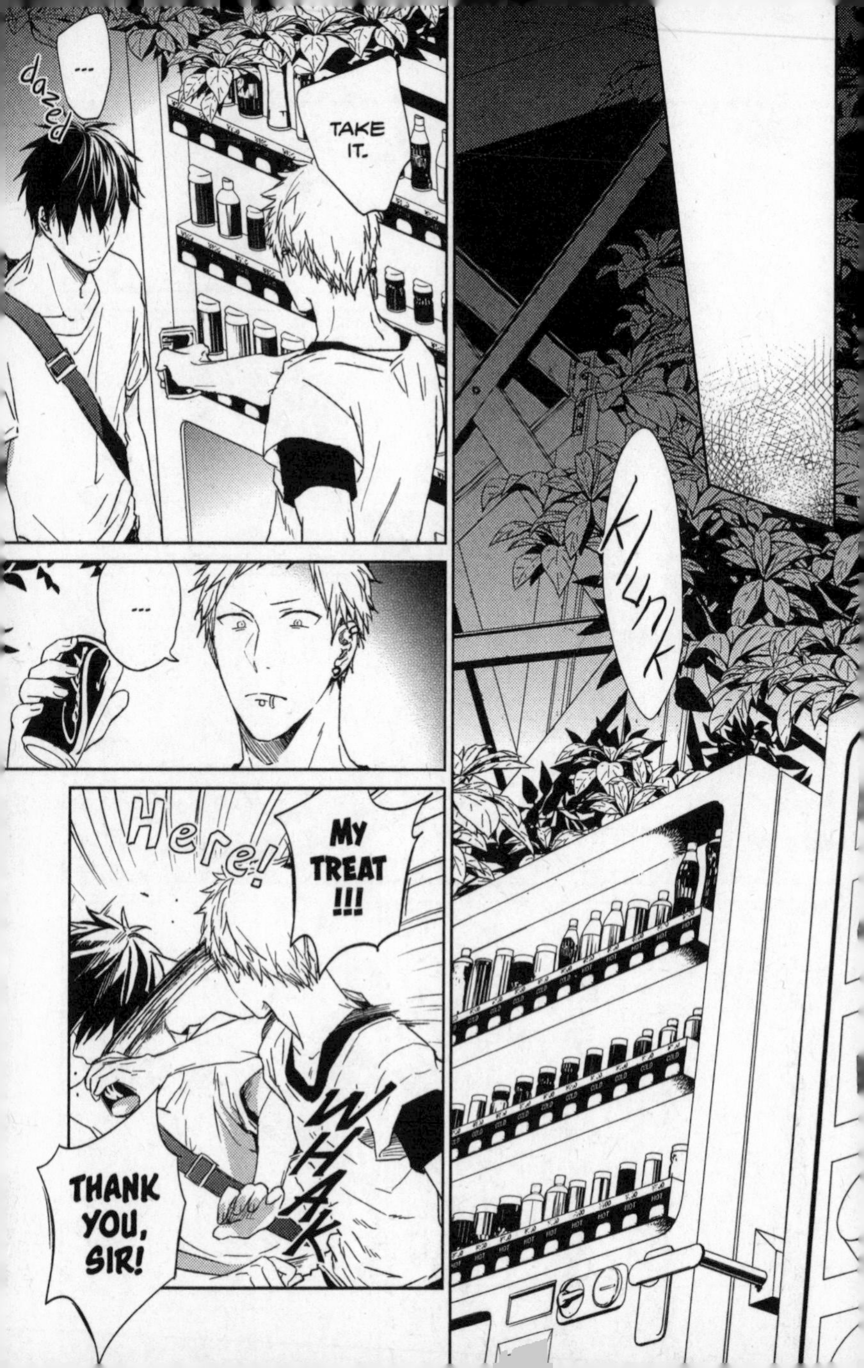
KLUNK
TAKE IT.
...
dazed
...
MY TREAT !!!
Here!
WHAK
THANK YOU, SIR!

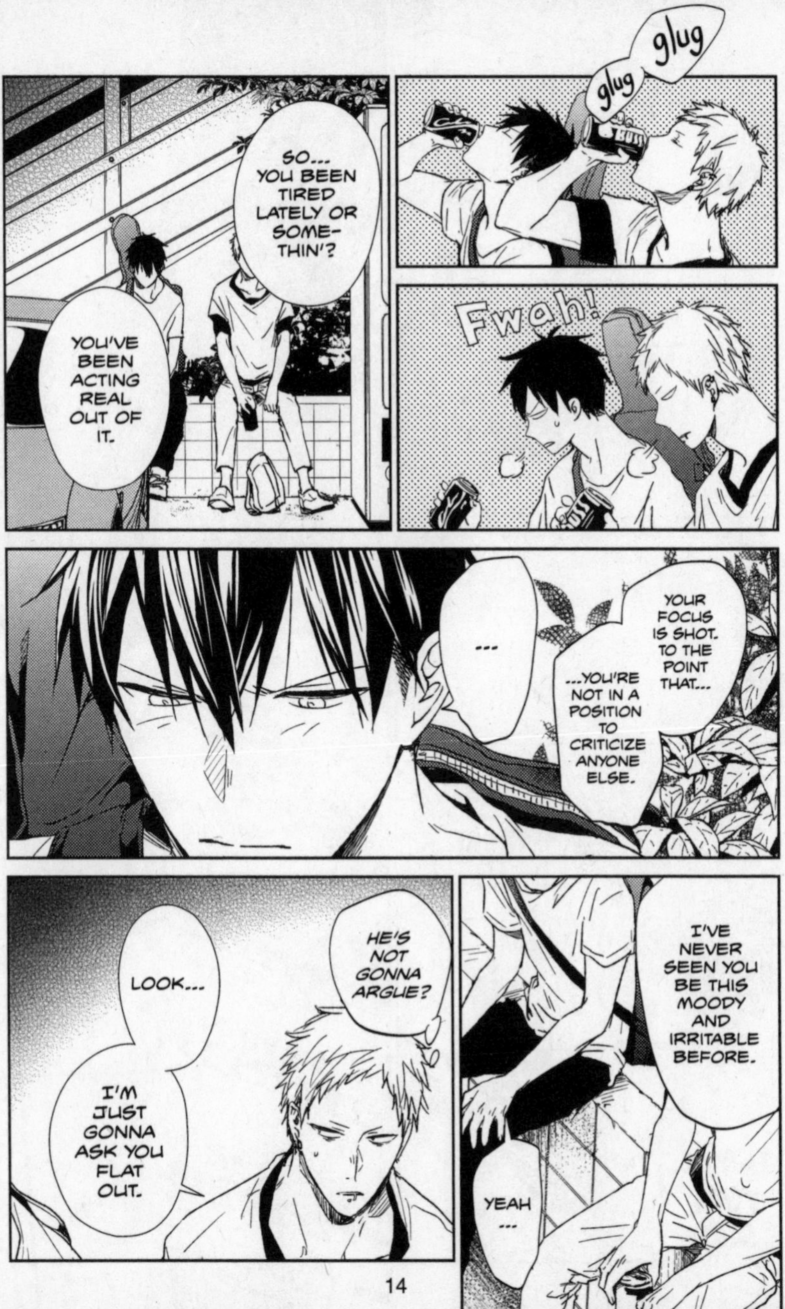
glug
glug
Fwah!
SO... YOU BEEN TIRED LATELY OR SOME-THIN'?
YOU'VE BEEN ACTING REAL OUT OF IT.
YOUR FOCUS IS SHOT. TO THE POINT THAT...
...YOU'RE NOT IN A POSITION TO CRITICIZE ANYONE ELSE.
...
I'VE NEVER SEEN YOU BE THIS MOODY AND IRRITABLE BEFORE.
YEAH...
HE'S NOT GONNA ARGUE?
LOOK...
I'M JUST GONNA ASK YOU FLAT OUT.

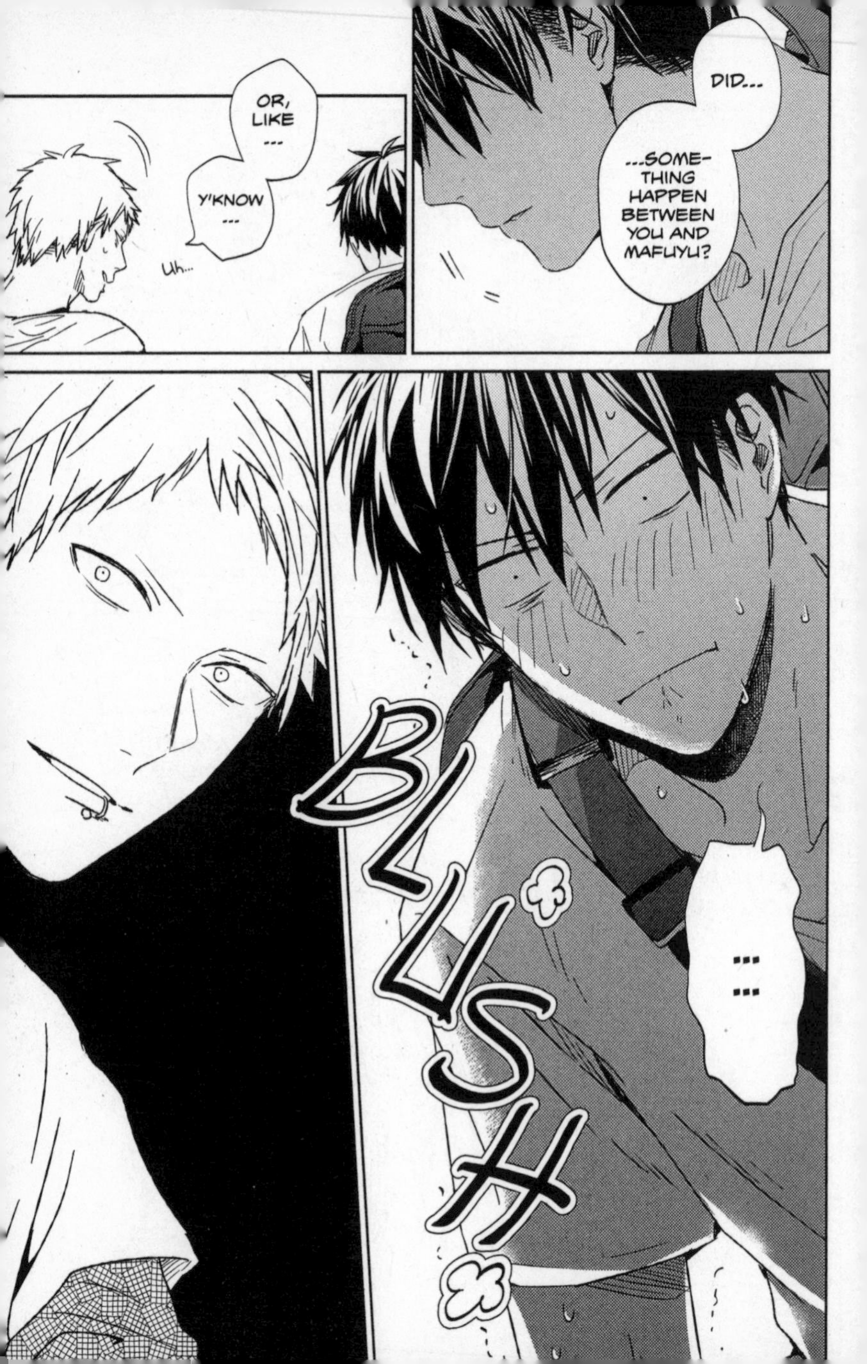
DID...
...SOME-THING HAPPEN BETWEEN YOU AND MAFUYU?
OR, LIKE ...
Y'KNOW ...
Uh...
...
...
BLUSH

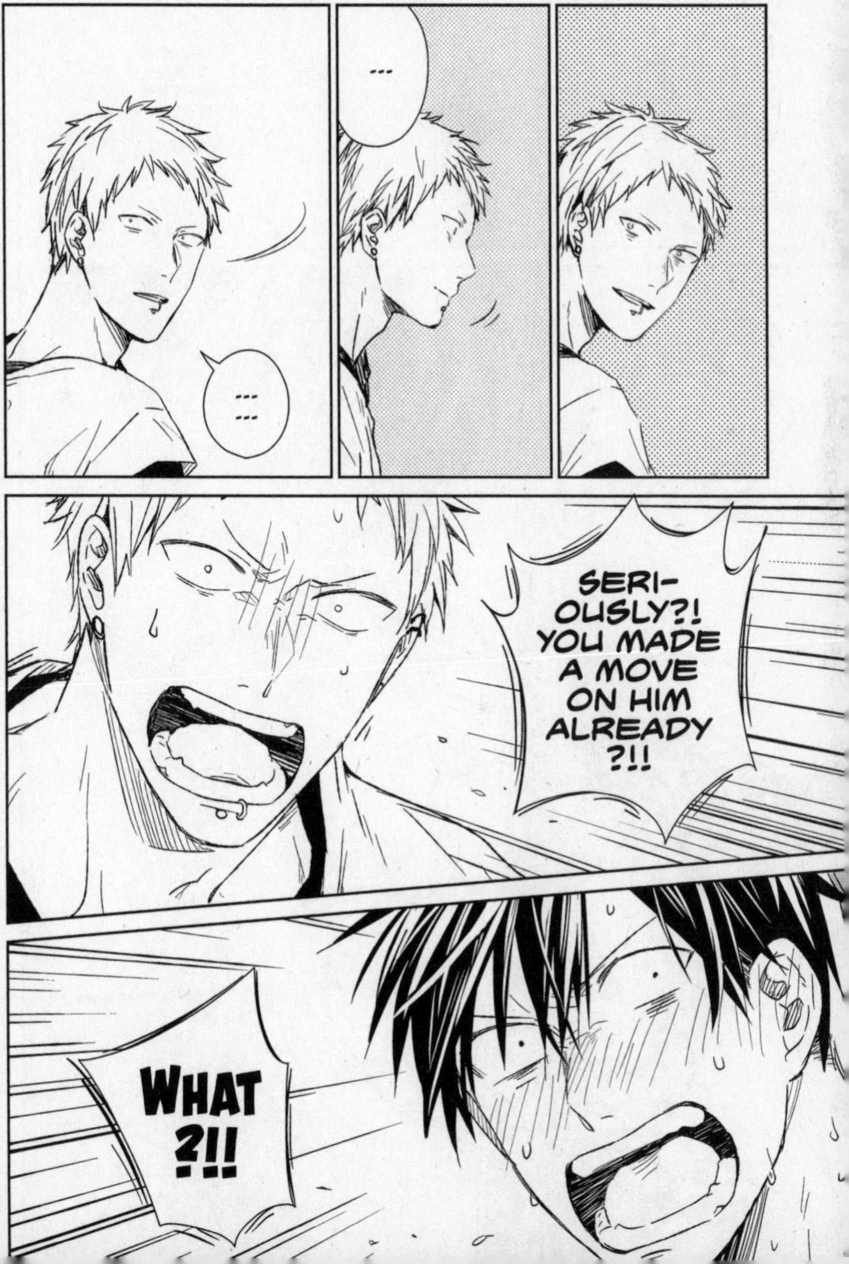
...
... ...
SERI-OUSLY?! YOU MADE A MOVE ON HIM ALREADY ?!!
WHAT ?!!

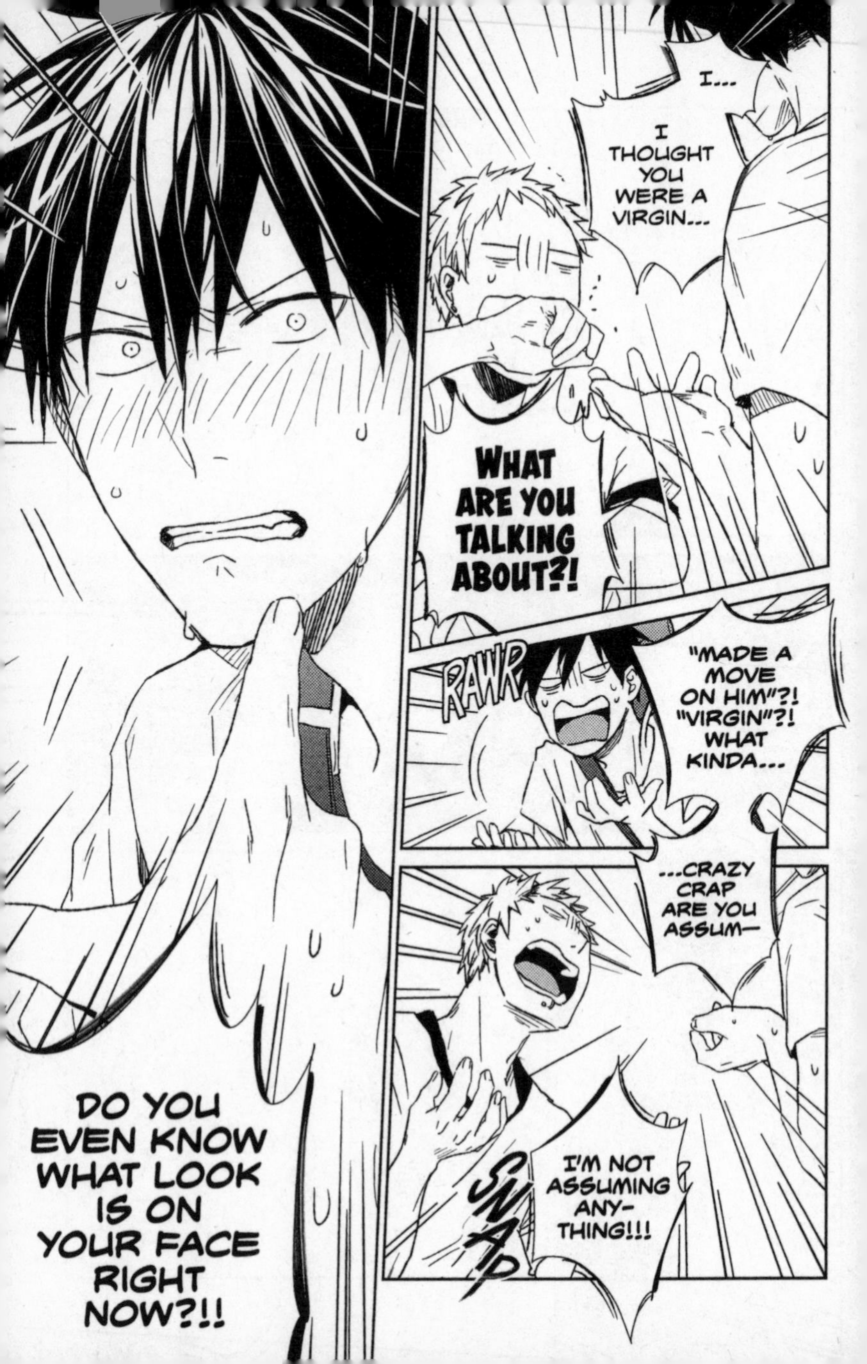
I...
I THOUGHT YOU WERE A VIRGIN...
WHAT ARE YOU TALKING ABOUT?!
RAWR
"MADE A MOVE ON HIM"?! "VIRGIN"?! WHAT KINDA...
...CRAZY CRAP ARE YOU ASSUM—
SNAP
I'M NOT ASSUMING ANY-THING!!!
DO YOU EVEN KNOW WHAT LOOK IS ON YOUR FACE RIGHT NOW?!!

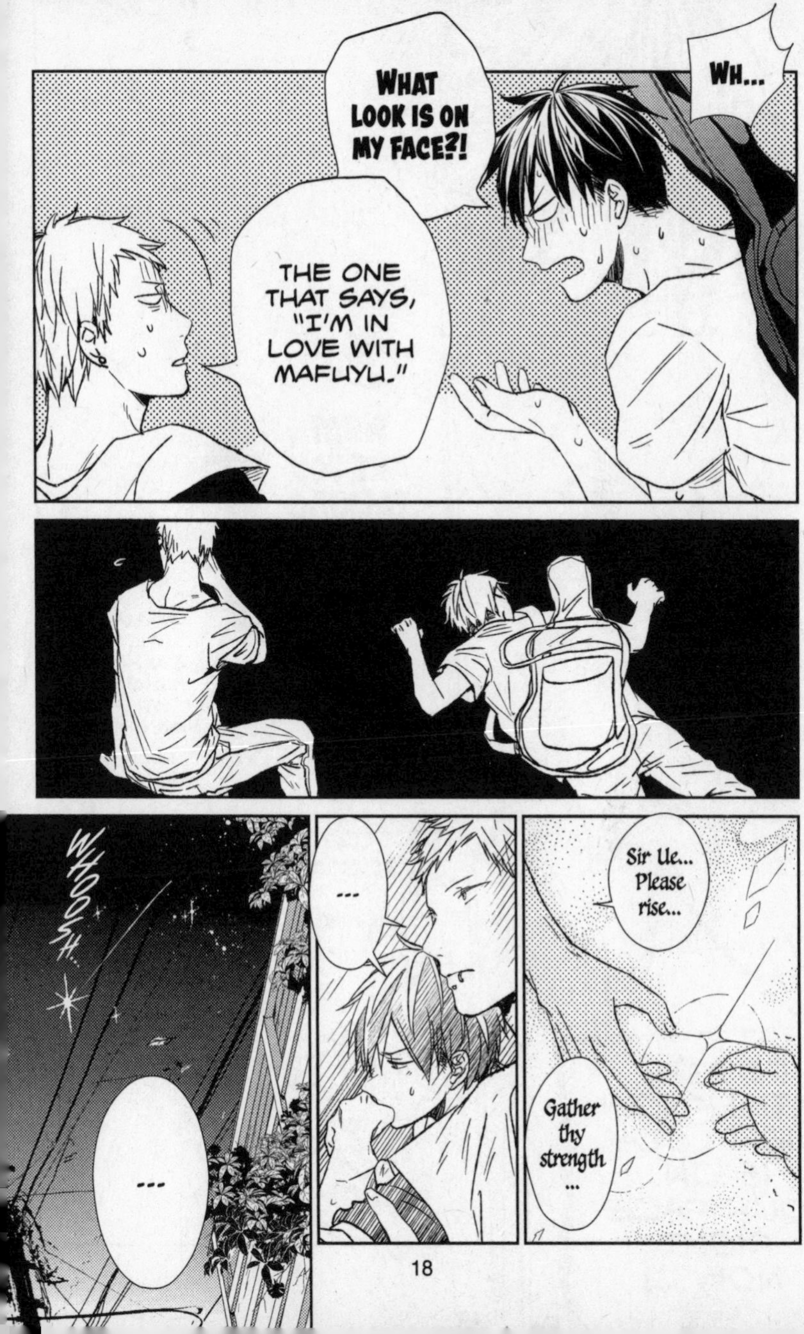
WH...
WHAT LOOK IS ON MY FACE?!
THE ONE THAT SAYS, "I'M IN LOVE WITH MAFUYU."
Sir Ue... Please rise...
Gather thy strength ...
...
WHOOOSH...
...

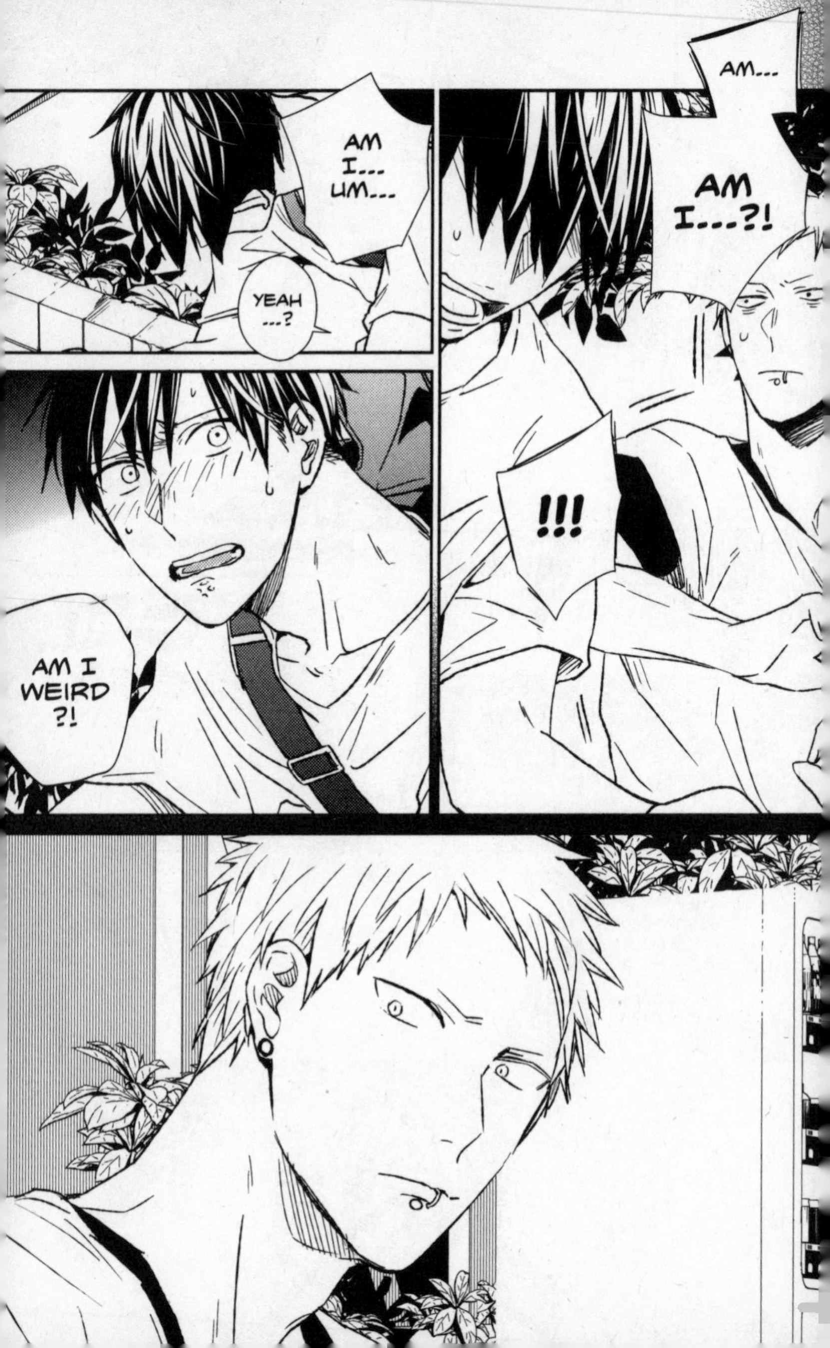
AM...
AM I...?!
!!!
AM I... UM...
YEAH ...?
AM I WEIRD ?!

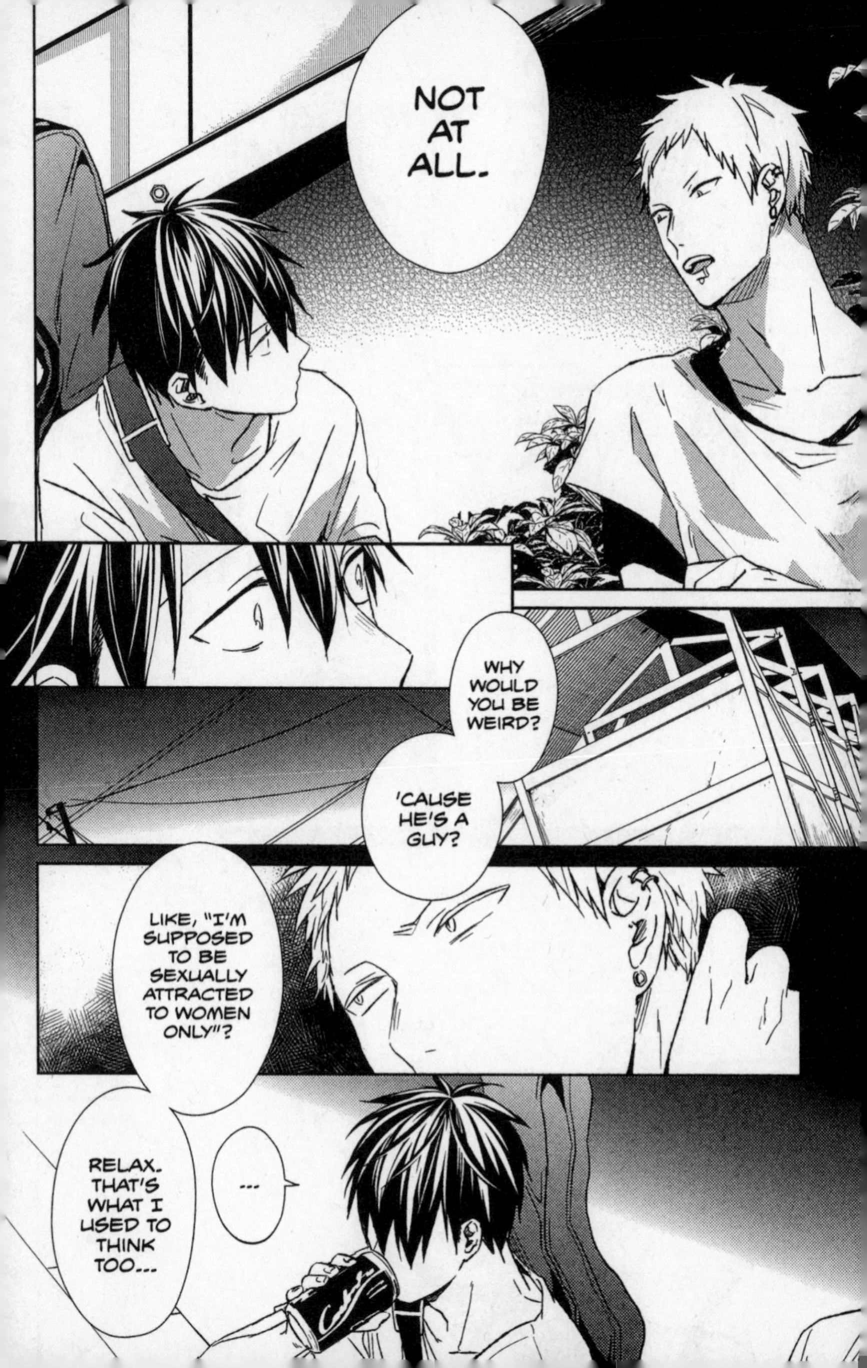
NOT AT ALL.
WHY WOULD YOU BE WEIRD?
'CAUSE HE'S A GUY?
LIKE, "I'M SUPPOSED TO BE SEXUALLY ATTRACTED TO WOMEN ONLY"?
...
RELAX. THAT'S WHAT I USED TO THINK TOO...

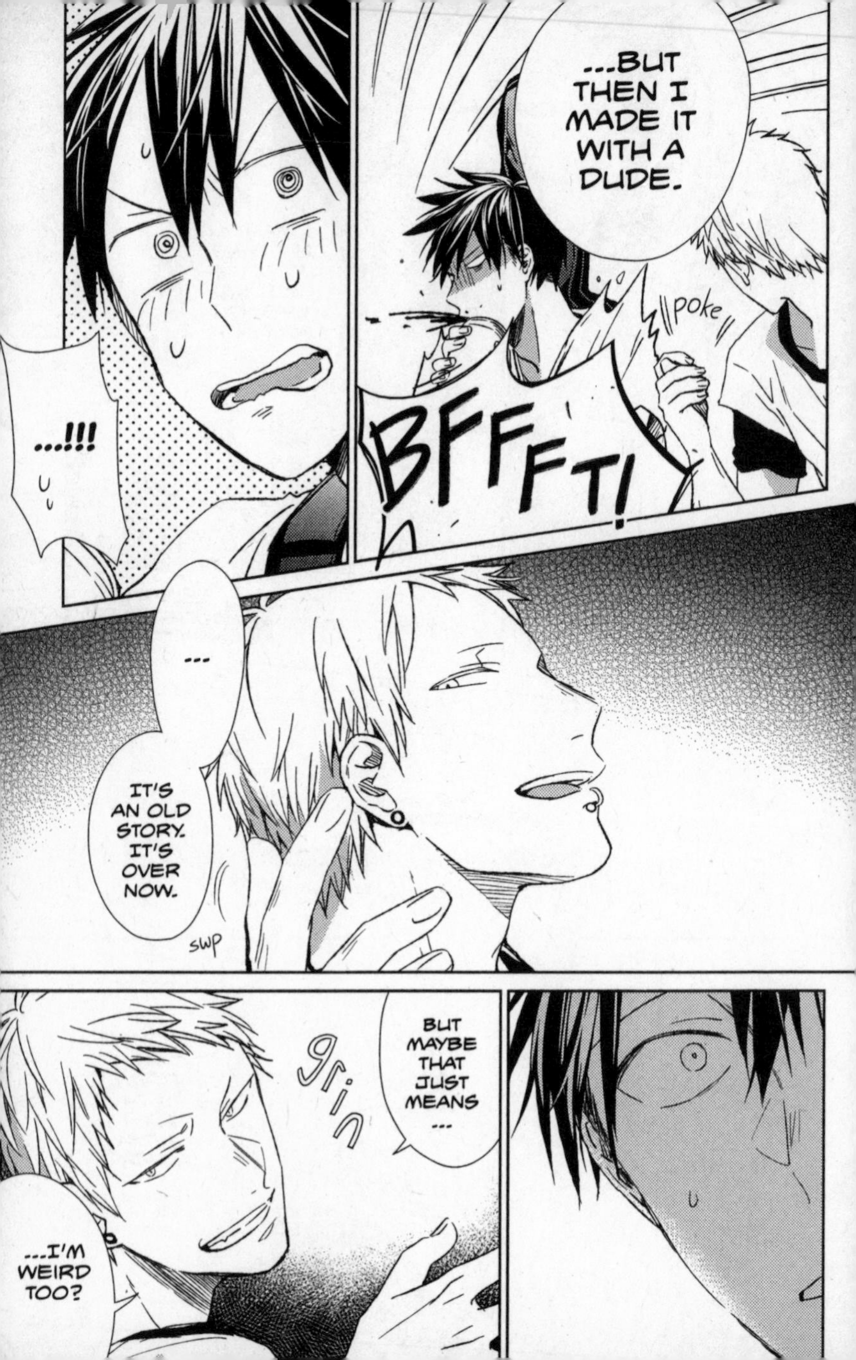
...BUT THEN I MADE IT WITH A DUDE.
poke
BFFFT!
...!!!
...
IT'S AN OLD STORY. IT'S OVER NOW.
swp
BUT MAYBE THAT JUST MEANS...
grin
...I'M WEIRD TOO?

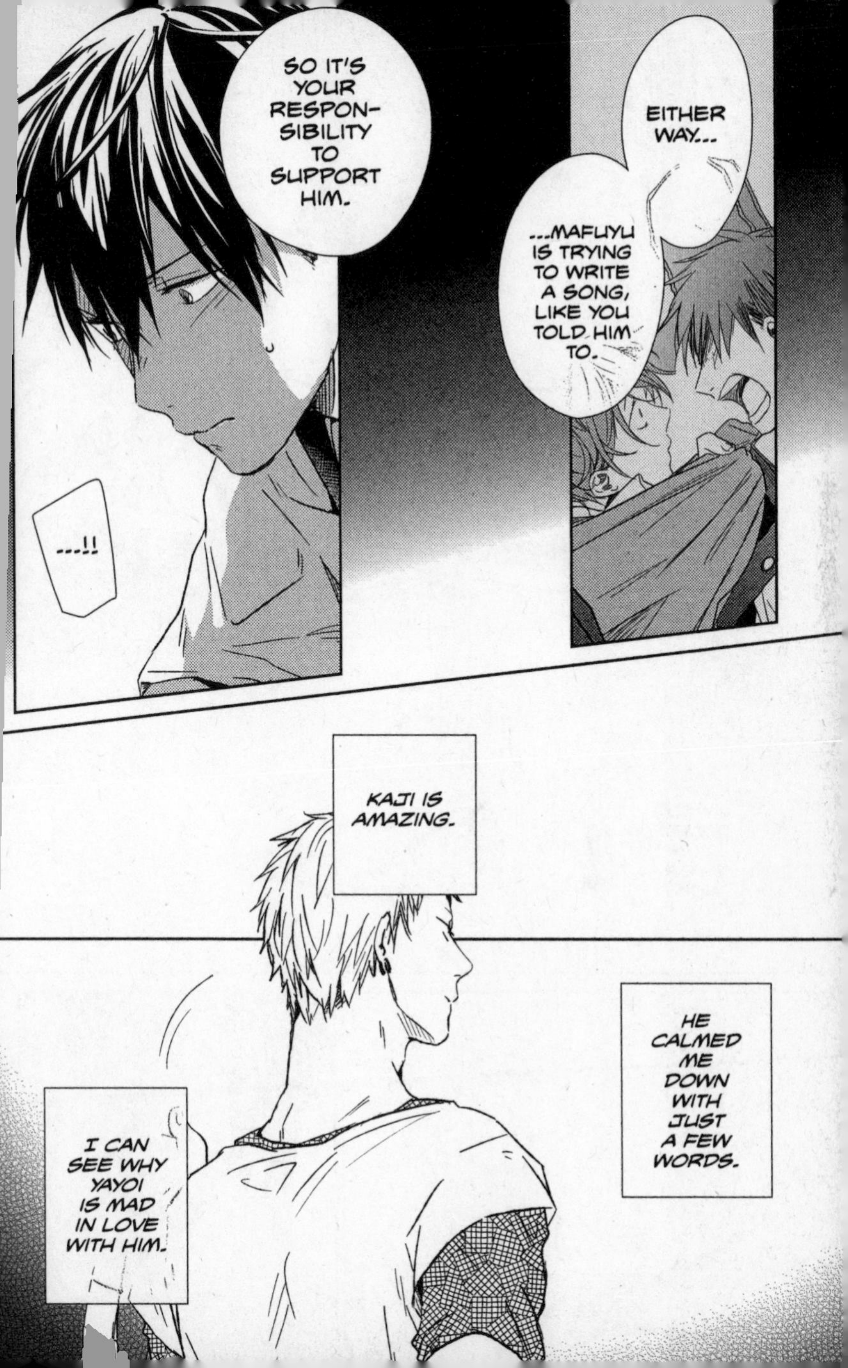
EITHER WAY...
...MAFUYU IS TRYING TO WRITE A SONG, LIKE YOU TOLD HIM TO.
SO IT'S YOUR RESPON-SIBILITY TO SUPPORT HIM.
...!!
KAJI IS AMAZING.
HE CALMED ME DOWN WITH JUST A FEW WORDS.
I CAN SEE WHY YAYOI IS MAD IN LOVE WITH HIM.

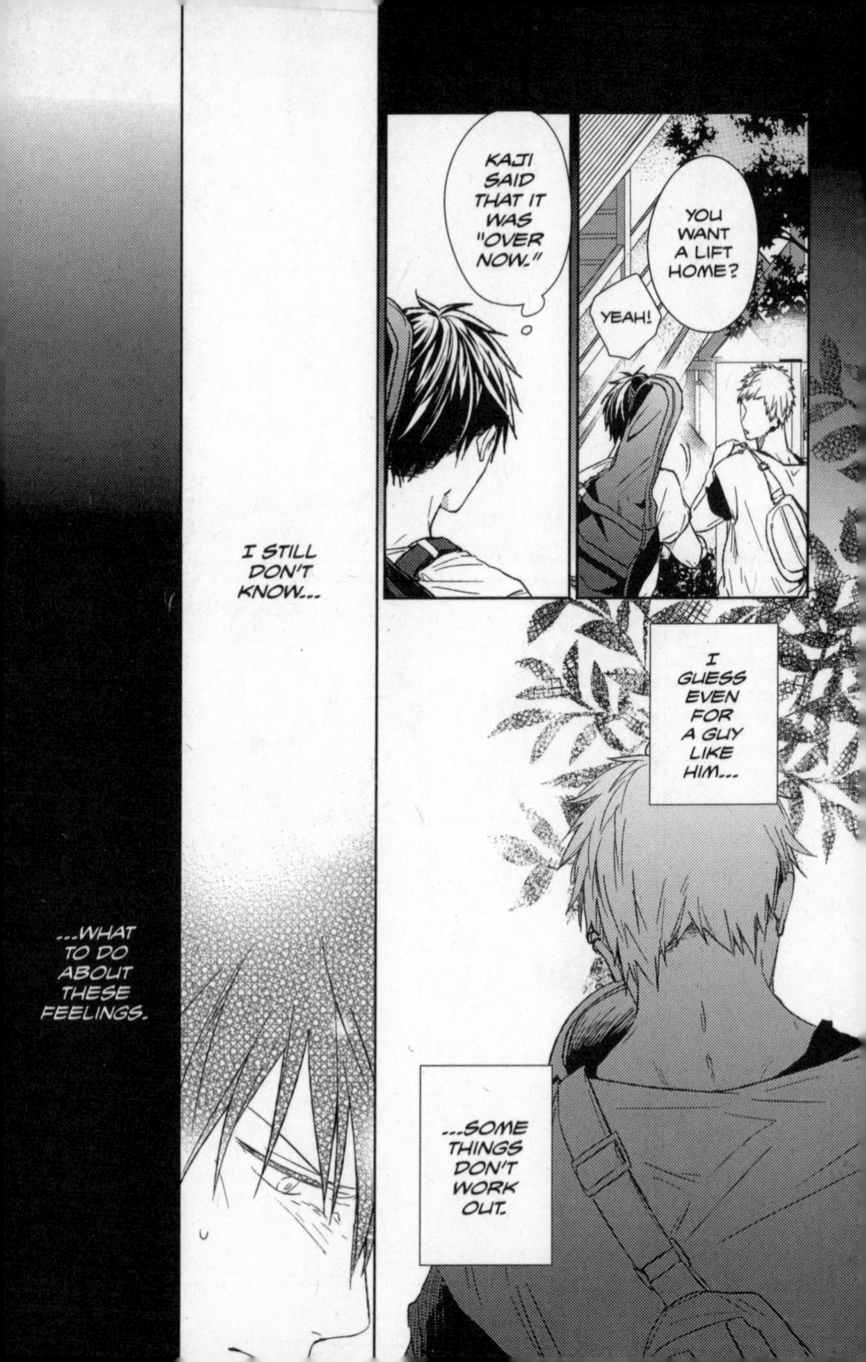
YOU WANT A LIFT HOME?
YEAH!
KAJI SAID THAT IT WAS "OVER NOW."
I GUESS EVEN FOR A GUY LIKE HIM...
...SOME THINGS DON'T WORK OUT.
I STILL DON'T KNOW...
...WHAT TO DO ABOUT THESE FEELINGS.

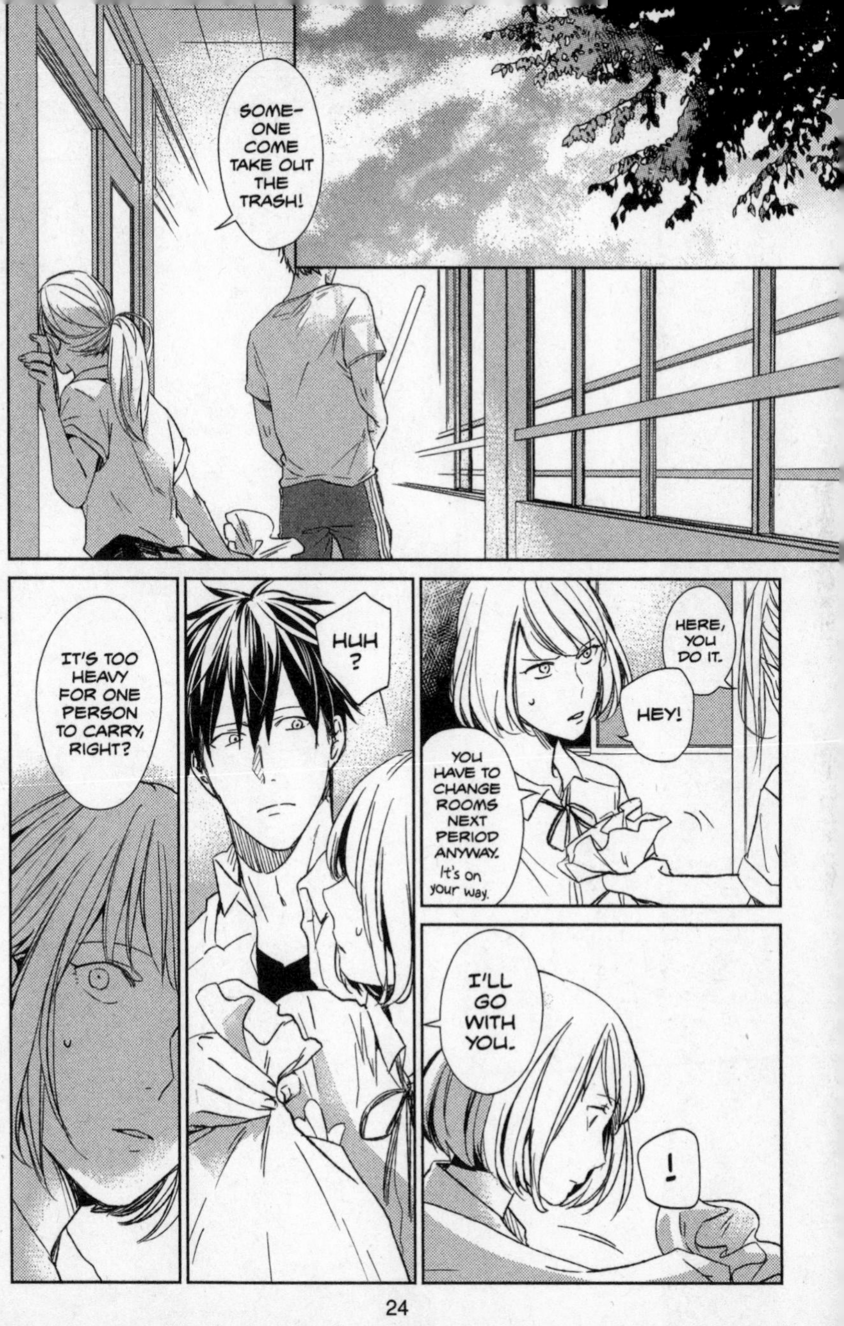
SOME-ONE COME TAKE OUT THE TRASH!
HERE, YOU DO IT.
HEY!
YOU HAVE TO CHANGE ROOMS NEXT PERIOD ANYWAY.
It's on your way.
I'LL GO WITH YOU.
!
HUH ?
IT'S TOO HEAVY FOR ONE PERSON TO CARRY, RIGHT?

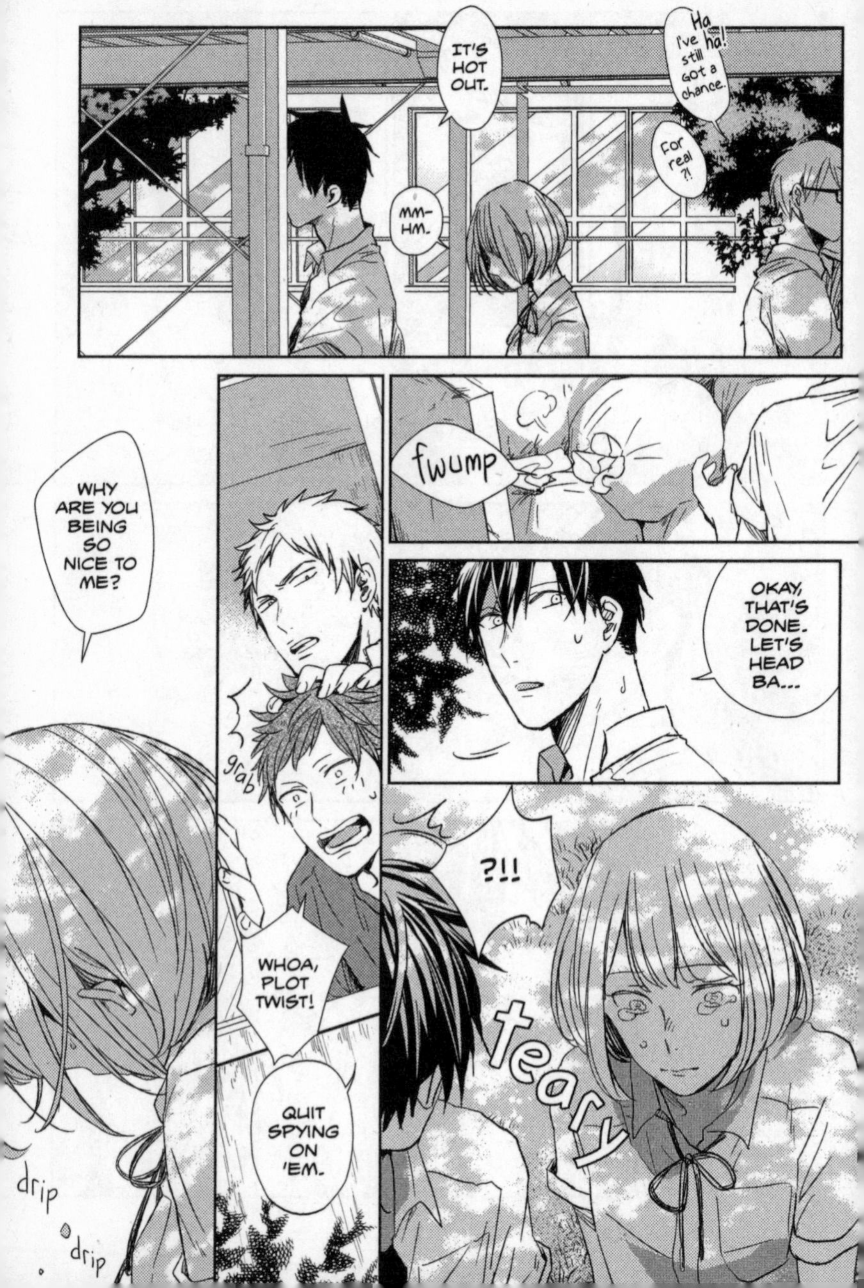
Ha ha! I've still got a chance.
For real ?!
IT'S HOT OUT.
MM-HM.
fwump
OKAY, THAT'S DONE. LET'S HEAD BA...
?!!
teary
WHY ARE YOU BEING SO NICE TO ME?
drip drip
grab
WHOA, PLOT TWIST!
QUIT SPYING ON 'EM.

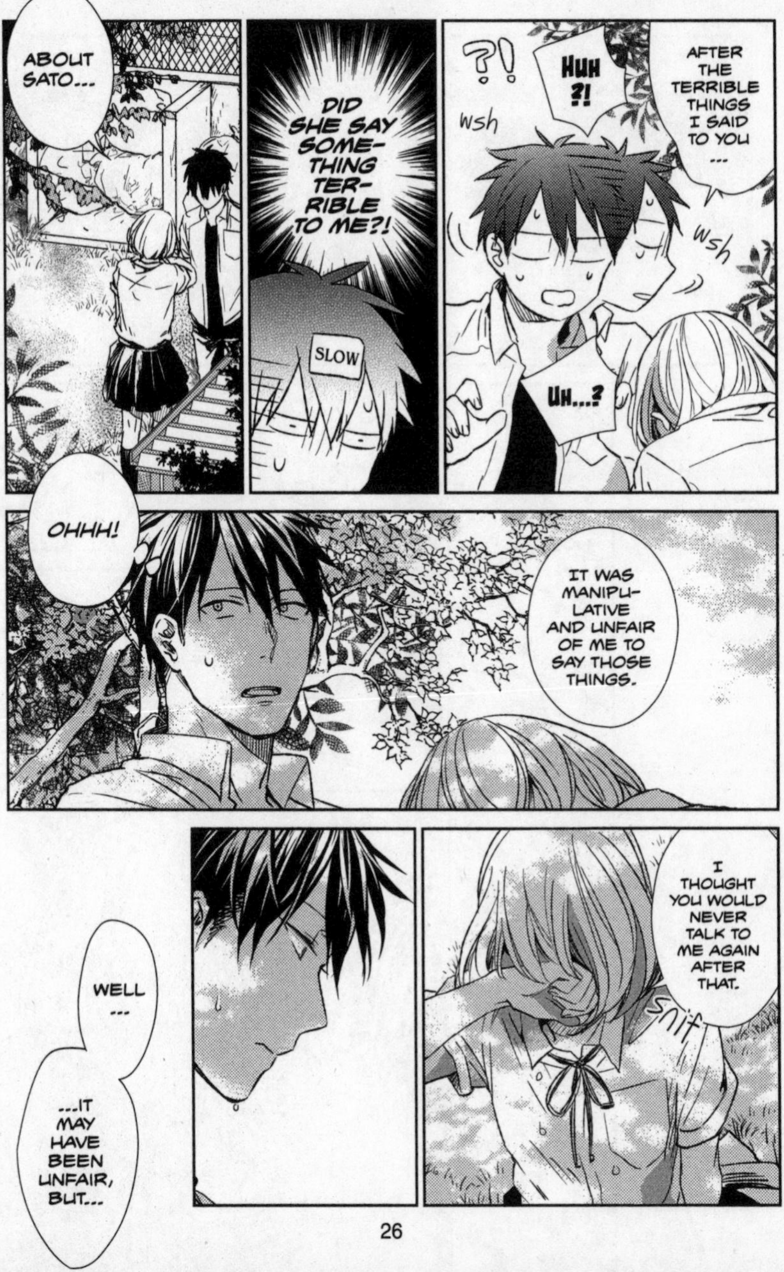
AFTER THE TERRIBLE THINGS I SAID TO YOU ...
wsh
?!
HUH ?!
wsh
UH...?
DID SHE SAY SOME-THING TER-RIBLE TO ME?!
SLOW
ABOUT SATO...
IT WAS MANIPU-LATIVE AND UNFAIR OF ME TO SAY THOSE THINGS.
OHHH!
I THOUGHT YOU WOULD NEVER TALK TO ME AGAIN AFTER THAT.
snif
WELL ...
...IT MAY HAVE BEEN UNFAIR, BUT...

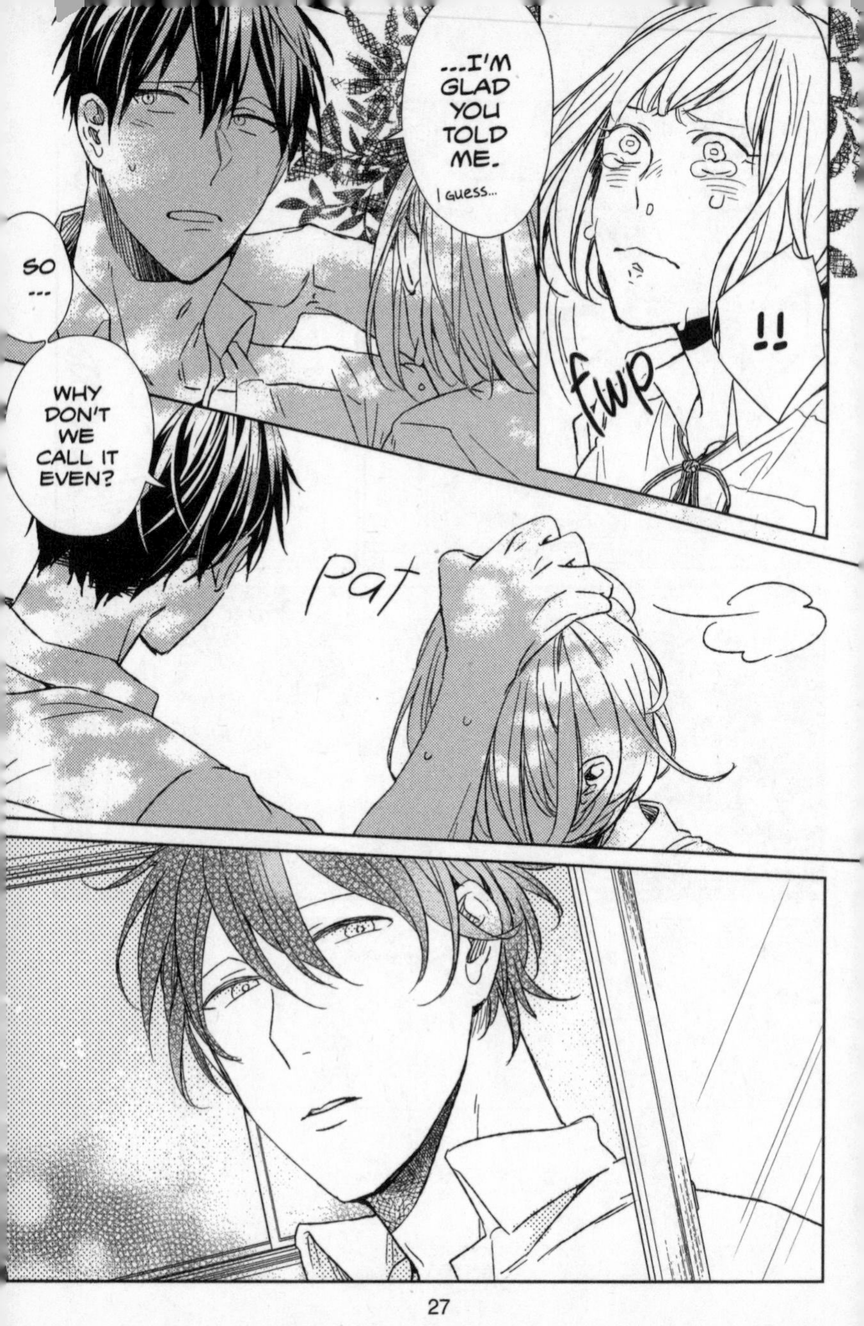
!!
fwp
...I'M GLAD YOU TOLD ME.
I guess...
SO ...
WHY DON'T WE CALL IT EVEN?
pat

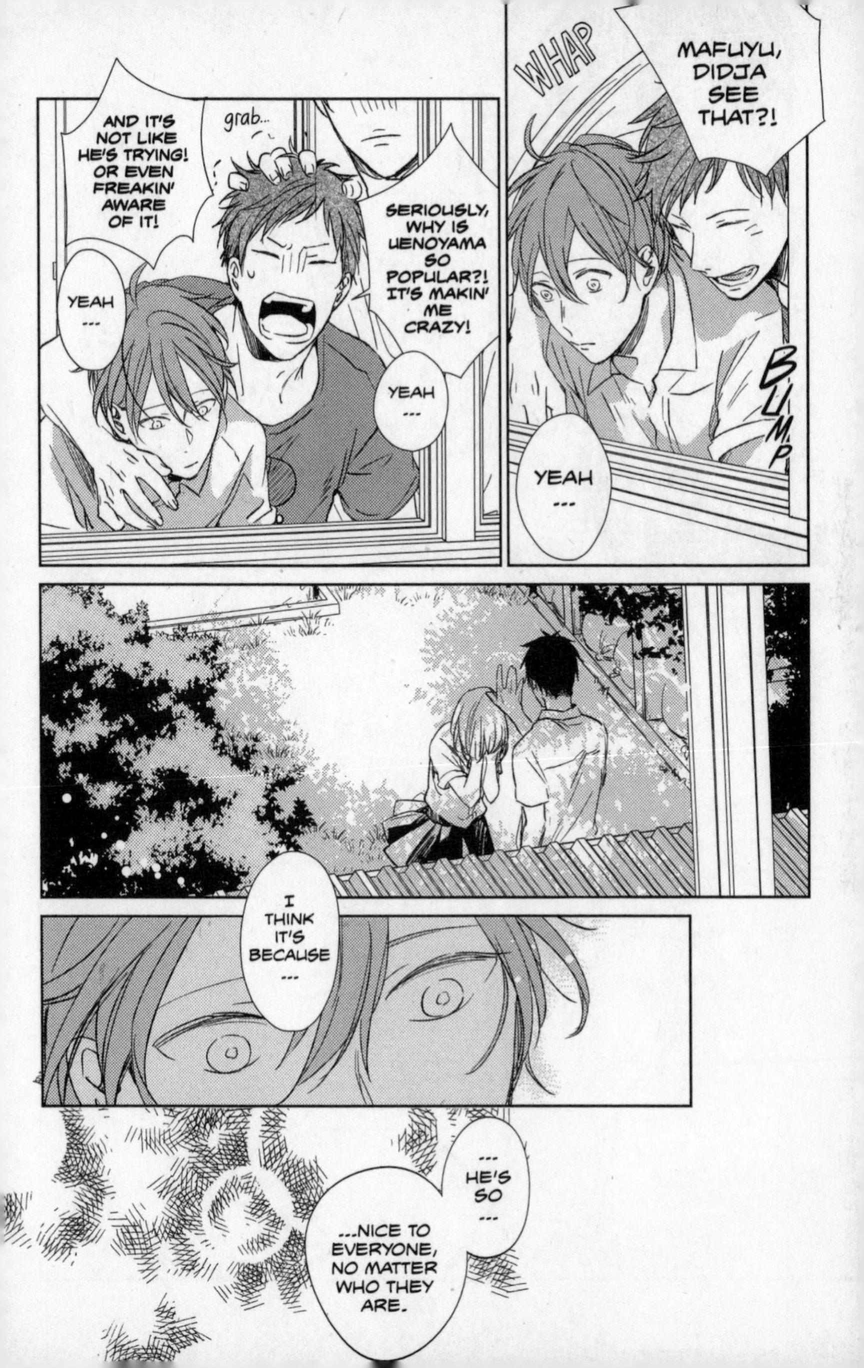
WHAP
MAFUYU, DIDJA SEE THAT?!
BUMP
YEAH ---
SERIOUSLY, WHY IS UENOYAMA SO POPULAR?! IT'S MAKIN' ME CRAZY!
grab...
AND IT'S NOT LIKE HE'S TRYING! OR EVEN FREAKIN' AWARE OF IT!
YEAH ---
YEAH ---
I THINK IT'S BECAUSE ---
--- HE'S SO ---
...NICE TO EVERYONE, NO MATTER WHO THEY ARE.

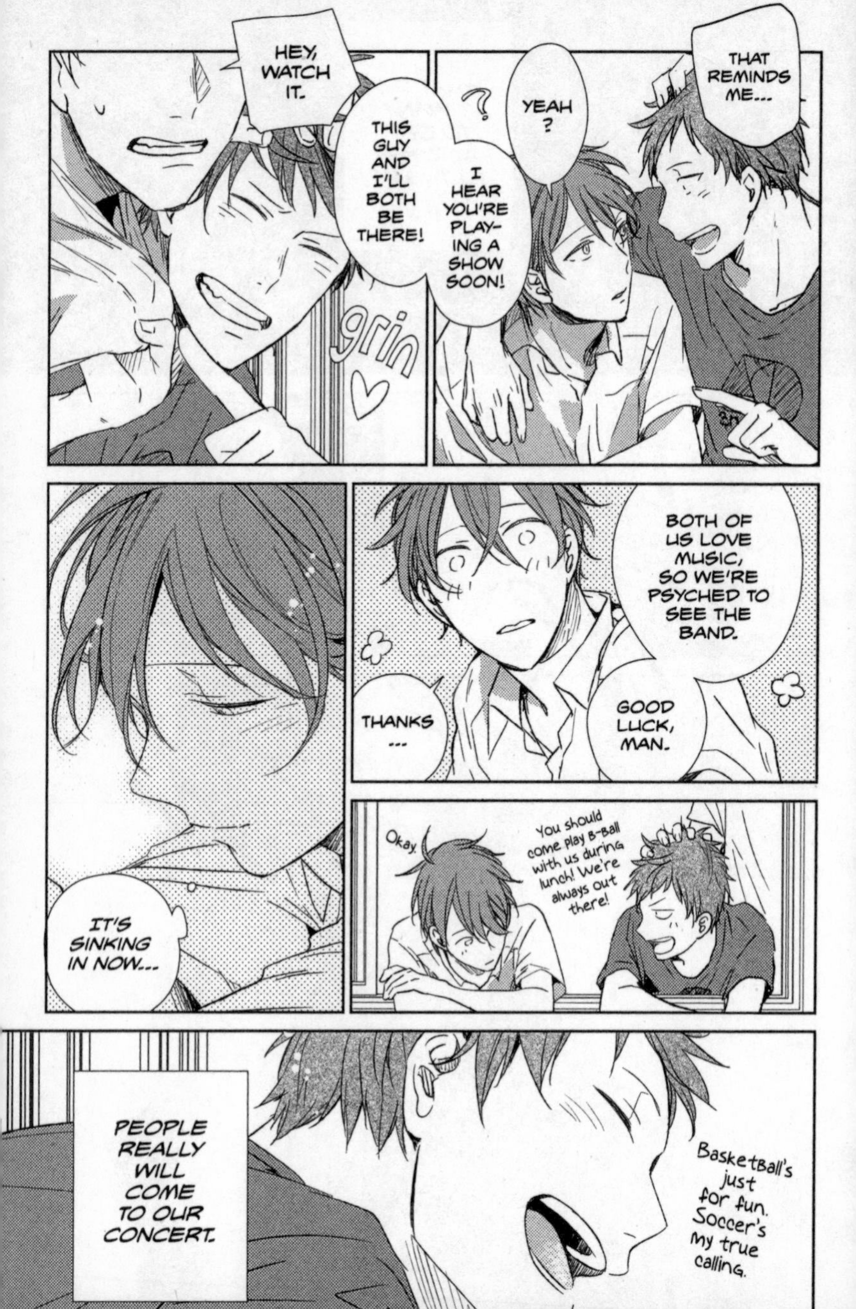
THAT REMINDS ME...
YEAH?
I HEAR YOU'RE PLAYING A SHOW SOON!
THIS GUY AND I'LL BOTH BE THERE!
HEY, WATCH IT.
grin
BOTH OF US LOVE MUSIC, SO WE'RE PSYCHED TO SEE THE BAND.
GOOD LUCK, MAN.
THANKS...
You should come play B-Ball with us during lunch! We're always out there!
Okay.
IT'S SINKING IN NOW...
Basketball's just for fun. Soccer's my true calling.
PEOPLE REALLY WILL COME TO OUR CONCERT.

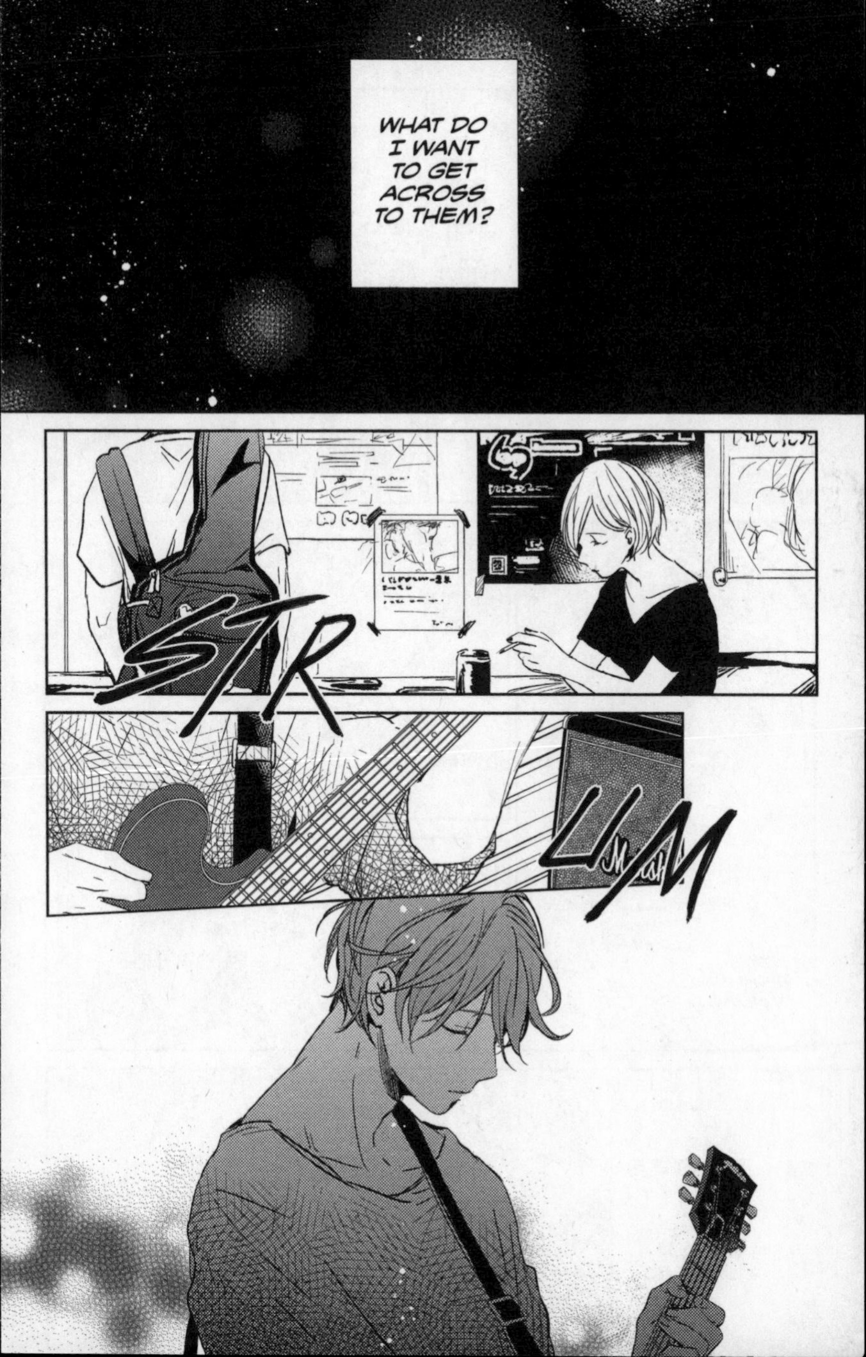
WHAT DO I WANT TO GET ACROSS TO THEM?
STR
UM

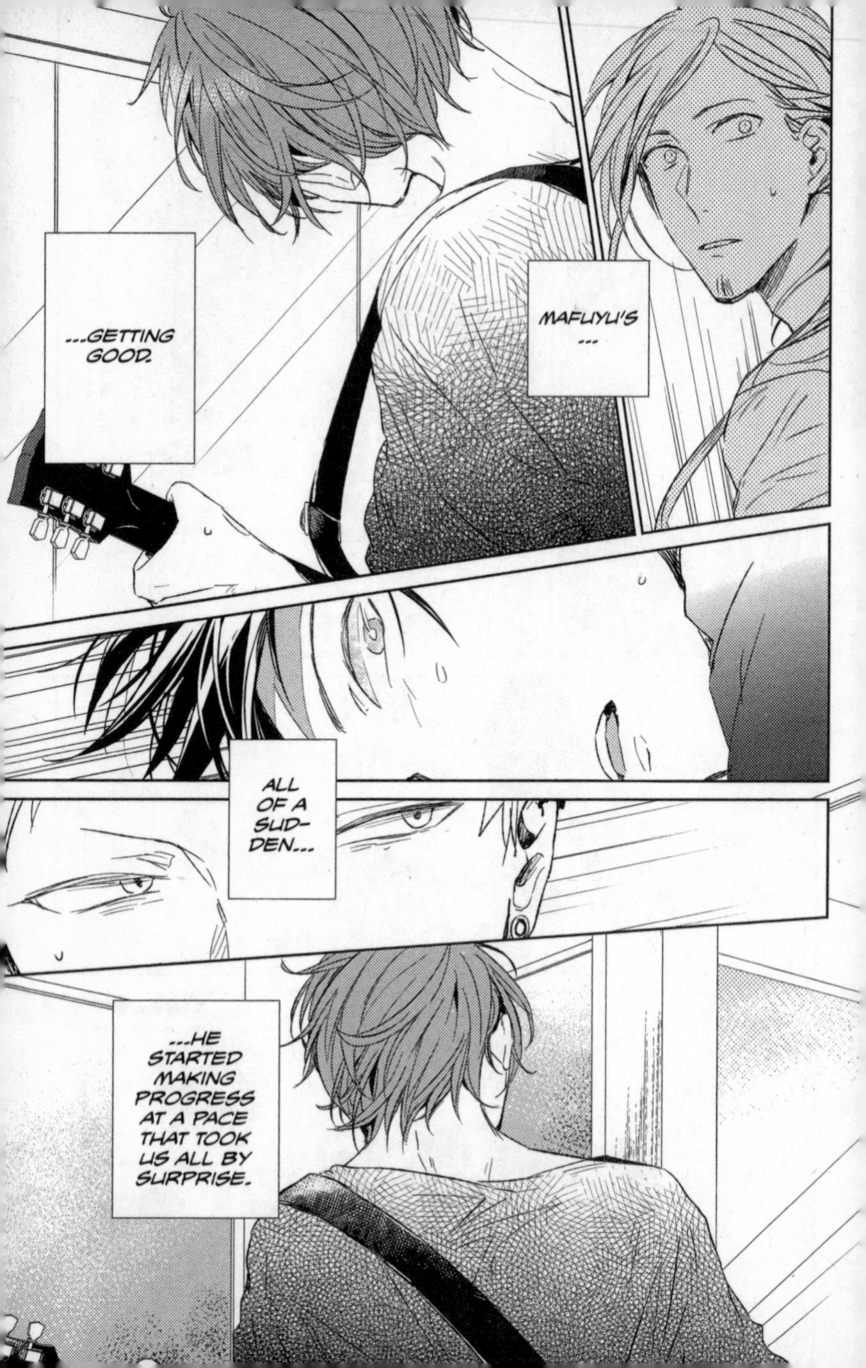
MAFUYU'S ...
...GETTING GOOD.
ALL OF A SUD-DEN...
...HE STARTED MAKING PROGRESS AT A PACE THAT TOOK US ALL BY SURPRISE.

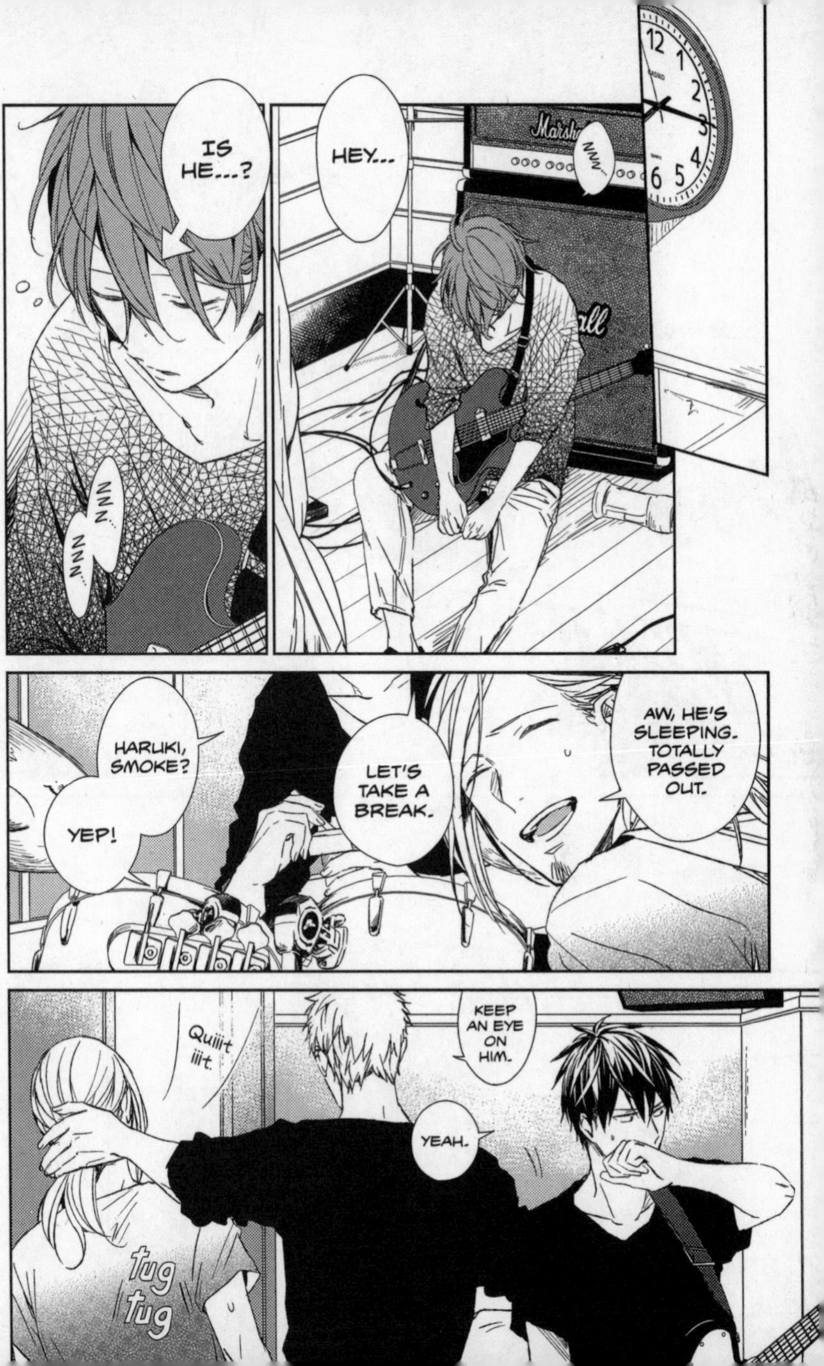
HEY...
ZZZ...
IS HE...?
ZZZ...
ZZZ...
AW, HE'S SLEEPING. TOTALLY PASSED OUT.
LET'S TAKE A BREAK.
HARUKI, SMOKE?
YEP!
KEEP AN EYE ON HIM.
YEAH.
Quiiit iiit.
tug tug

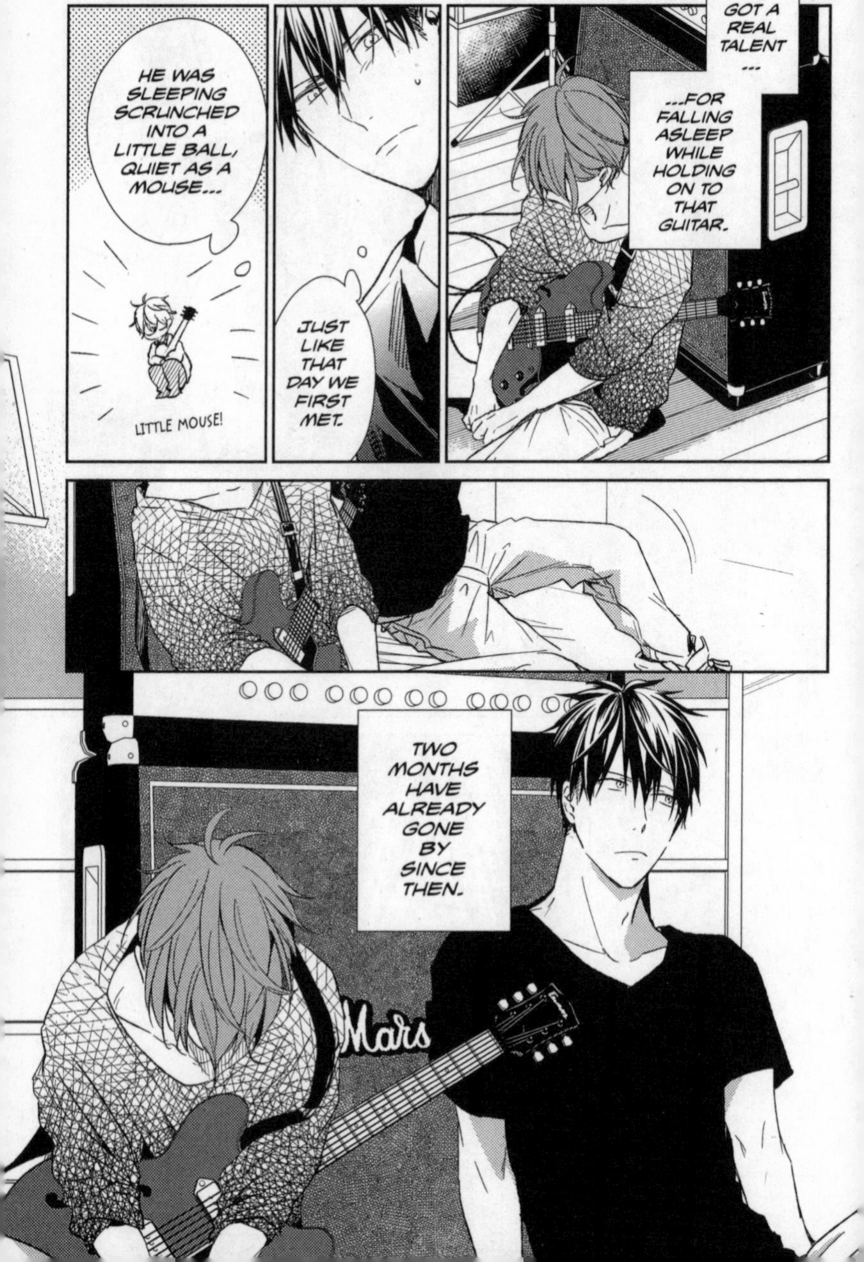
HE'S GOT A REAL TALENT ...
...FOR FALLING ASLEEP WHILE HOLDING ON TO THAT GUITAR.
JUST LIKE THAT DAY WE FIRST MET.
HE WAS SLEEPING SCRUNCHED INTO A LITTLE BALL, QUIET AS A MOUSE...
LITTLE MOUSE!
TWO MONTHS HAVE ALREADY GONE BY SINCE THEN.
Mars

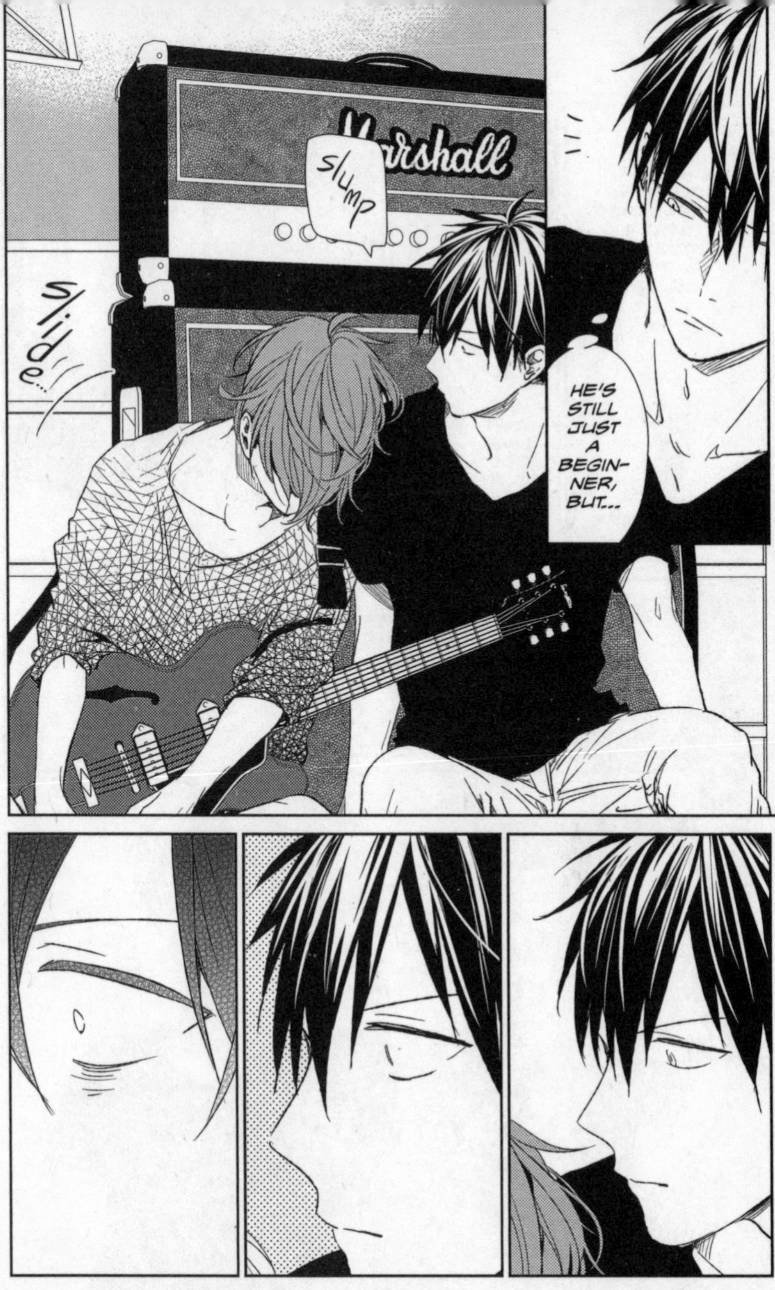
HE'S STILL JUST A BEGIN-NER, BUT...
slump
slide...

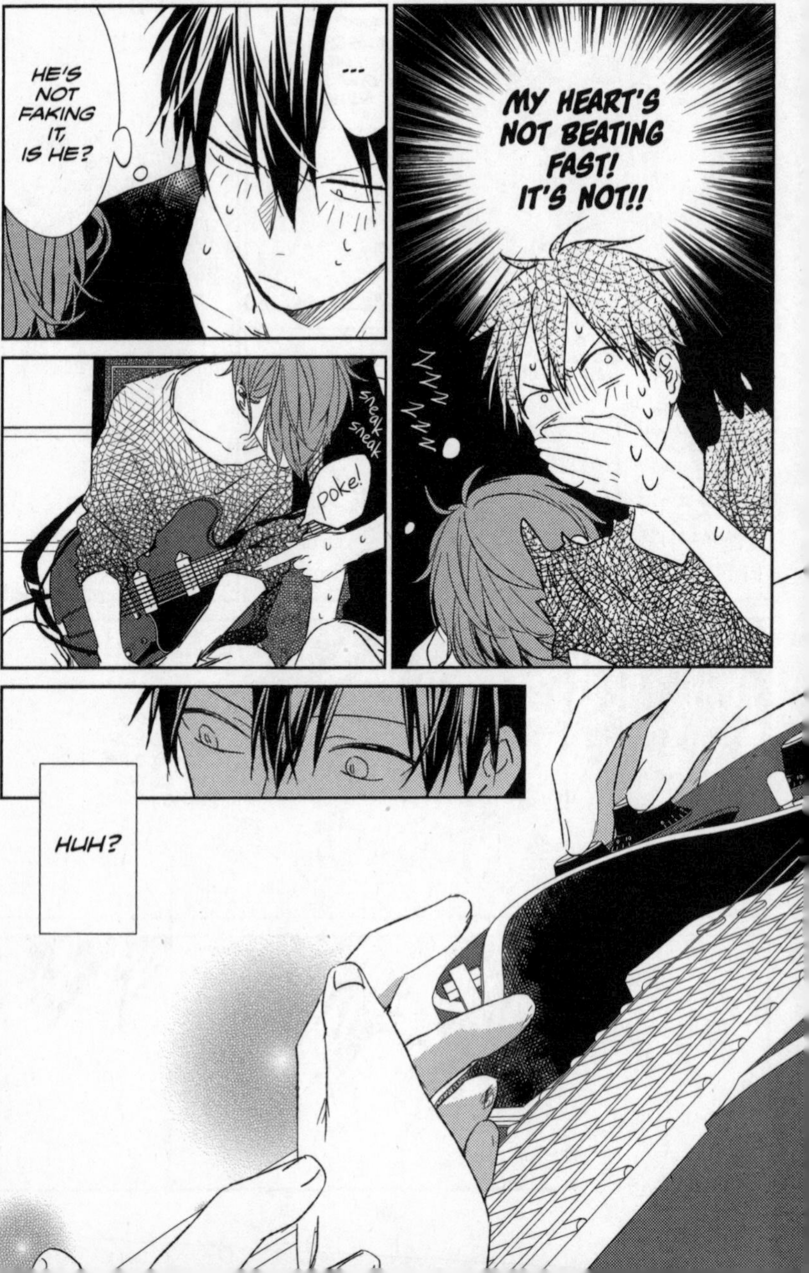
MY HEART'S NOT BEATING FAST! IT'S NOT!!
...
HE'S NOT FAKING IT, IS HE?
ZZZ ZZZ
sneak sneak
poke!
HUH?

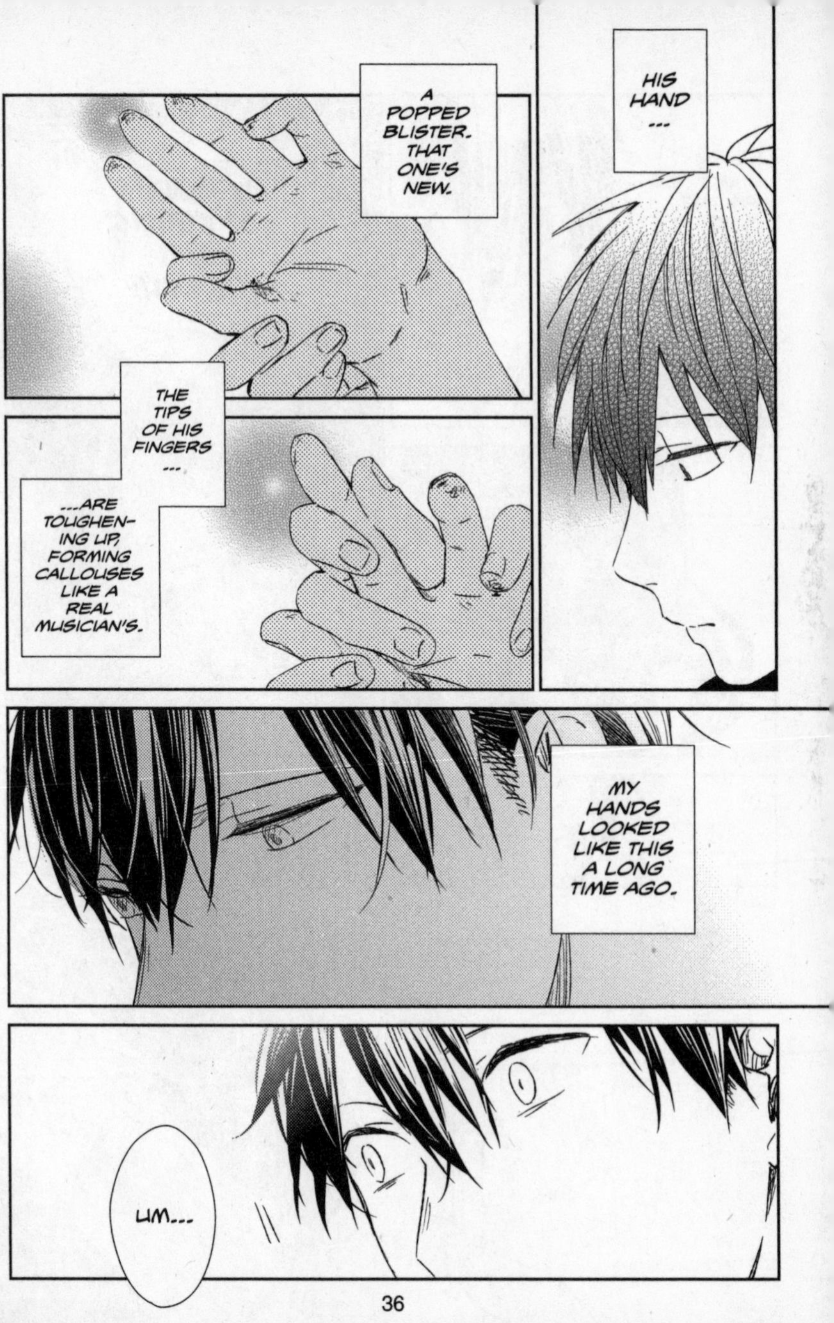
HIS HAND ...
A POPPED BLISTER. THAT ONE'S NEW.
THE TIPS OF HIS FINGERS ...
...ARE TOUGHENING UP, FORMING CALLOUSES LIKE A REAL MUSICIAN'S.
MY HANDS LOOKED LIKE THIS A LONG TIME AGO.
UM...

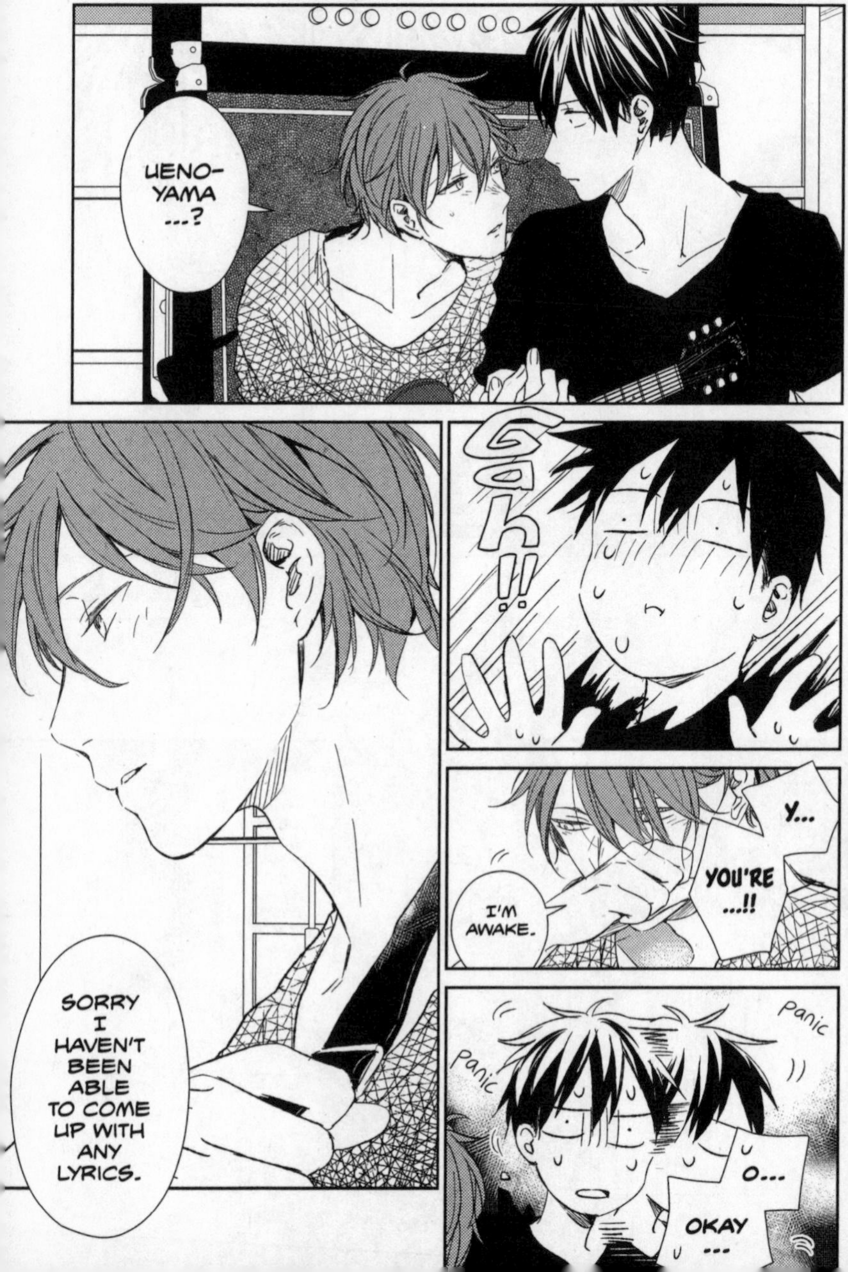
UENO-YAMA ...?
Y... YOU'RE ...!!
I'M AWAKE.
Panic
Panic
O... OKAY ...
SORRY I HAVEN'T BEEN ABLE TO COME UP WITH ANY LYRICS.

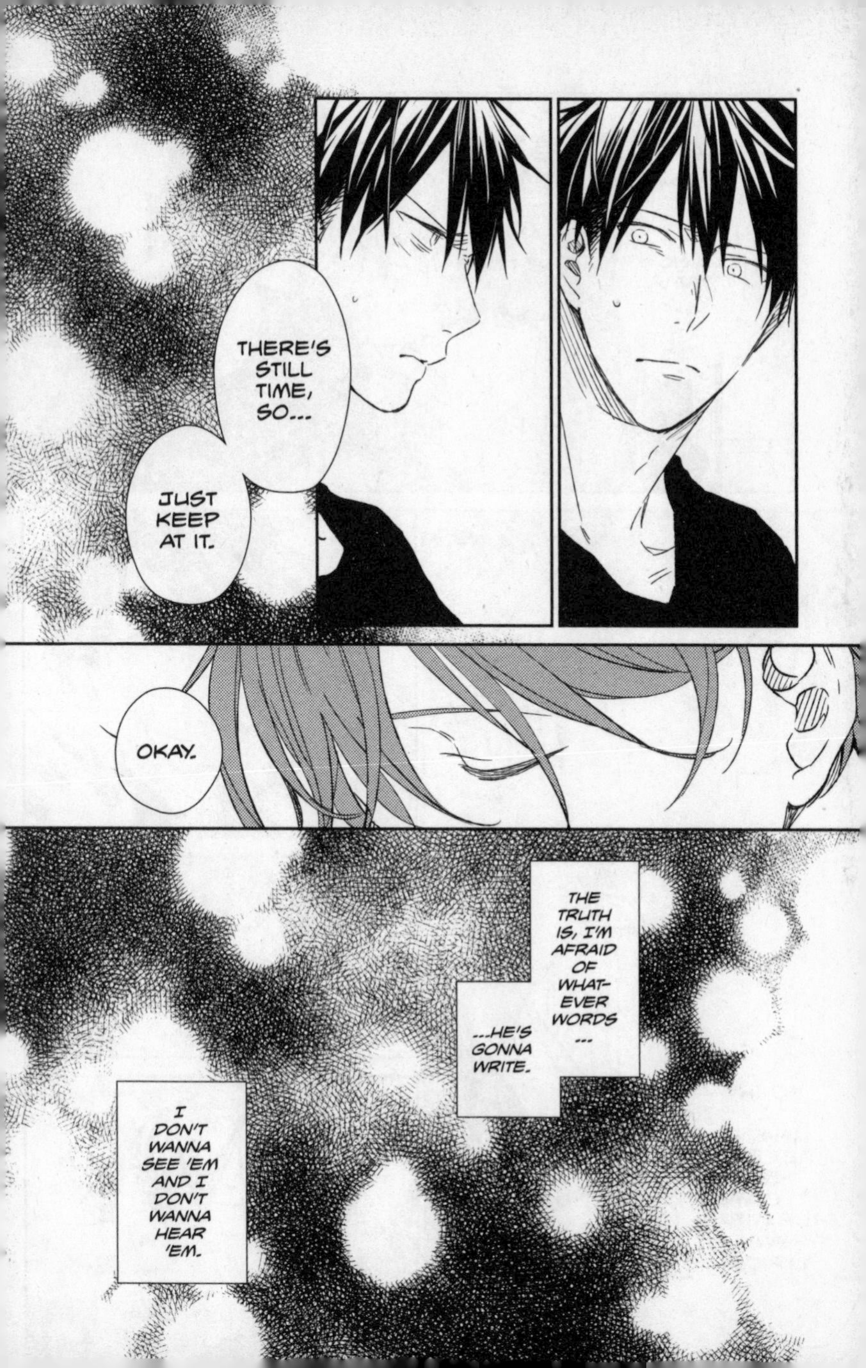
THERE'S STILL TIME, SO...
JUST KEEP AT IT.
OKAY.
THE TRUTH IS, I'M AFRAID OF WHATEVER WORDS...
...HE'S GONNA WRITE.
I DON'T WANNA SEE 'EM AND I DON'T WANNA HEAR 'EM.

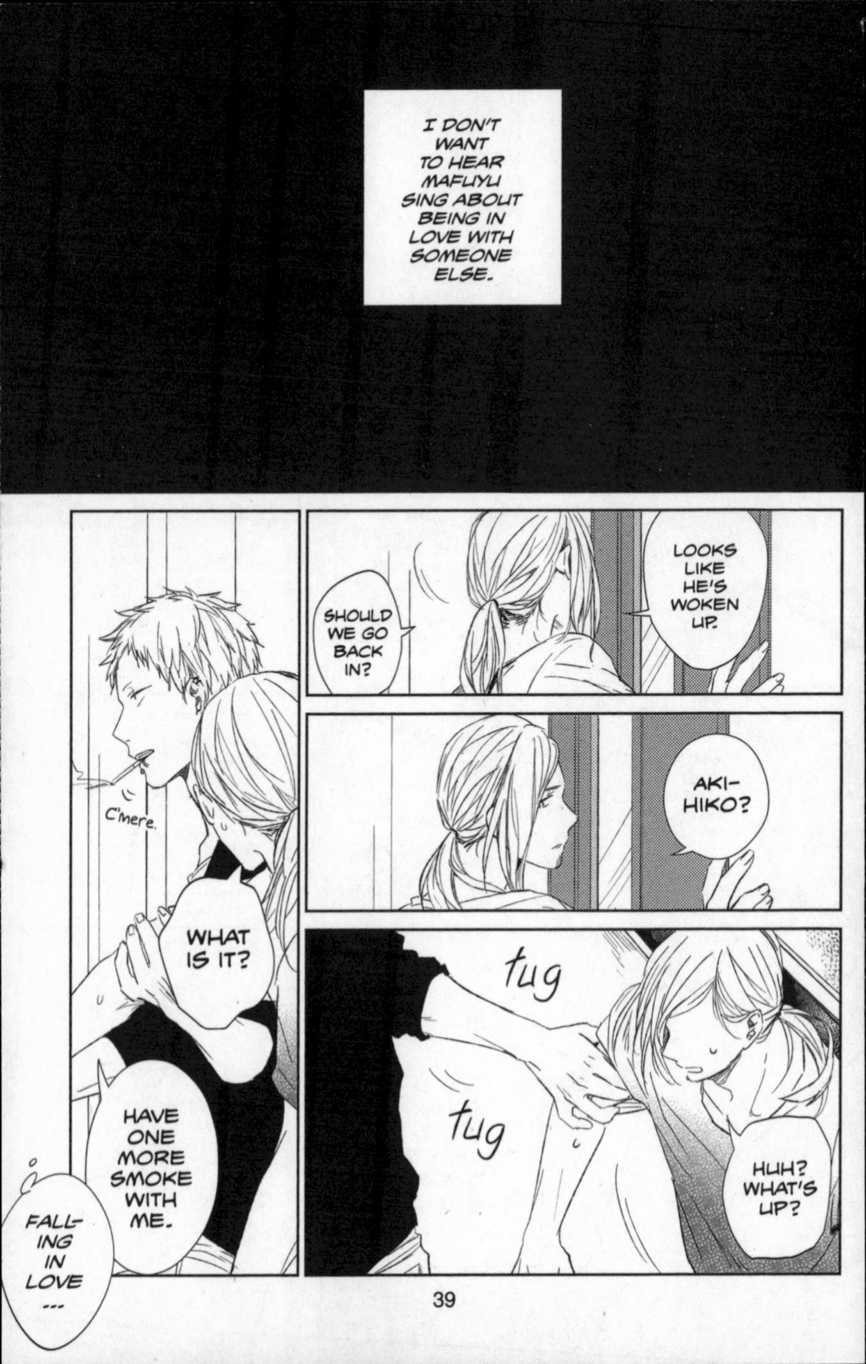
I DON'T WANT TO HEAR MAFUYU SING ABOUT BEING IN LOVE WITH SOMEONE ELSE.
LOOKS LIKE HE'S WOKEN UP.
SHOULD WE GO BACK IN?
AKI-HIKO?
tug
tug
HUH? WHAT'S UP?
C'mere.
WHAT IS IT?
HAVE ONE MORE SMOKE WITH ME.
FALL-ING IN LOVE ...

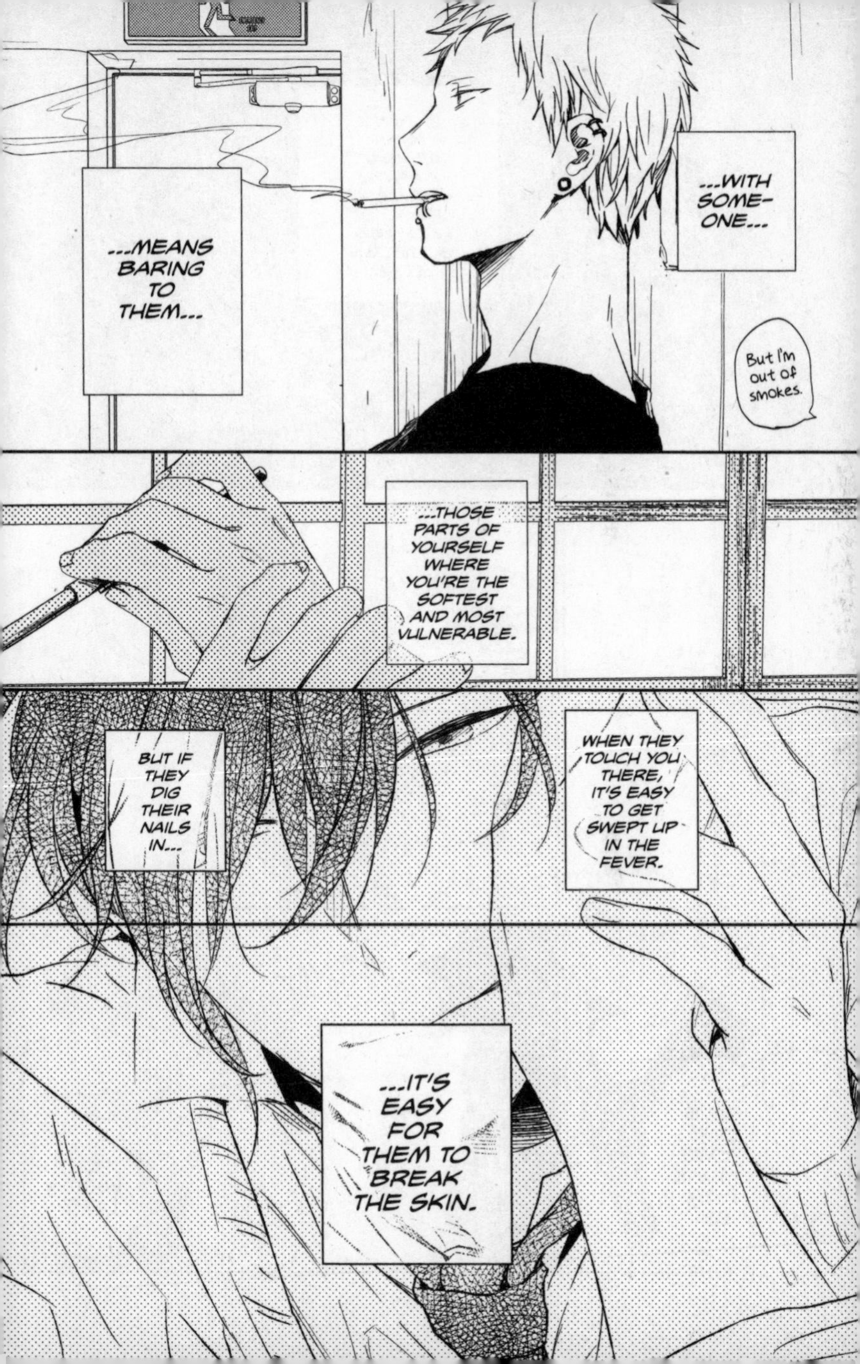
...WITH SOME-ONE...
...MEANS BARING TO THEM...
But I'm out of smokes.
...THOSE PARTS OF YOURSELF WHERE YOU'RE THE SOFTEST AND MOST VULNERABLE.
WHEN THEY TOUCH YOU THERE, IT'S EASY TO GET SWEPT UP IN THE FEVER.
BUT IF THEY DIG THEIR NAILS IN...
...IT'S EASY FOR THEM TO BREAK THE SKIN.

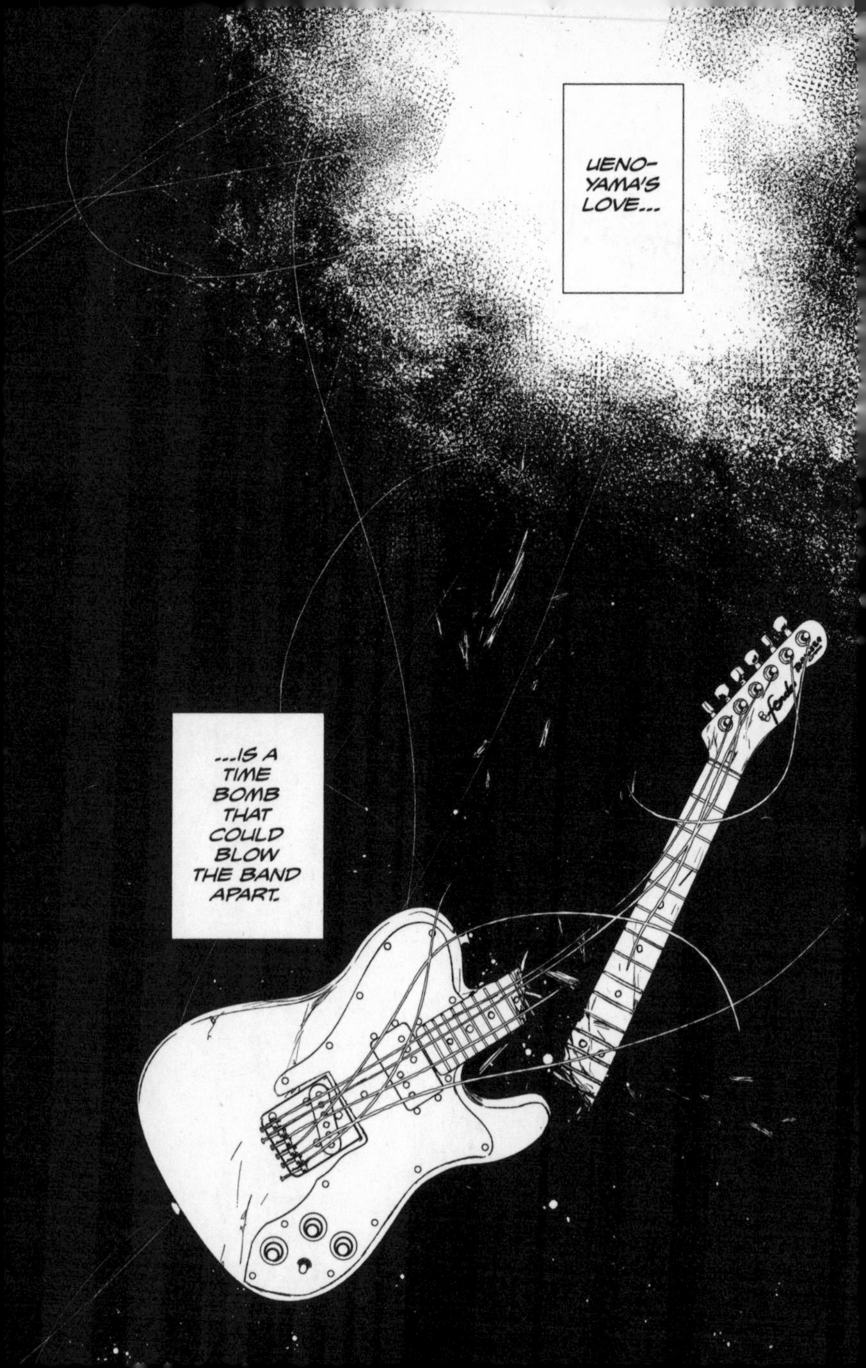
UENO-YAMA'S LOVE...
...IS A TIME BOMB THAT COULD BLOW THE BAND APART.

Shogo Itaya (17)

176 cm

(Second-year high school student)

Birthday: 5/20 Sign: Taurus

Blood Type: O

Soccer Club, Forward

Likes all ball sports.

(Soccer, basketball, baseball, volleyball, tennis, handball, etc.)

Music freak.

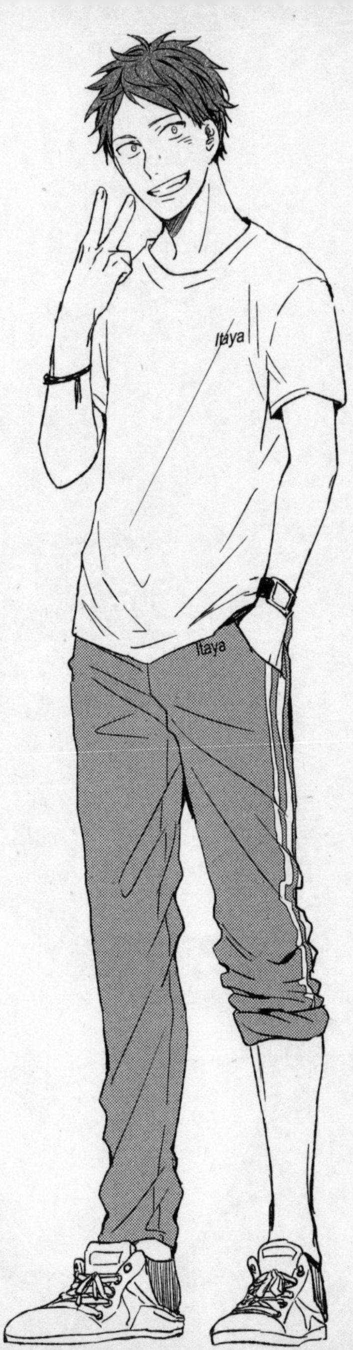
Itaya
Itaya

Itaya's True Calling

WHAT?! ITAYA?!
HM? YEAH.
ITAYA, FROM THE SOCCER CLUB?! *THAT* ITAYA?!
YOU KNOW HIM?
DO I KNOW HIM?! I'M IN THE SOCCER CLUB. OF COURSE I KNOW HIM!
HUH. HE'S GOT THAT MUCH OF A REP?
HOW DO YOU NOT KNOW THIS?! YOU'RE HIS FRIEND, AREN'T YOU?!
HE'S FAMOUS ALL OVER THE KANTO REGION AS A TOP STRIKER!!
Wh... Whaat?
No way...
Let's play...
...B-Ball!
YOU'RE HOPE-LESS!
Days Later
THE ITAYA I KNOW...
...ISN'T THAT COOL! HE'S A GIANT DORK!!!
IT'S TRUE.
DON'T BE RUDE.

given

by Natsuki Kizu

chapter 8
given

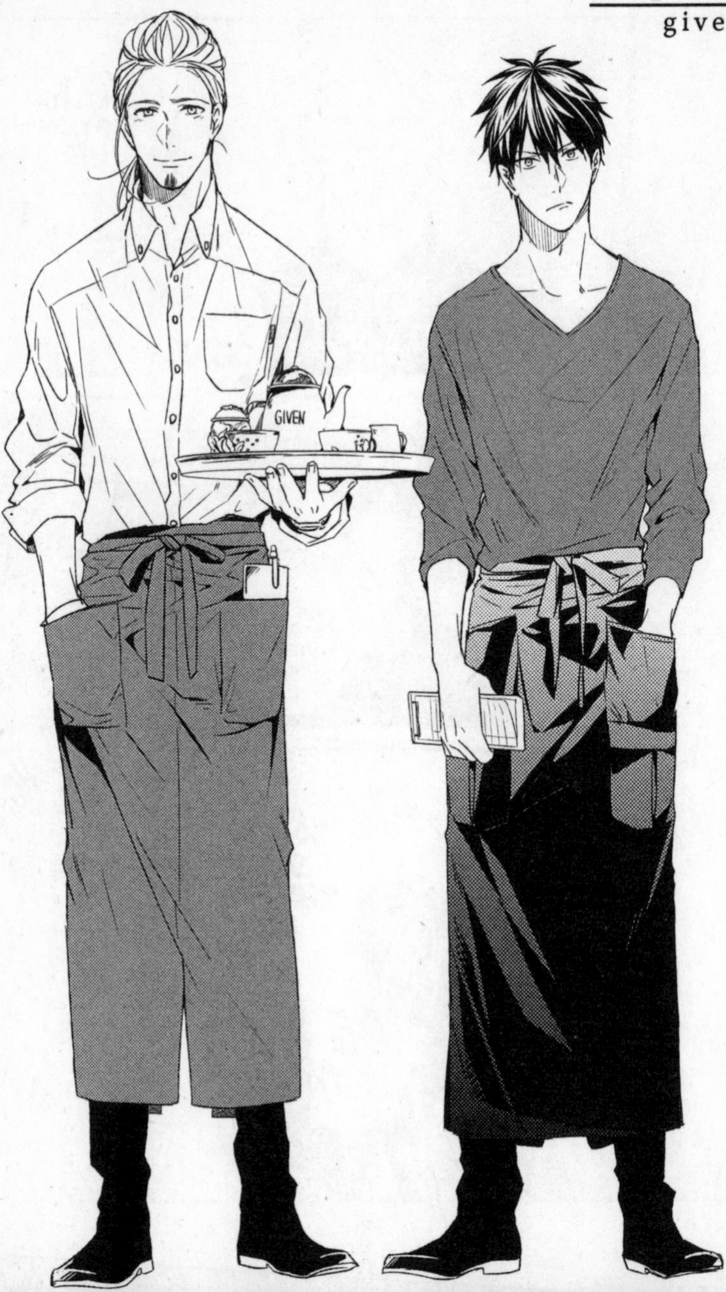
GIVEN

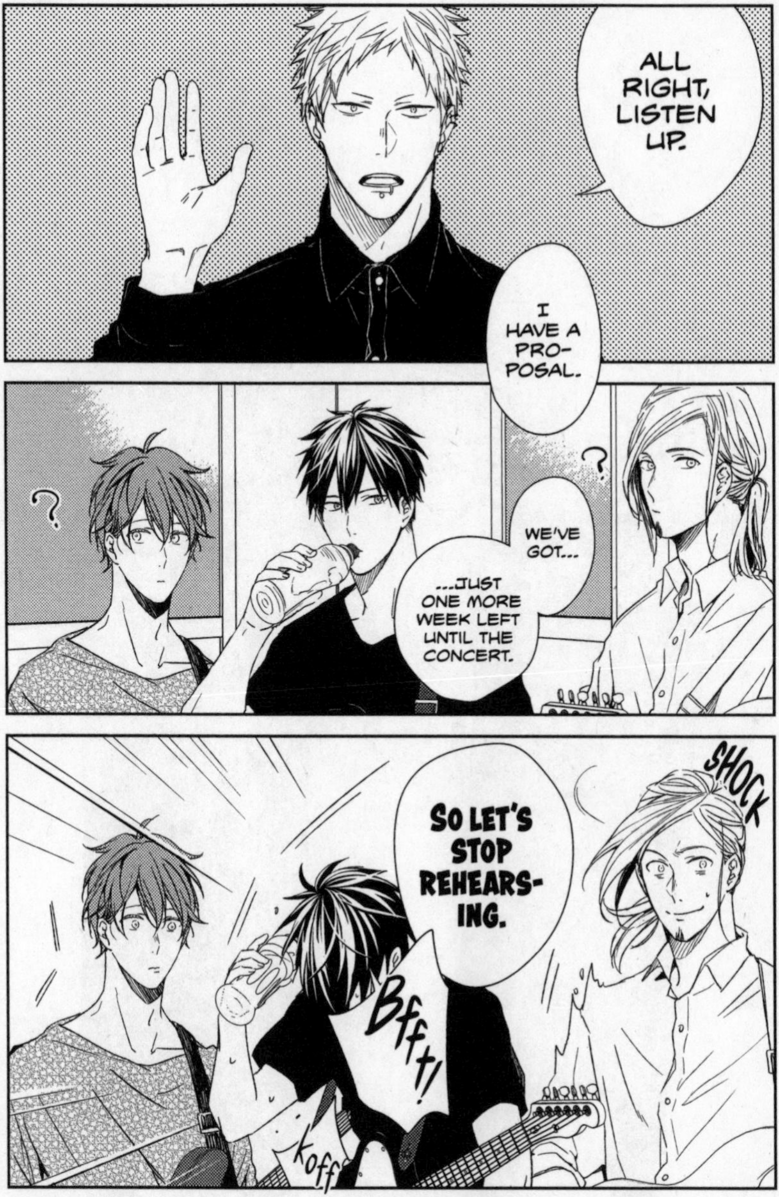
ALL RIGHT, LISTEN UP.
I HAVE A PRO-POSAL.
WE'VE GOT...
...JUST ONE MORE WEEK LEFT UNTIL THE CONCERT.
SHOCK
SO LET'S STOP REHEARS-ING.
Bfft!
koff

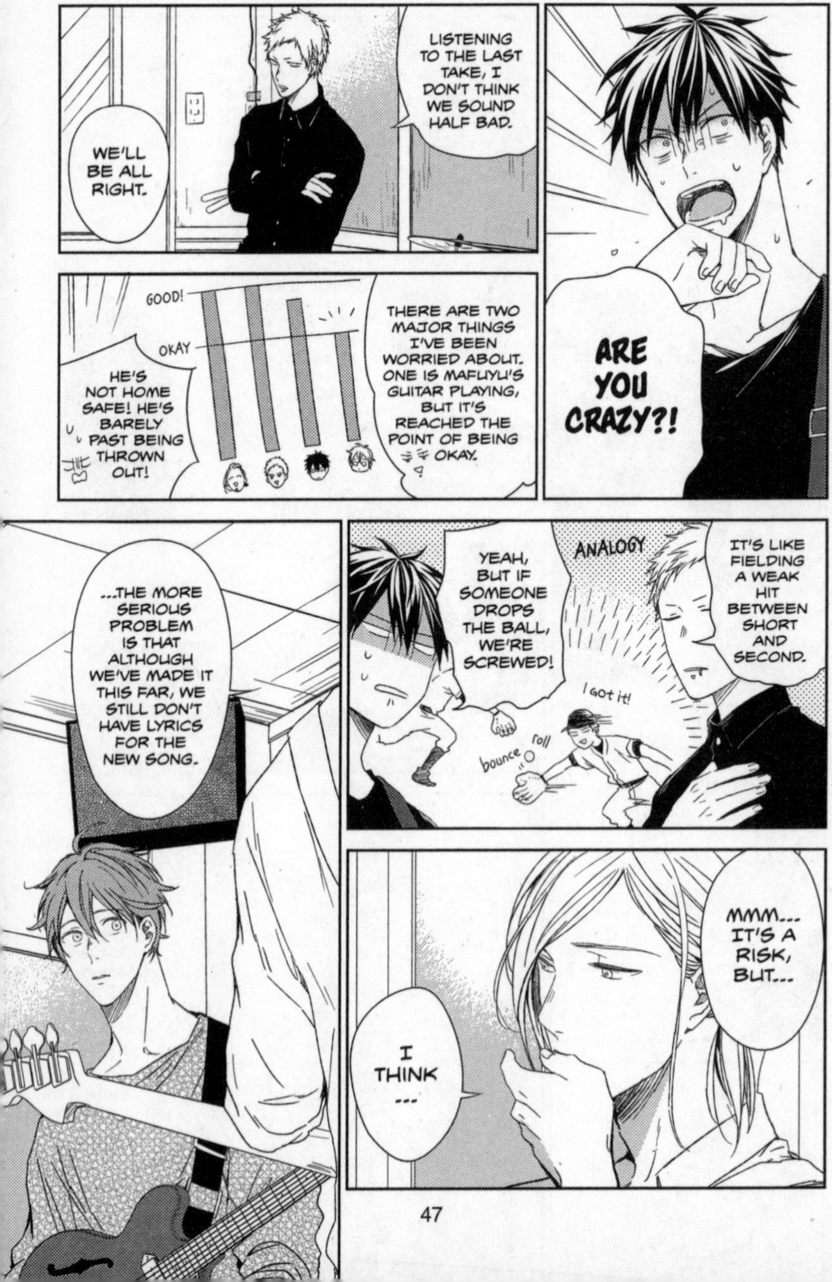
ARE YOU CRAZY?!
LISTENING TO THE LAST TAKE, I DON'T THINK WE SOUND HALF BAD.
WE'LL BE ALL RIGHT.
THERE ARE TWO MAJOR THINGS I'VE BEEN WORRIED ABOUT. ONE IS MAFUYU'S GUITAR PLAYING, BUT IT'S REACHED THE POINT OF BEING OKAY.
GOOD!
OKAY
HE'S NOT HOME SAFE! HE'S BARELY PAST BEING THROWN OUT!
IT'S LIKE FIELDING A WEAK HIT BETWEEN SHORT AND SECOND.
ANALOGY
YEAH, BUT IF SOMEONE DROPS THE BALL, WE'RE SCREWED!
I got it!
roll
bounce
MMM... IT'S A RISK, BUT...
I THINK ...
...THE MORE SERIOUS PROBLEM IS THAT ALTHOUGH WE'VE MADE IT THIS FAR, WE STILL DON'T HAVE LYRICS FOR THE NEW SONG.

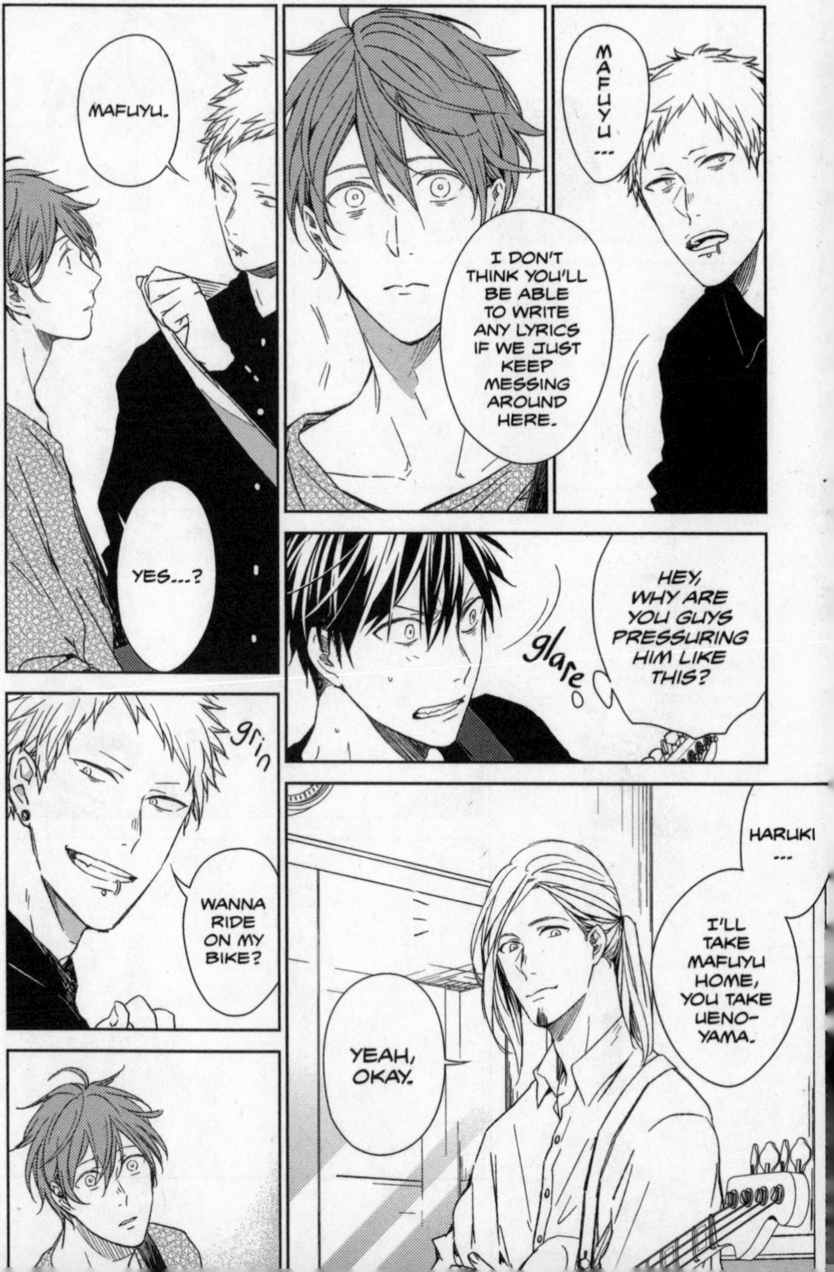
MAFUYU...
I DON'T THINK YOU'LL BE ABLE TO WRITE ANY LYRICS IF WE JUST KEEP MESSING AROUND HERE.
HEY, WHY ARE YOU GUYS PRESSURING HIM LIKE THIS?
glare
MAFUYU.
YES...?
HARUKI...
I'LL TAKE MAFUYU HOME, YOU TAKE UENO-YAMA.
YEAH, OKAY.
grin
WANNA RIDE ON MY BIKE?

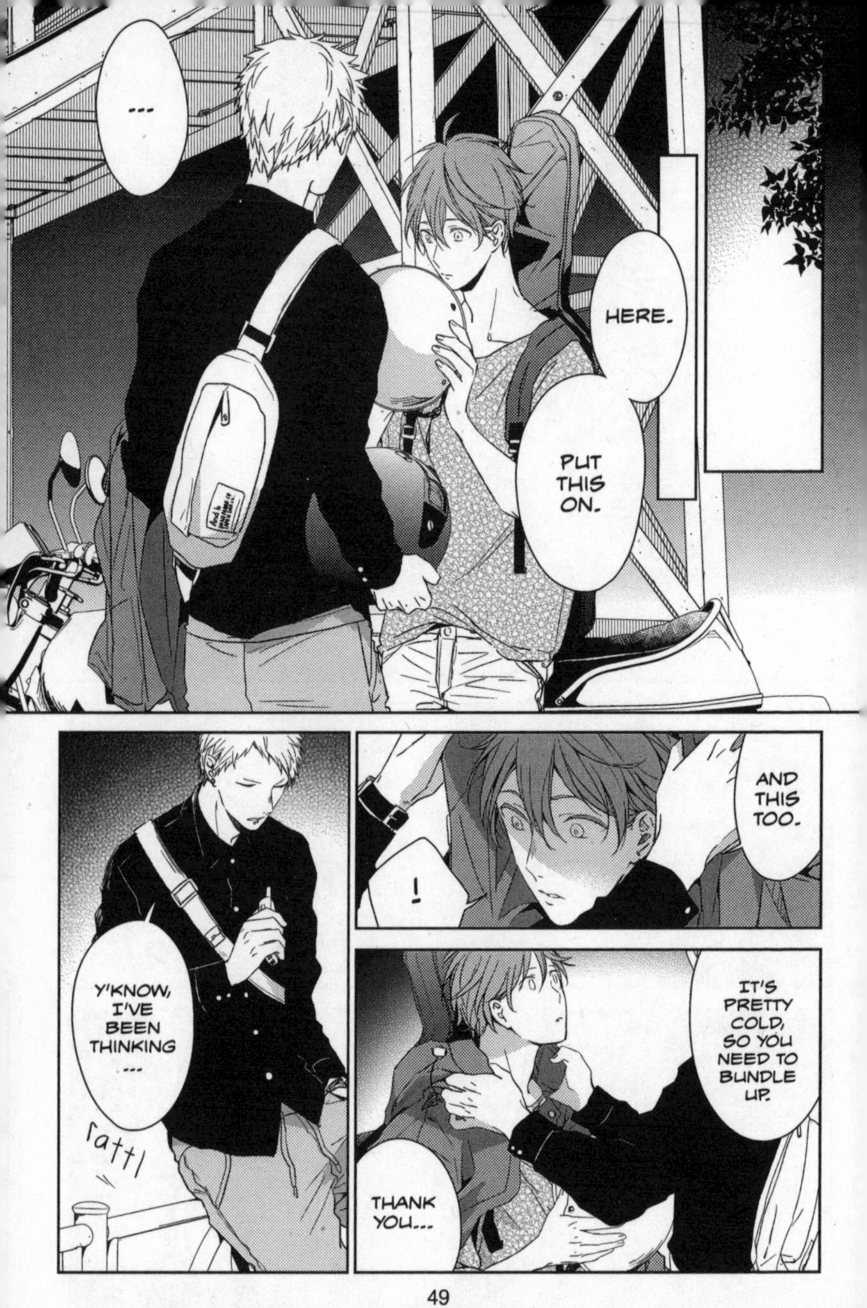
HERE.
PUT THIS ON.
...
AND THIS TOO.
!
IT'S PRETTY COLD, SO YOU NEED TO BUNDLE UP.
THANK YOU...
Y'KNOW, I'VE BEEN THINKING...
rattl

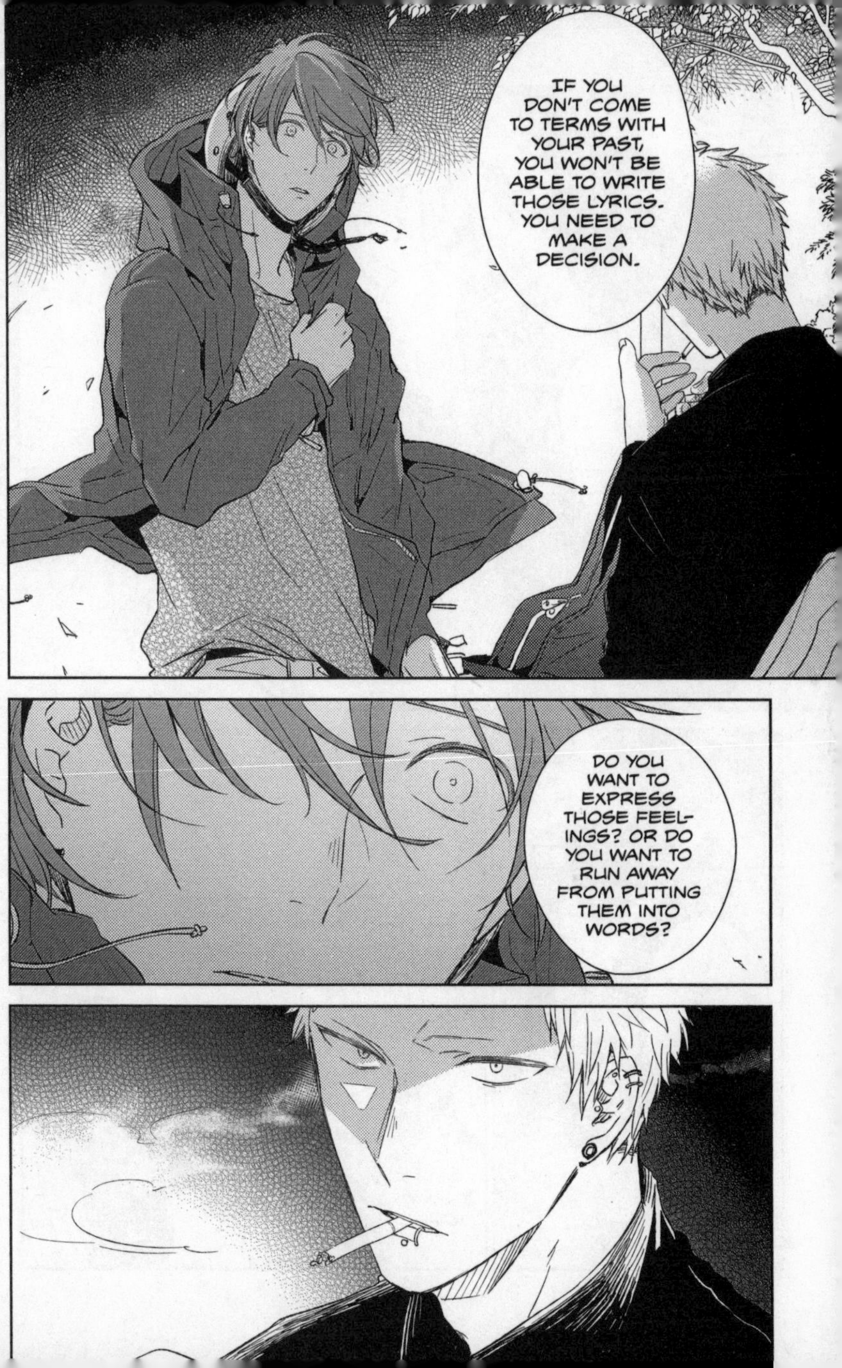
IF YOU DON'T COME TO TERMS WITH YOUR PAST, YOU WON'T BE ABLE TO WRITE THOSE LYRICS. YOU NEED TO MAKE A DECISION.
DO YOU WANT TO EXPRESS THOSE FEEL-INGS? OR DO YOU WANT TO RUN AWAY FROM PUTTING THEM INTO WORDS?

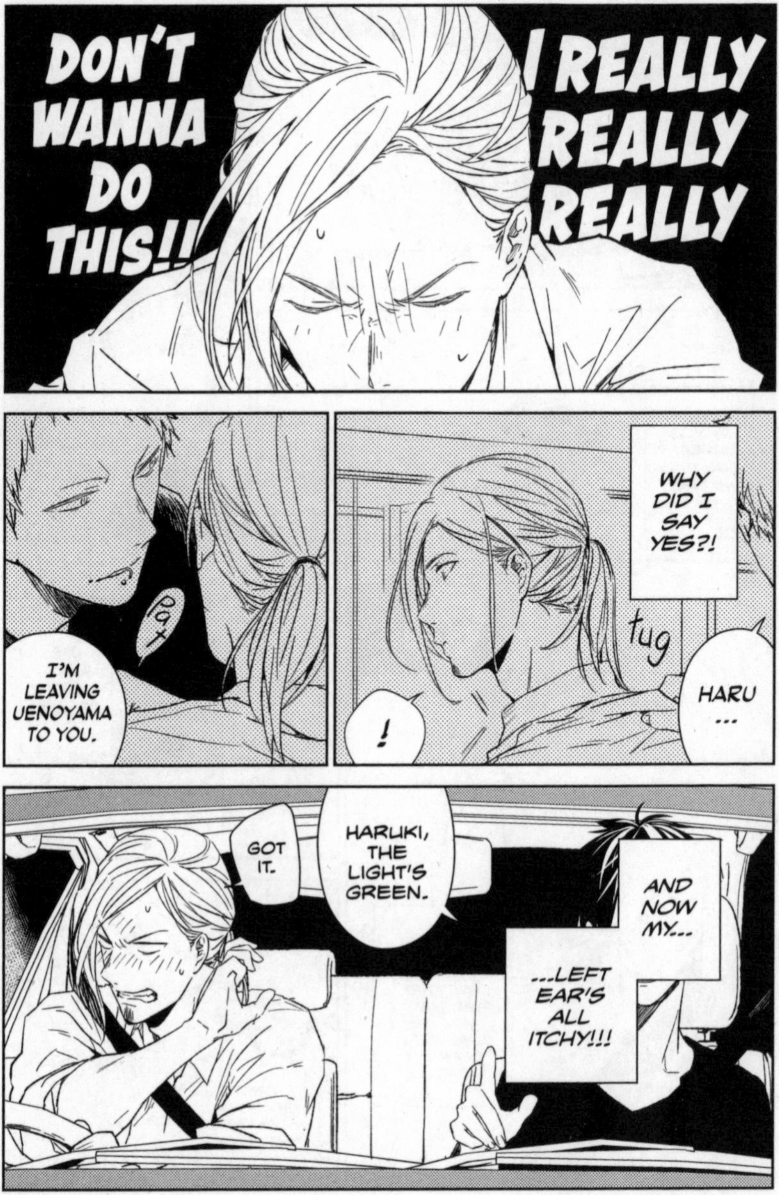
I REALLY REALLY REALLY
DON'T WANNA DO THIS!!!
WHY DID I SAY YES?!
tug
HARU...
!
pat
I'M LEAVING UENOYAMA TO YOU.
AND NOW MY...
...LEFT EAR'S ALL ITCHY!!!
HARUKI, THE LIGHT'S GREEN.
GOT IT.

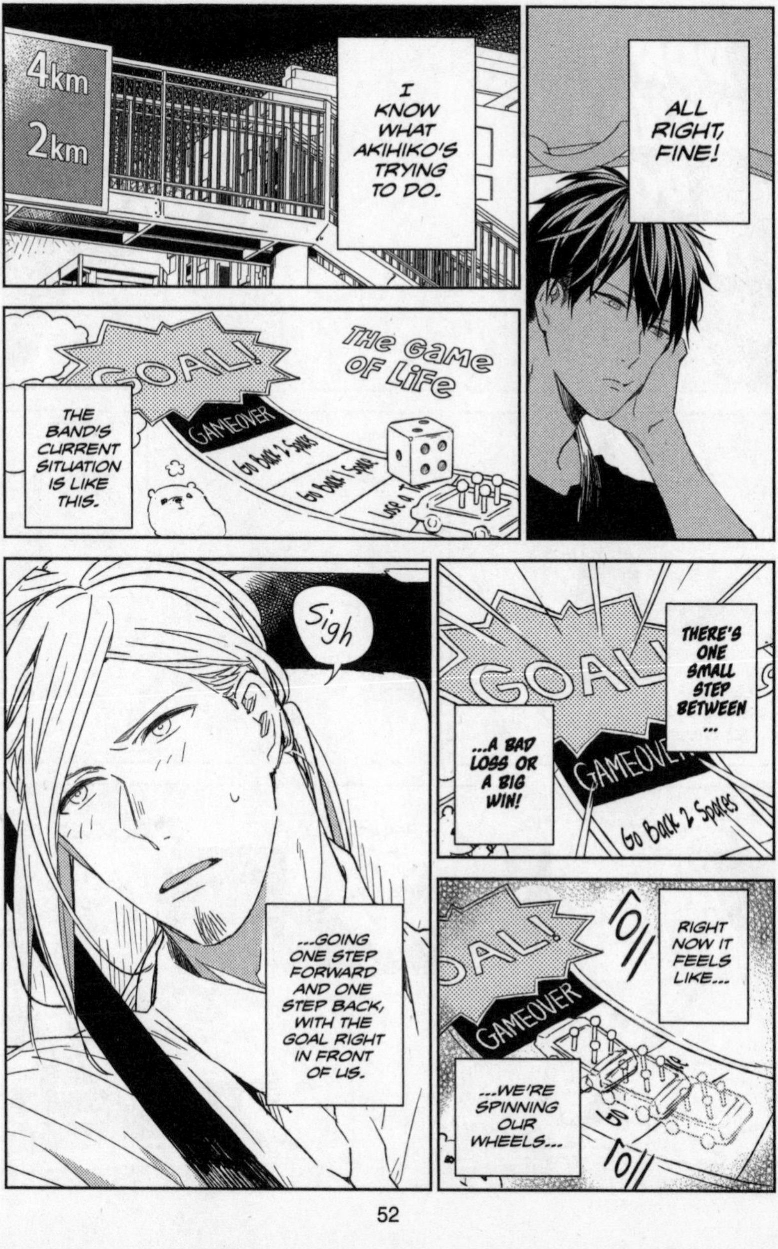

ALL RIGHT, FINE!
I KNOW WHAT AKIHIKO'S TRYING TO DO.
4km
2km
The Game of Life
GOAL!
GAMEOVER
Go Back 2 Spaces
Go Back 1 Space
THE BAND'S CURRENT SITUATION IS LIKE THIS.
THERE'S ONE SMALL STEP BETWEEN...
GOAL!
...A BAD LOSS OR A BIG WIN!
GAMEOVER
Go Back 2 Spaces
RIGHT NOW IT FEELS LIKE...
GOAL!
GAMEOVER
...WE'RE SPINNING OUR WHEELS...
Sigh
...GOING ONE STEP FORWARD AND ONE STEP BACK, WITH THE GOAL RIGHT IN FRONT OF US.

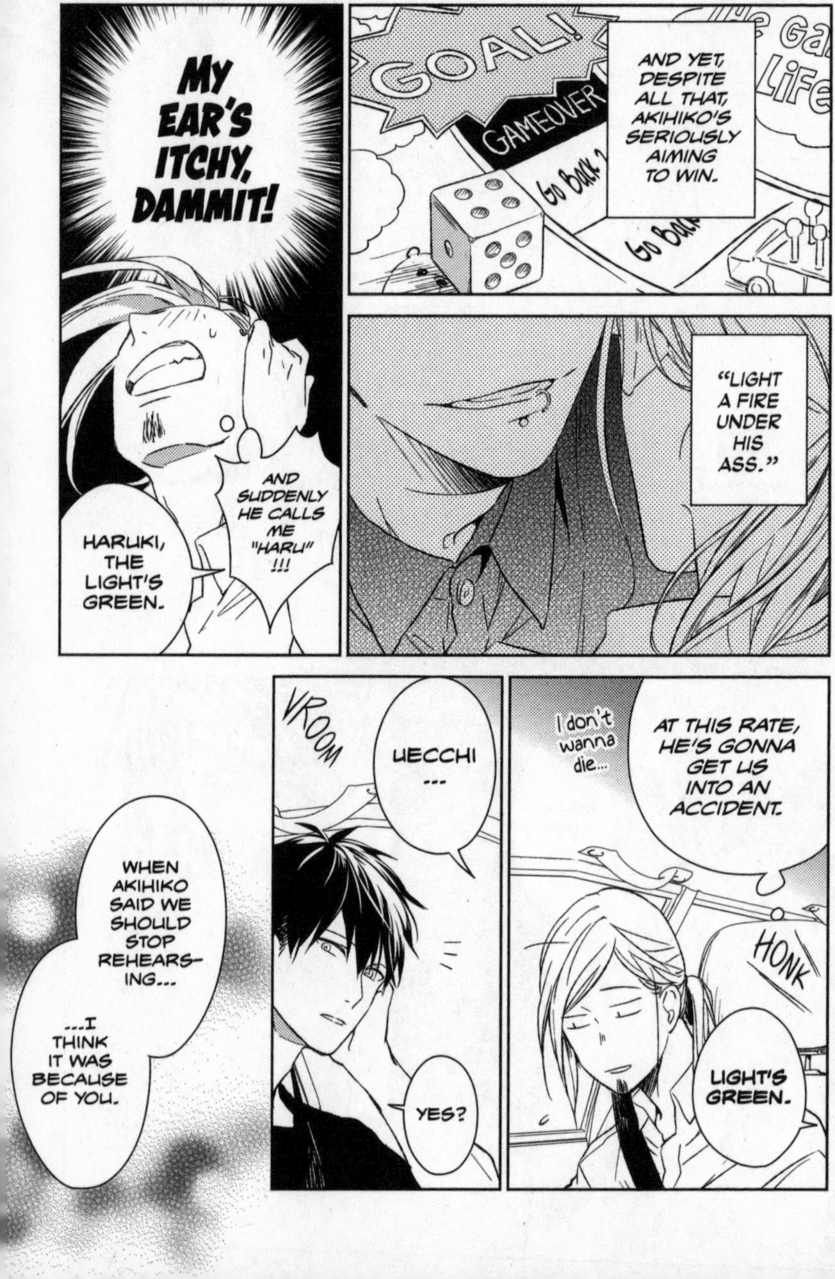
GOAL!
GAMEOVER
AND YET, DESPITE ALL THAT, AKIHIKO'S SERIOUSLY AIMING TO WIN.
"LIGHT A FIRE UNDER HIS ASS."
MY EAR'S ITCHY, DAMMIT!
AND SUDDENLY HE CALLS ME "HARU" !!!
HARUKI, THE LIGHT'S GREEN.
AT THIS RATE, HE'S GONNA GET US INTO AN ACCIDENT.
I don't wanna die...
HONK
LIGHT'S GREEN.
UECCHI ...
VROOM
YES?
WHEN AKIHIKO SAID WE SHOULD STOP REHEARS-ING...
...I THINK IT WAS BECAUSE OF YOU.

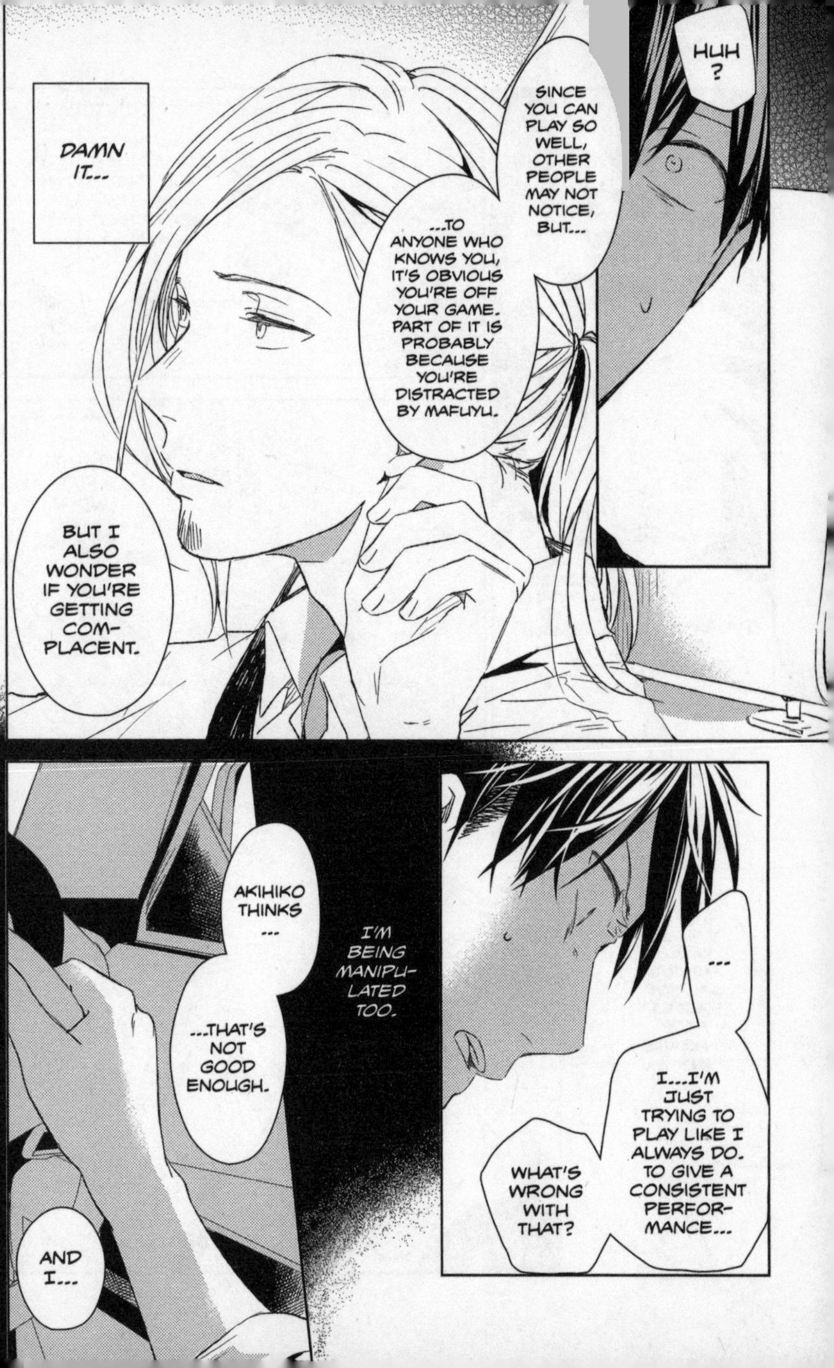
HUH?
SINCE YOU CAN PLAY SO WELL, OTHER PEOPLE MAY NOT NOTICE, BUT...
...TO ANYONE WHO KNOWS YOU, IT'S OBVIOUS YOU'RE OFF YOUR GAME. PART OF IT IS PROBABLY BECAUSE YOU'RE DISTRACTED BY MAFUYU.
DAMN IT...
BUT I ALSO WONDER IF YOU'RE GETTING COM-PLACENT.
...
I...I'M JUST TRYING TO PLAY LIKE I ALWAYS DO. TO GIVE A CONSISTENT PERFOR-MANCE...
WHAT'S WRONG WITH THAT?
AKIHIKO THINKS...
...THAT'S NOT GOOD ENOUGH.
AND I...
I'M BEING MANIPU-LATED TOO.

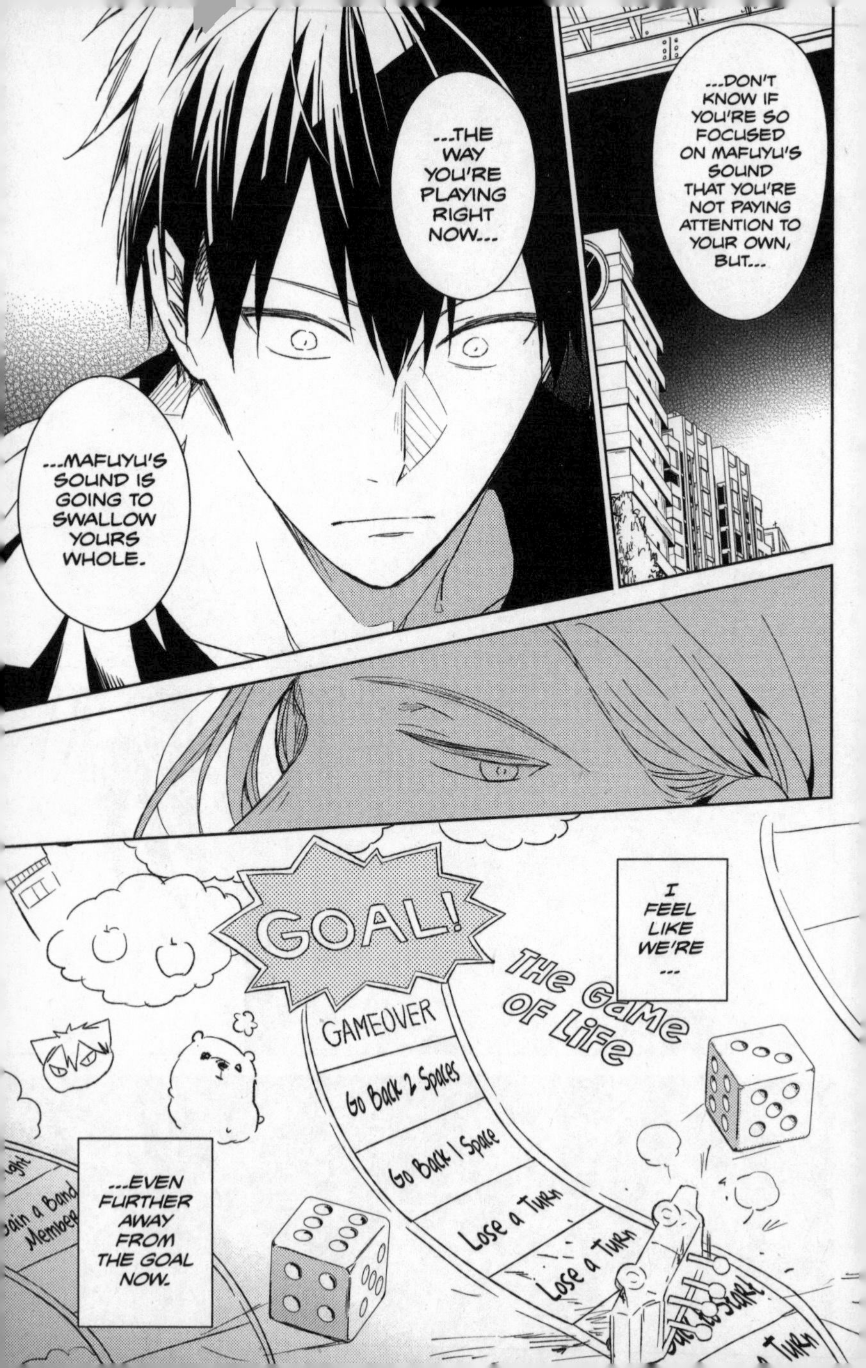
...DON'T KNOW IF YOU'RE SO FOCUSED ON MAFUYU'S SOUND THAT YOU'RE NOT PAYING ATTENTION TO YOUR OWN, BUT...
...THE WAY YOU'RE PLAYING RIGHT NOW...
...MAFUYU'S SOUND IS GOING TO SWALLOW YOURS WHOLE.
I FEEL LIKE WE'RE ...
GOAL!
The Game of Life
GAMEOVER
Go Back 2 Spaces
Go Back 1 Space
Lose a Turn
Lose a Turn
...EVEN FURTHER AWAY FROM THE GOAL NOW.

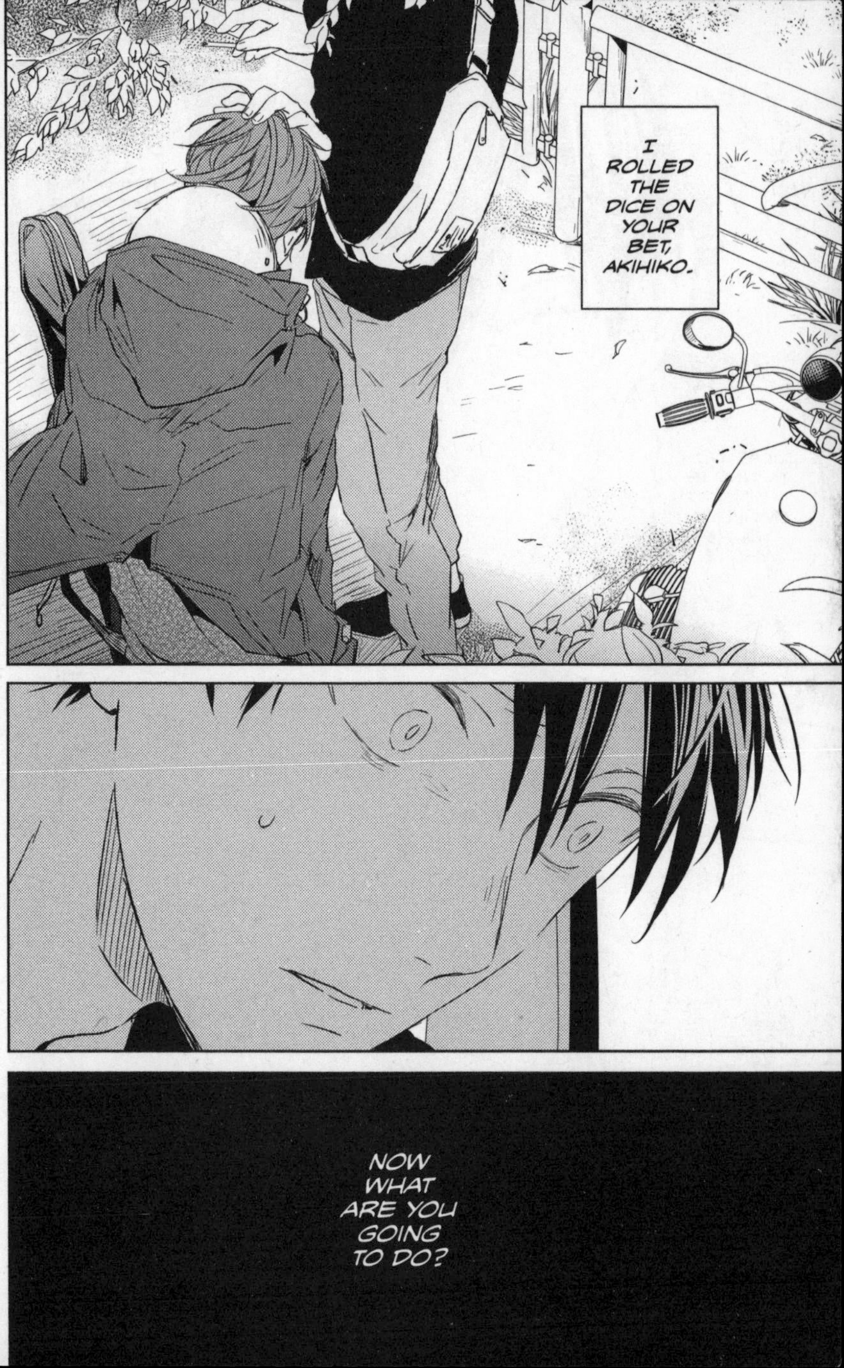
I ROLLED THE DICE ON YOUR BET, AKIHIKO.
NOW WHAT ARE YOU GOING TO DO?

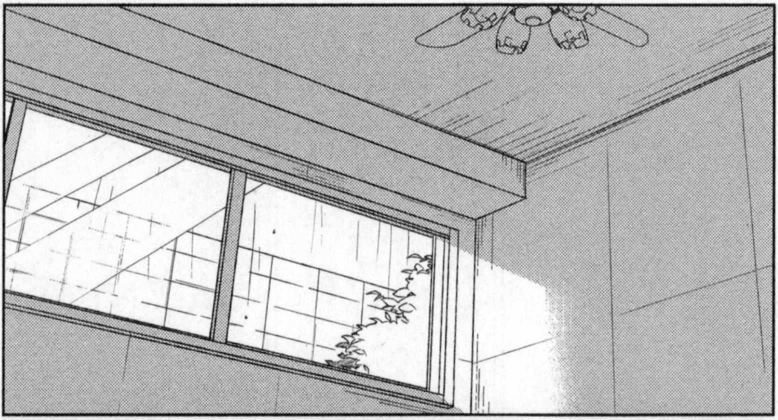

Seven Days Until the Concert

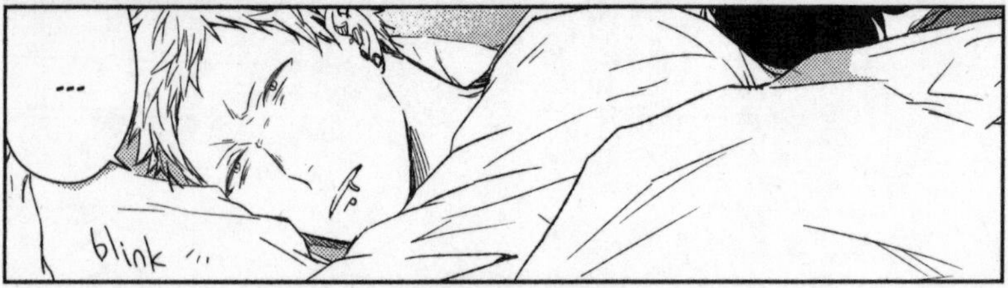
...
blink ...

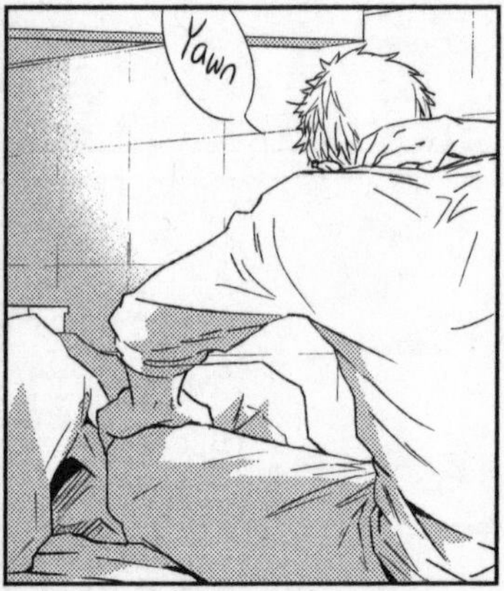
Yawn

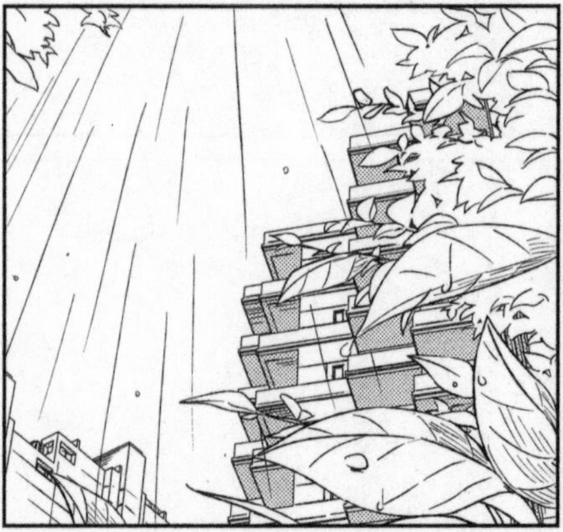

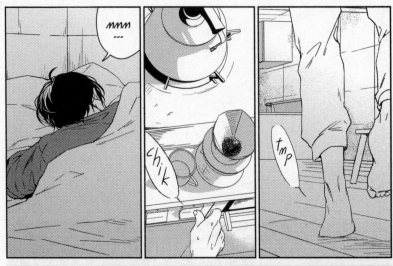

mmm ---

chik

tmp

The approach of a low-pressure front this morn- ing...

...will mean heavy rain for the Kanto

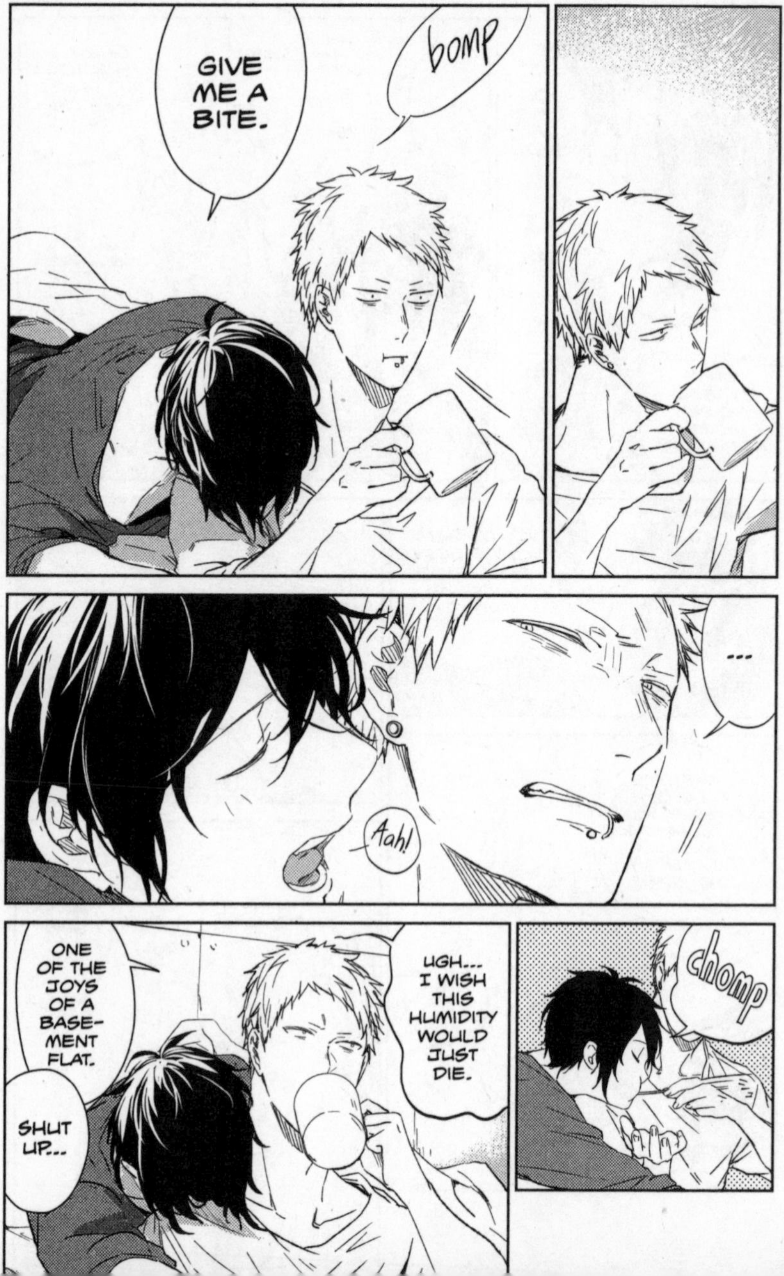
bomp
GIVE ME A BITE.
...
Aah!
chomp
UGH... I WISH THIS HUMIDITY WOULD JUST DIE.
ONE OF THE JOYS OF A BASEMENT FLAT.
SHUT UP...

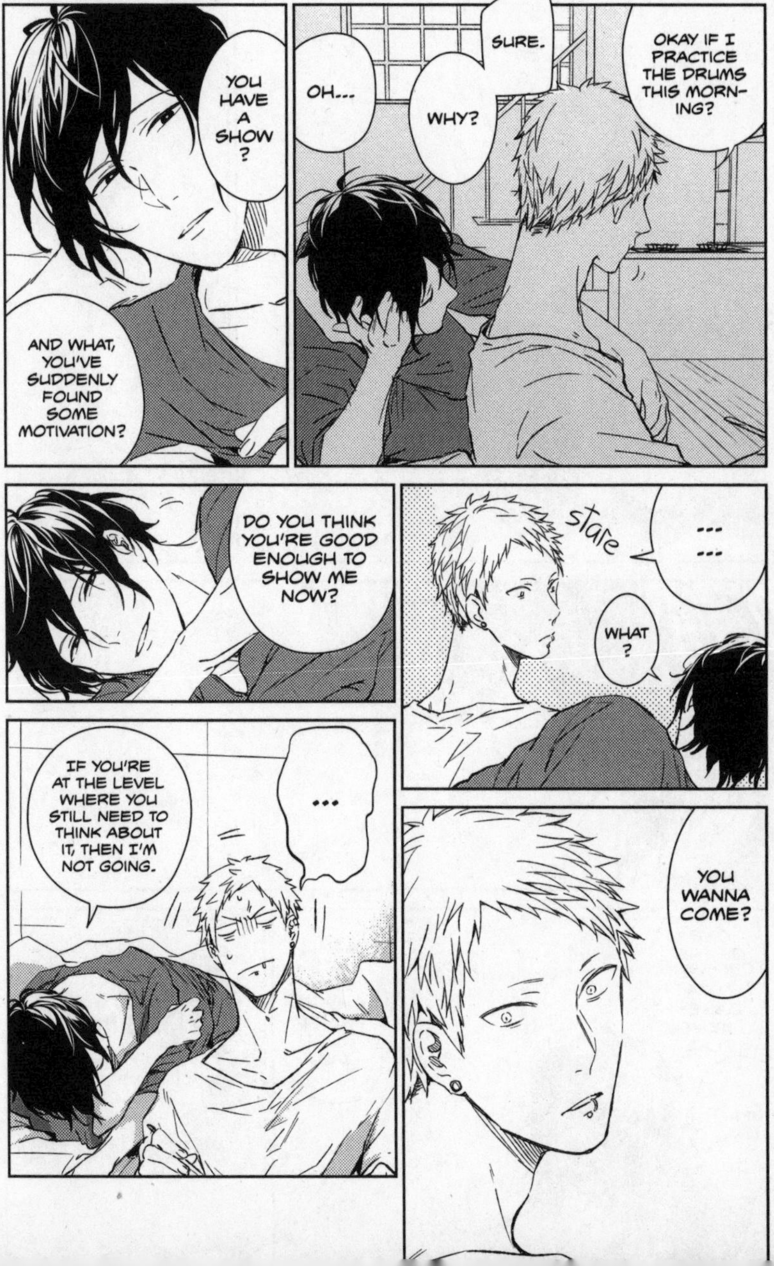
OKAY IF I PRACTICE THE DRUMS THIS MORNING?
SURE.
WHY?
OH...
YOU HAVE A SHOW?
AND WHAT, YOU'VE SUDDENLY FOUND SOME MOTIVATION?
stare
... ...
WHAT?
DO YOU THINK YOU'RE GOOD ENOUGH TO SHOW ME NOW?
YOU WANNA COME?
IF YOU'RE AT THE LEVEL WHERE YOU STILL NEED TO THINK ABOUT IT, THEN I'M NOT GOING.
...

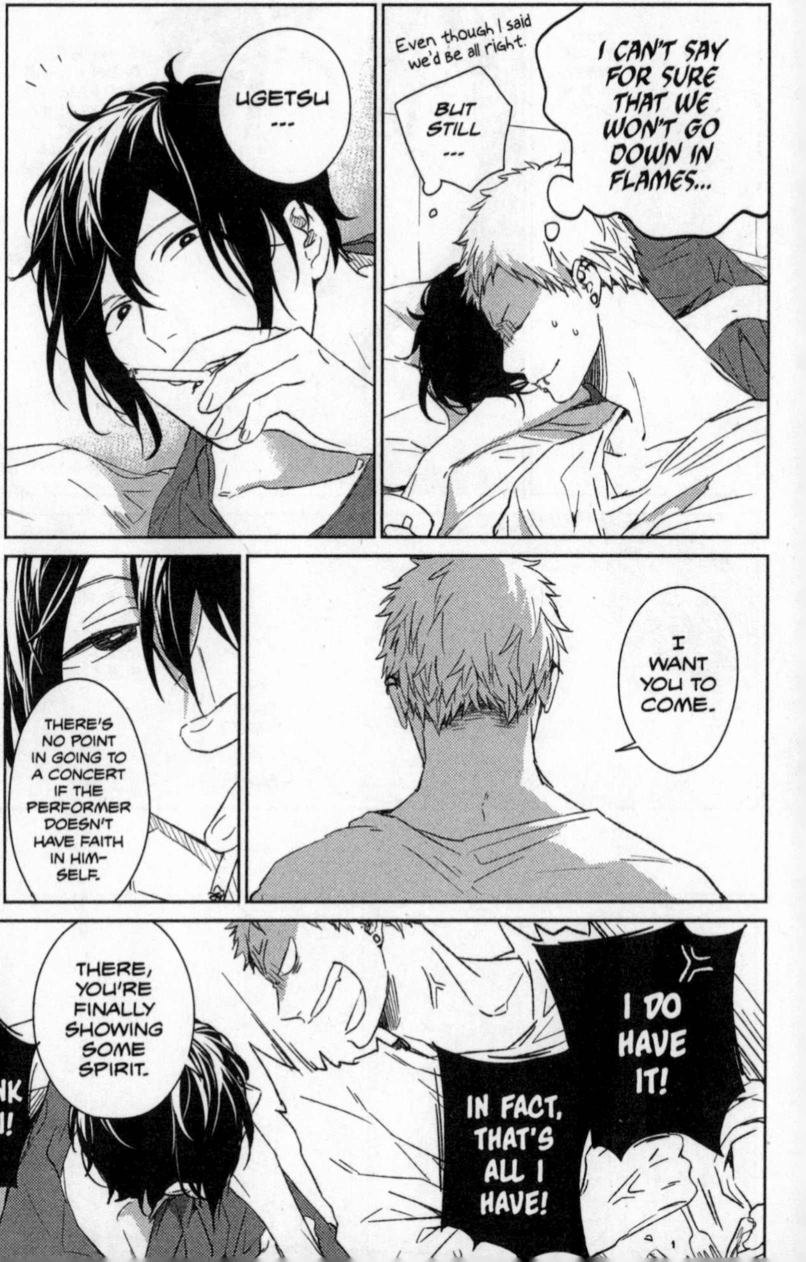
I CAN'T SAY FOR SURE THAT WE WON'T GO DOWN IN FLAMES...
Even though I said we'd be all right.
BUT STILL ---
UGETSU ---
I WANT YOU TO COME.
THERE'S NO POINT IN GOING TO A CONCERT IF THE PERFORMER DOESN'T HAVE FAITH IN HIM-SELF.
I DO HAVE IT!
IN FACT, THAT'S ALL I HAVE!
THERE, YOU'RE FINALLY SHOWING SOME SPIRIT.
THANK YOU!

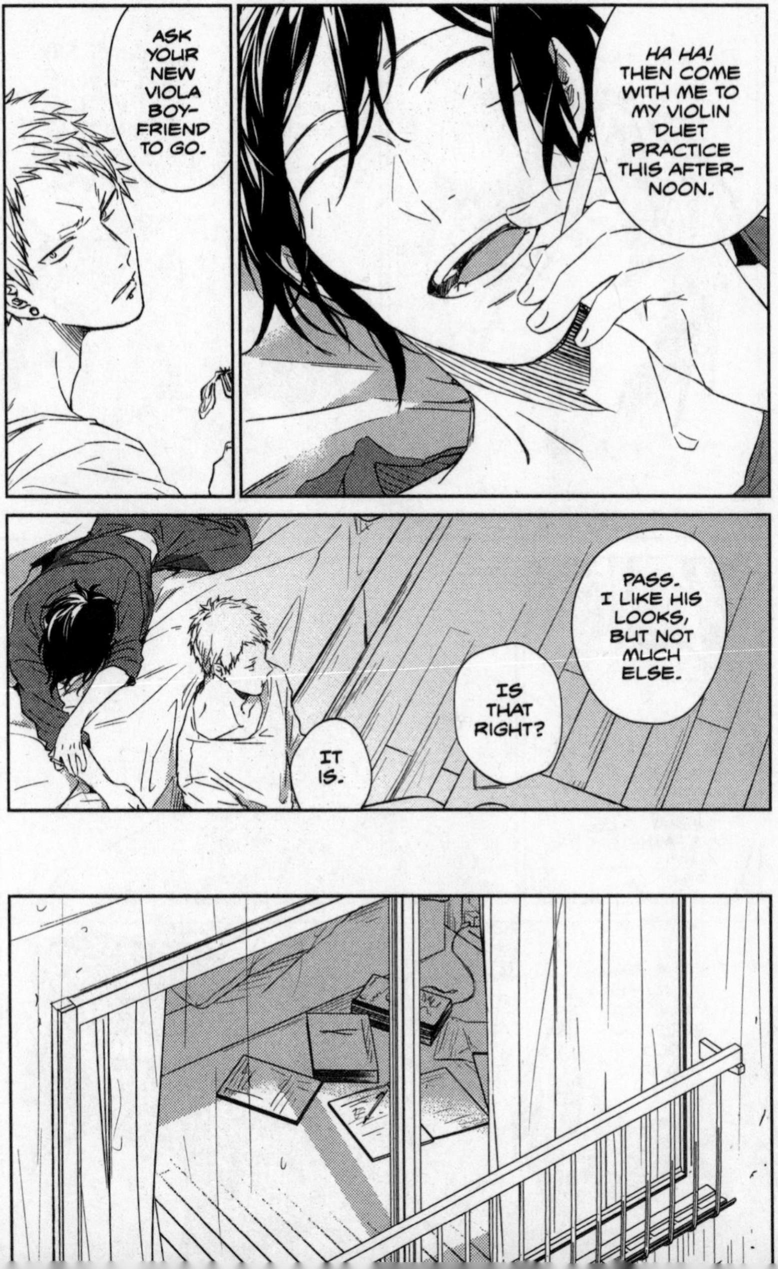
HA HA! THEN COME WITH ME TO MY VIOLIN DUET PRACTICE THIS AFTER-NOON.
ASK YOUR NEW VIOLA BOY-FRIEND TO GO.
PASS. I LIKE HIS LOOKS, BUT NOT MUCH ELSE.
IS THAT RIGHT?
IT IS.

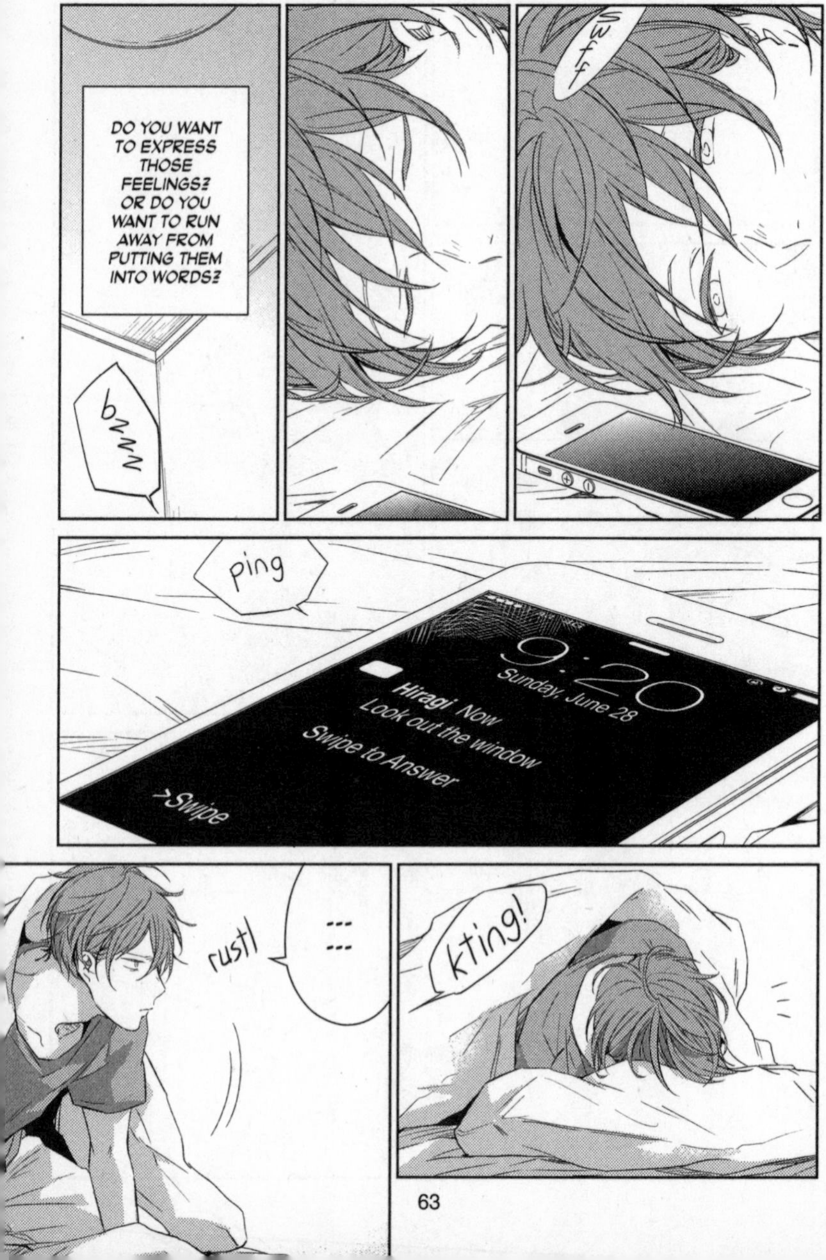
swff
DO YOU WANT TO EXPRESS THOSE FEELINGS? OR DO YOU WANT TO RUN AWAY FROM PUTTING THEM INTO WORDS?
bzzz
ping
9:20
Sunday, June 28
Hiragi Now
Look out the window
Swipe to Answer
>Swipe
kting!
......
rustl

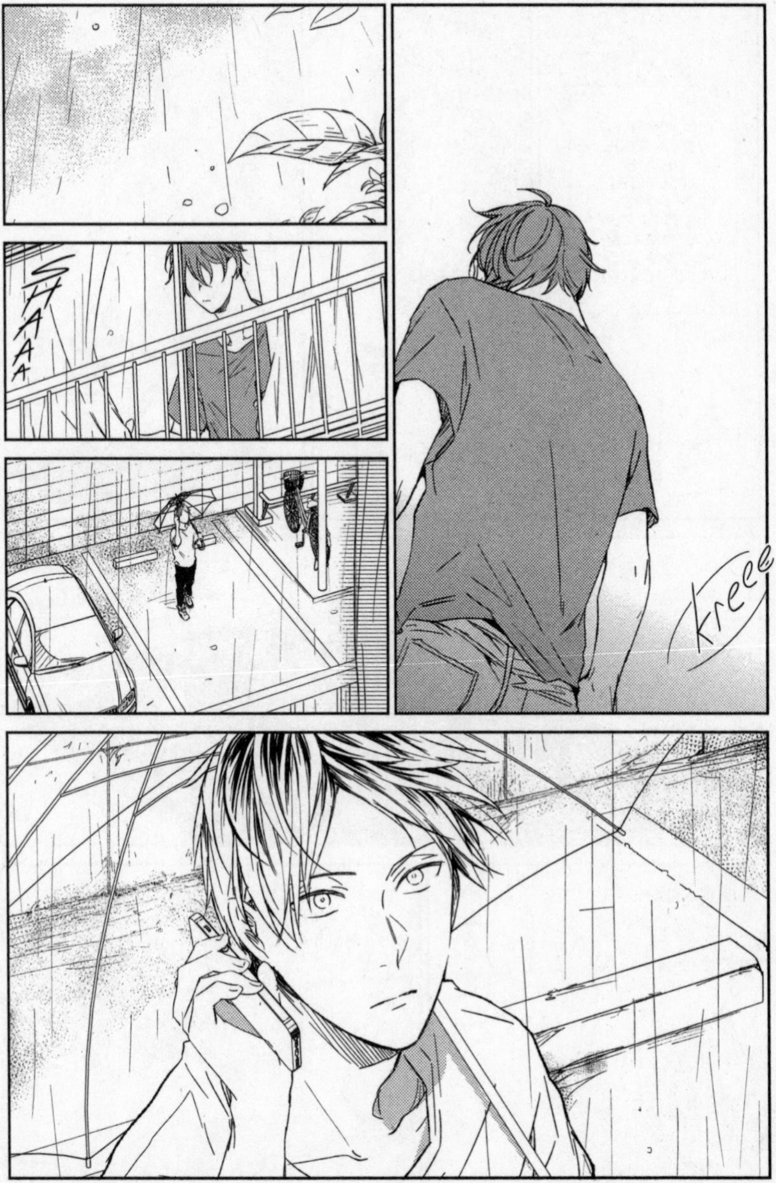
kreee
SHAAAA

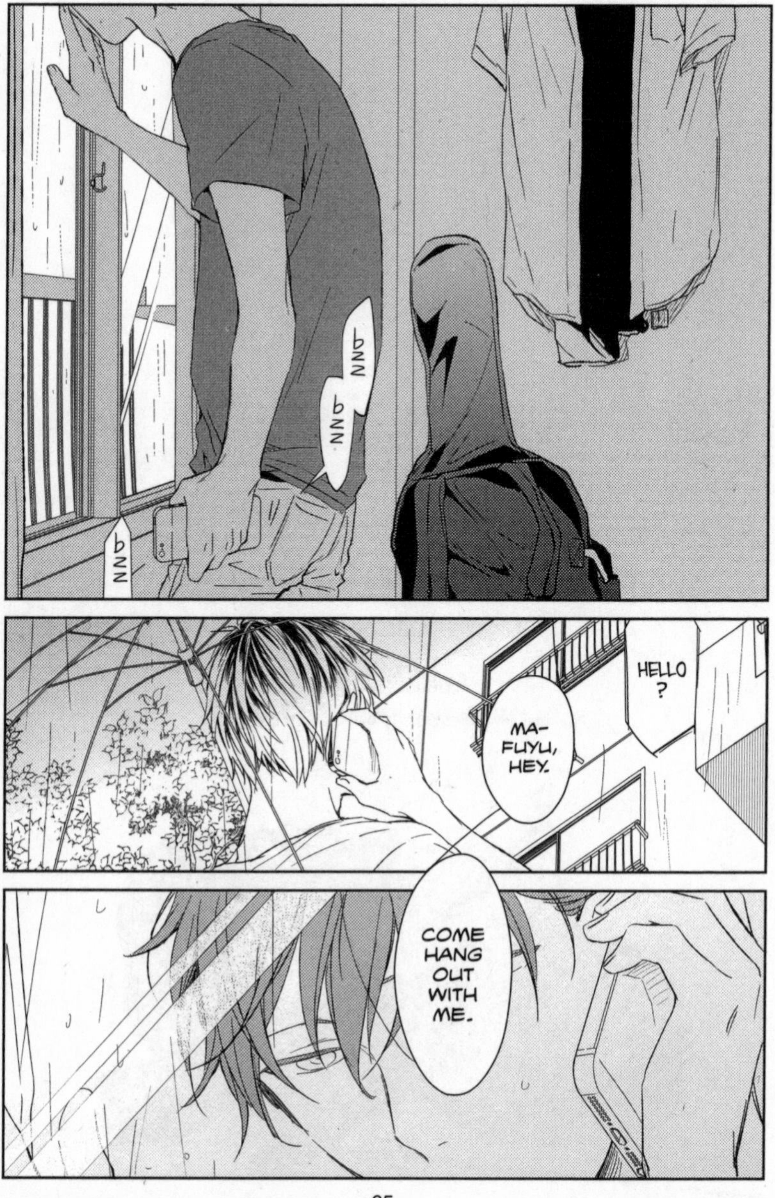
bzz
bzz
bzz
HELLO?
MA-FUYU, HEY.
COME HANG OUT WITH ME.

Ugetsu Murata (21)

175 cm
(Akihiko's classmate)

Birthday: 6/6 Sign: Gemini Blood Type: O

Violinist

Akihiko's roommate,
but he's frequently out of the country.

A Day in the Life (of Roommates)

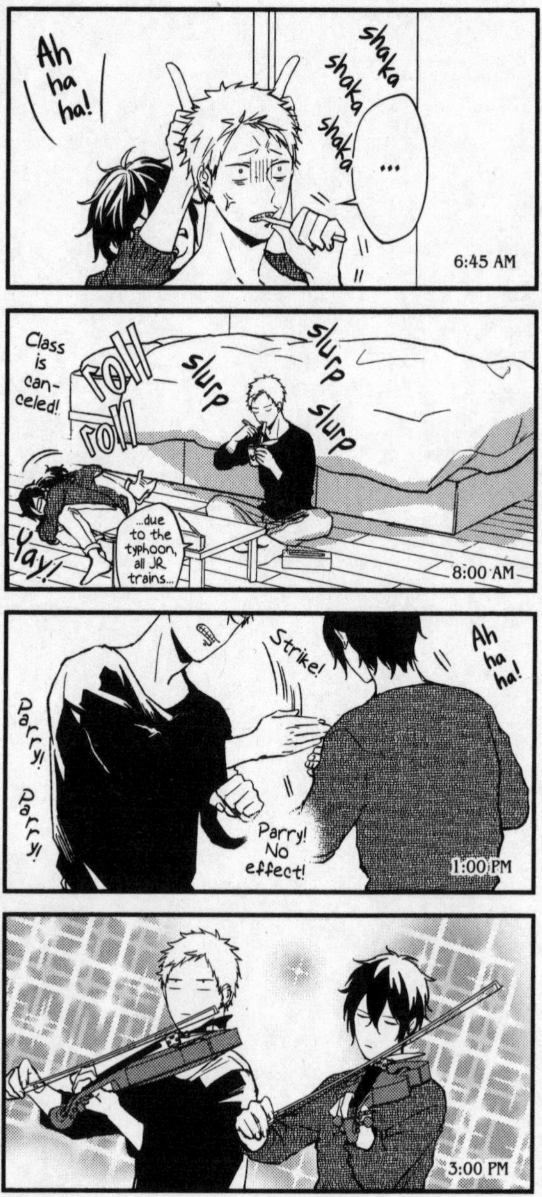
shaka
shaka
shaka
...
Ah ha ha!
6:45 AM
slurp
slurp
slurp
Class is can-celed!
roll
roll
...due to the typhoon, all JR trains...
Yay!
8:00 AM
Ah ha ha!
Strike!
Parry! No effect!
Parry!
Parry!
1:00 PM
3:00 PM

given

by Natsuki Kizu

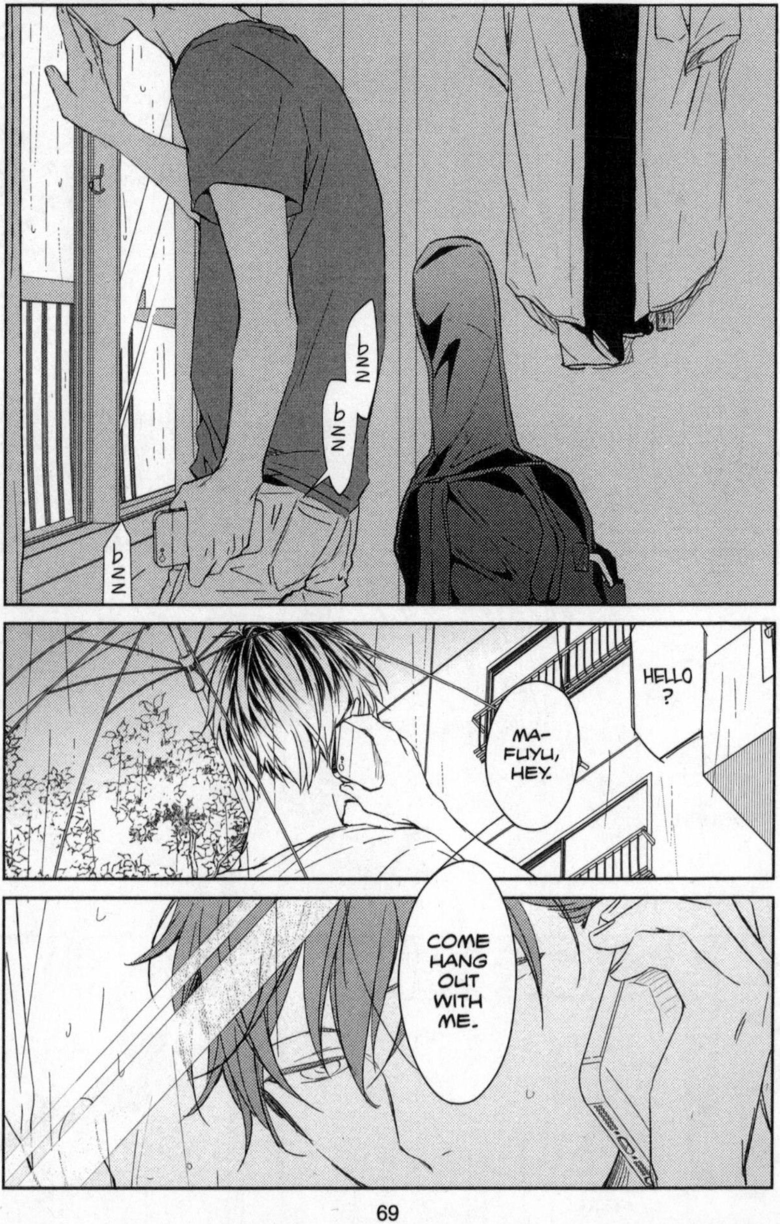
bzz
bzz
bzz
HELLO?
MA-FUYU, HEY.
COME HANG OUT WITH ME.

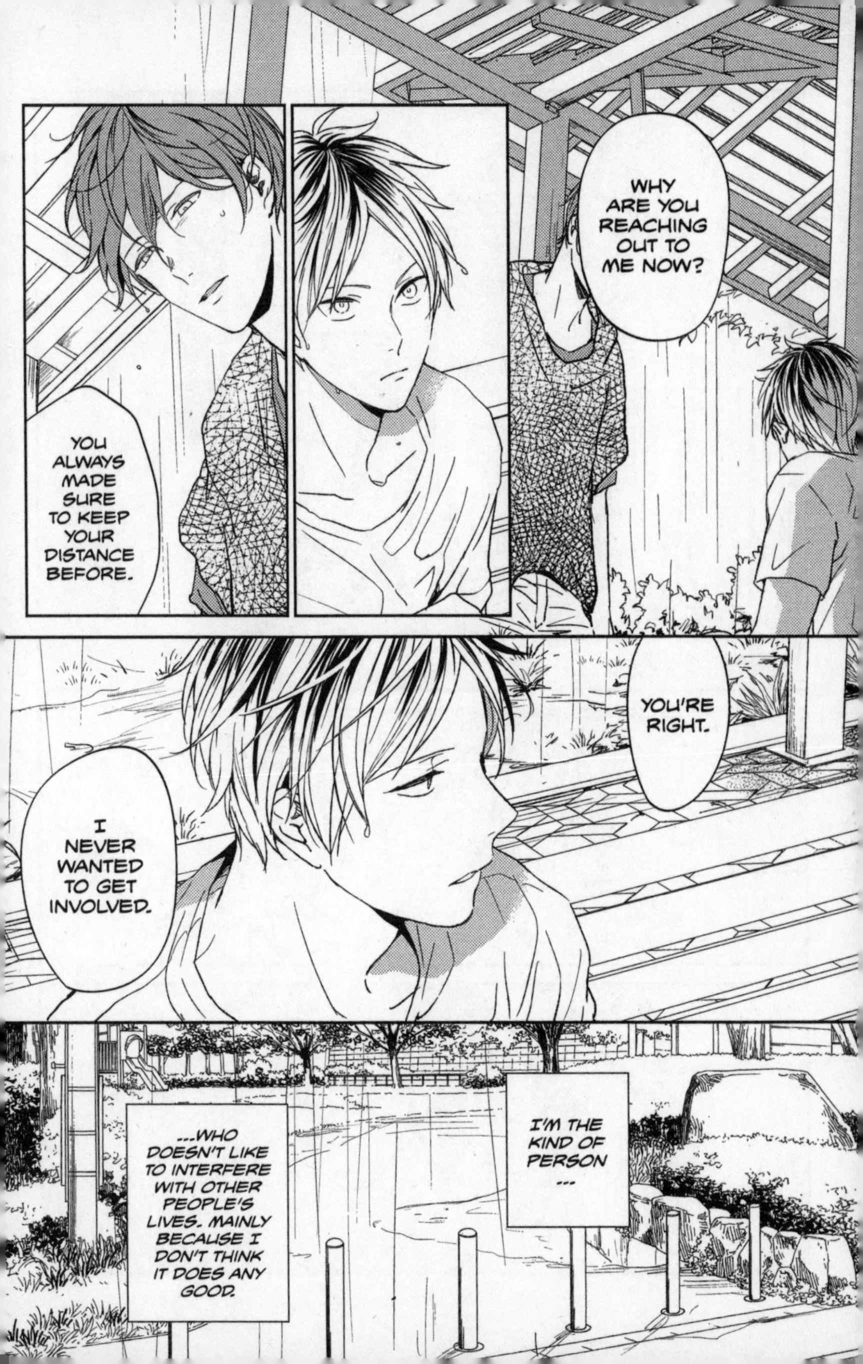
WHY ARE YOU REACHING OUT TO ME NOW?
YOU ALWAYS MADE SURE TO KEEP YOUR DISTANCE BEFORE.
YOU'RE RIGHT.
I NEVER WANTED TO GET INVOLVED.
I'M THE KIND OF PERSON ...
...WHO DOESN'T LIKE TO INTERFERE WITH OTHER PEOPLE'S LIVES. MAINLY BECAUSE I DON'T THINK IT DOES ANY GOOD.

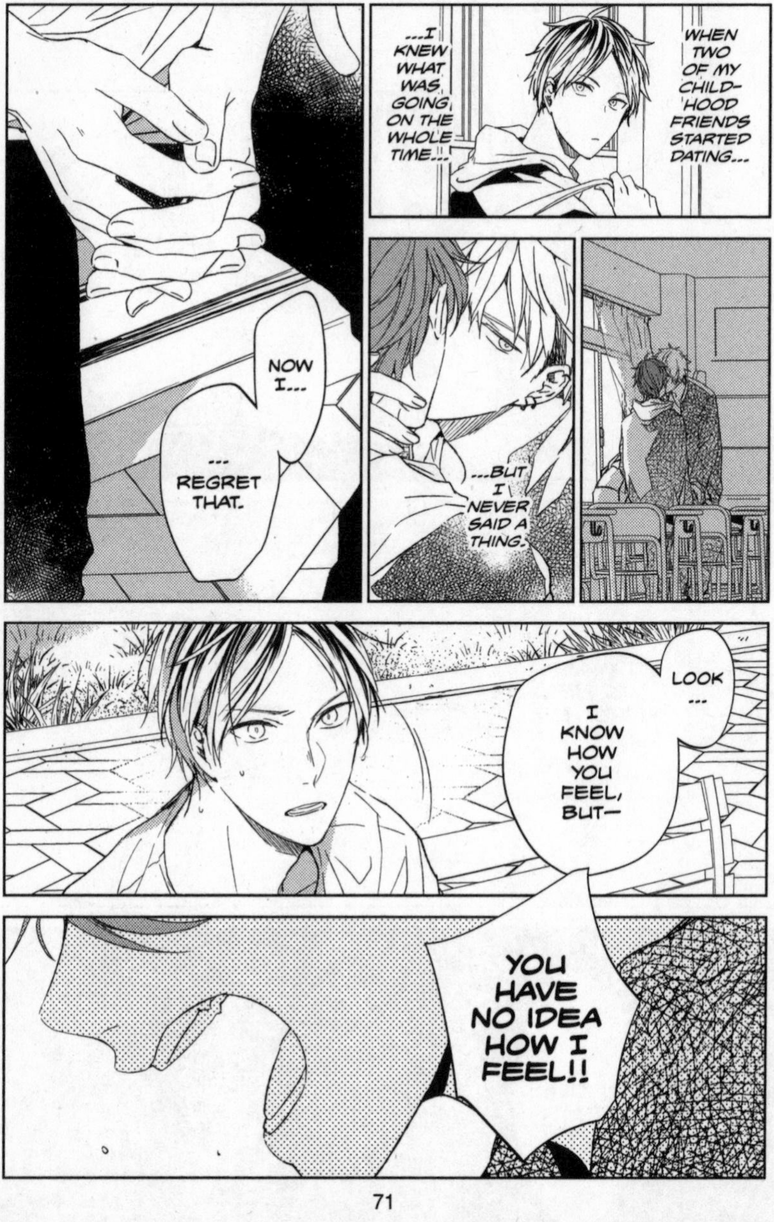
WHEN TWO OF MY CHILDHOOD FRIENDS STARTED DATING...
...I KNEW WHAT WAS GOING ON THE WHOLE TIME...
...BUT I NEVER SAID A THING.
NOW I...
...REGRET THAT.
LOOK...
I KNOW HOW YOU FEEL, BUT—
YOU HAVE NO IDEA HOW I FEEL!!

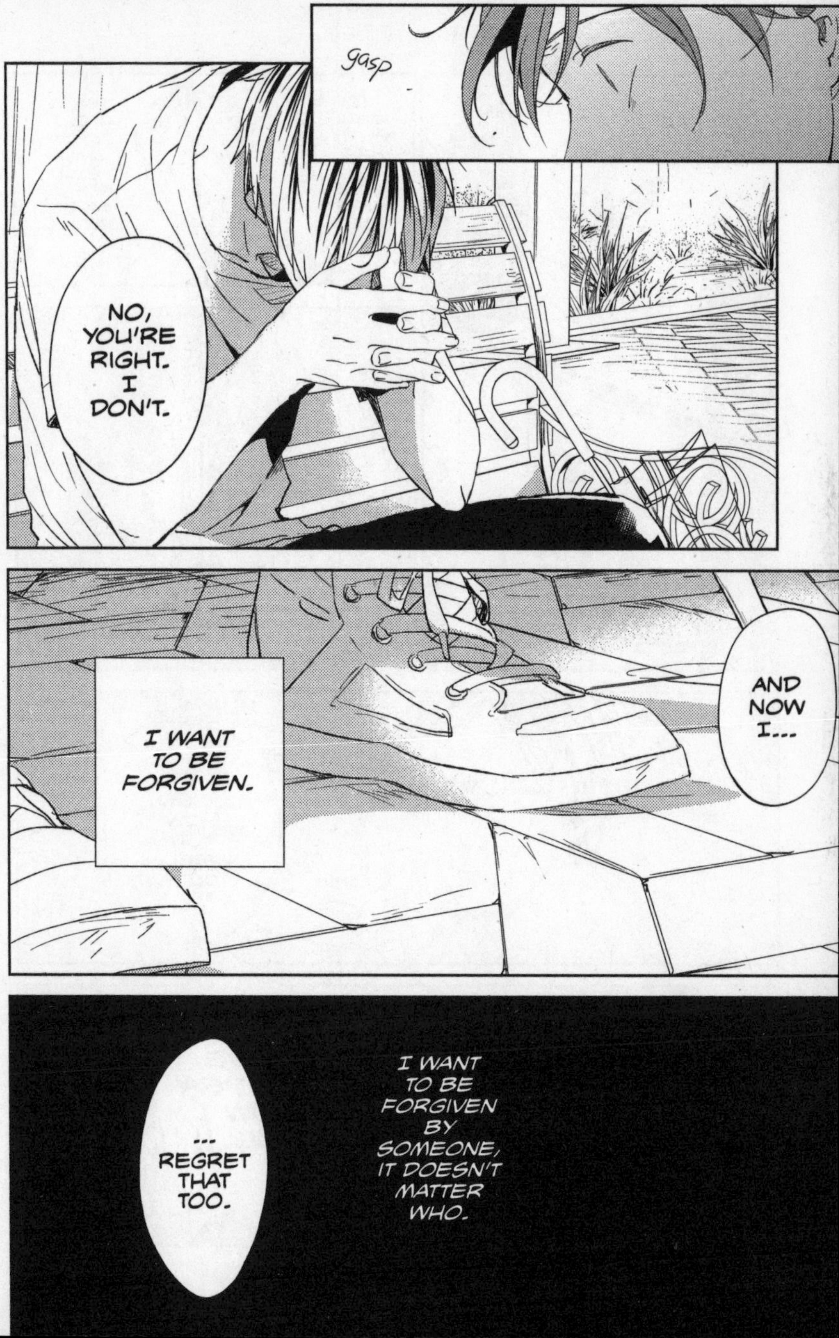
gasp
NO, YOU'RE RIGHT. I DON'T.
AND NOW I...
I WANT TO BE FORGIVEN.
I WANT TO BE FORGIVEN BY SOMEONE, IT DOESN'T MATTER WHO.
...REGRET THAT TOO.

chapter 9

given

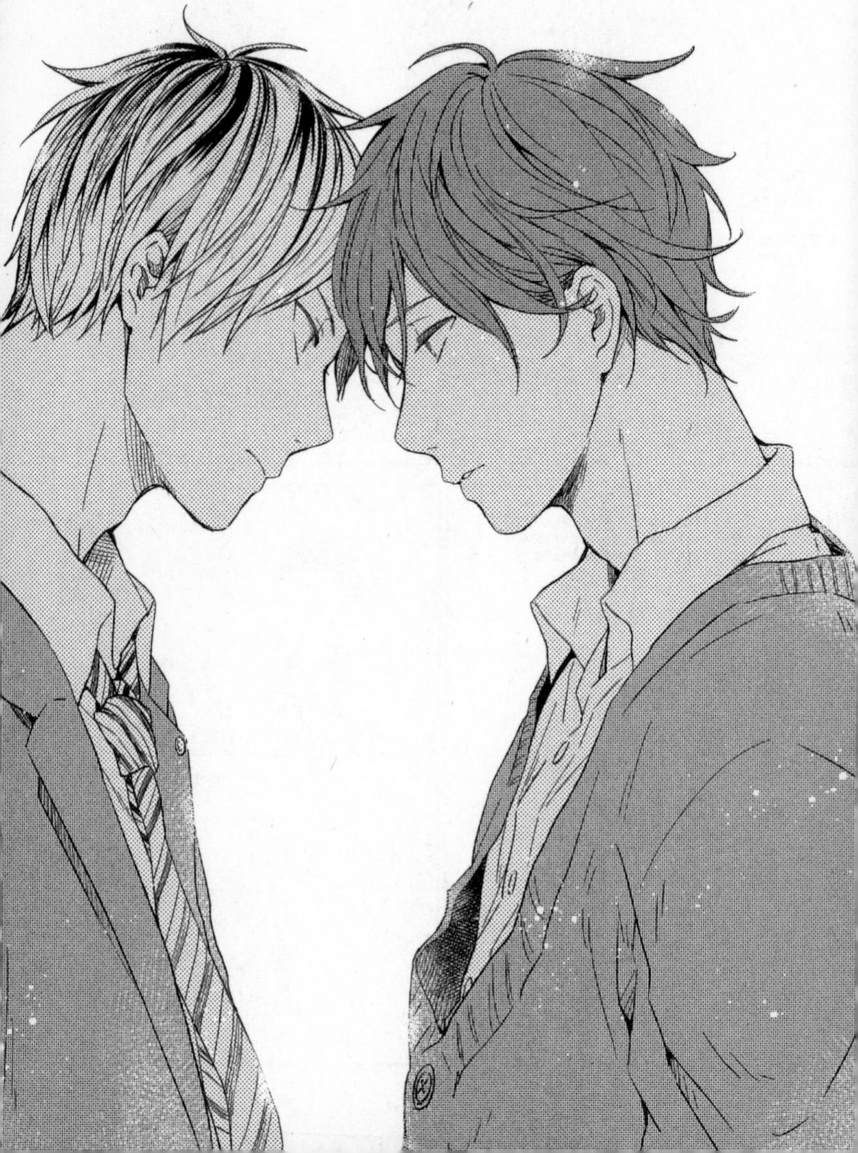

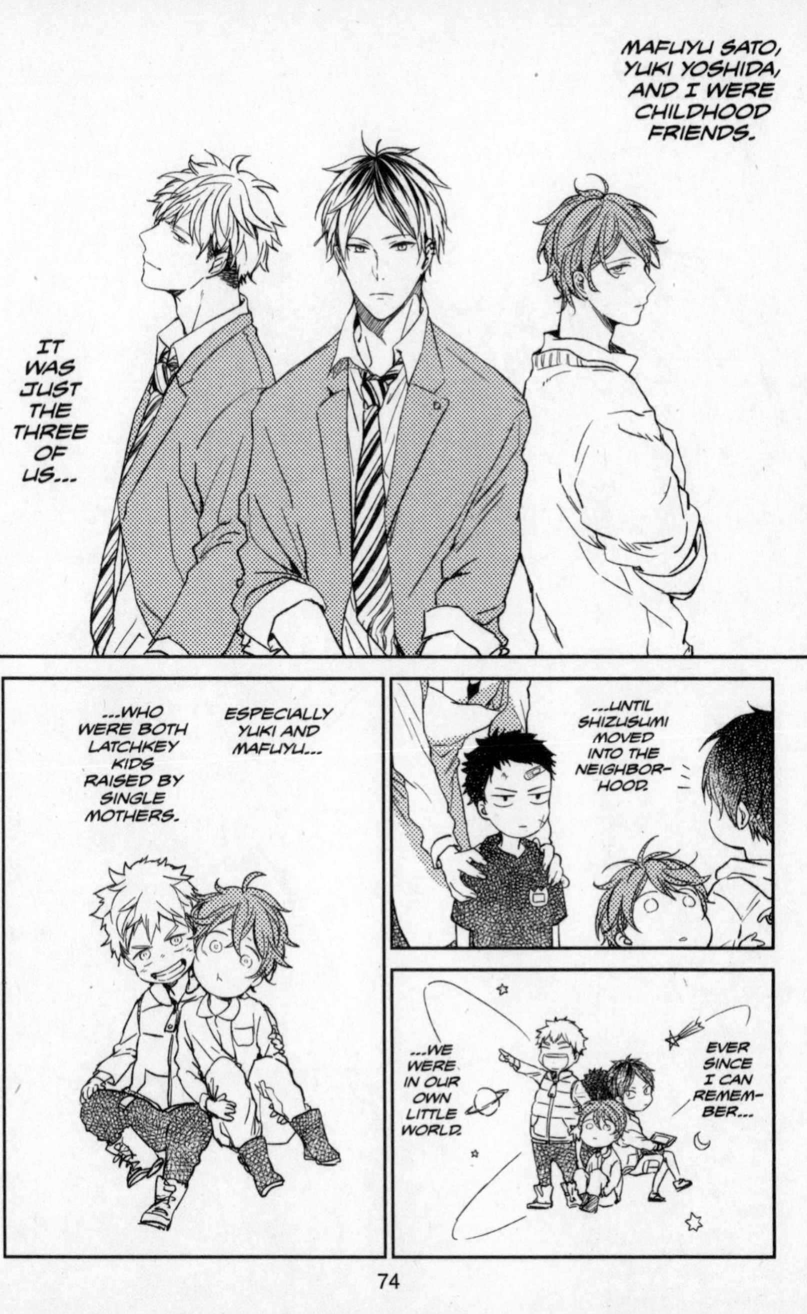
MAFUYU SATO, YUKI YOSHIDA, AND I WERE CHILDHOOD FRIENDS.
IT WAS JUST THE THREE OF US...
...UNTIL SHIZUSUMI MOVED INTO THE NEIGHBOR-HOOD.
EVER SINCE I CAN REMEM-BER...
...WE WERE IN OUR OWN LITTLE WORLD.
ESPECIALLY YUKI AND MAFUYU...
...WHO WERE BOTH LATCHKEY KIDS RAISED BY SINGLE MOTHERS.

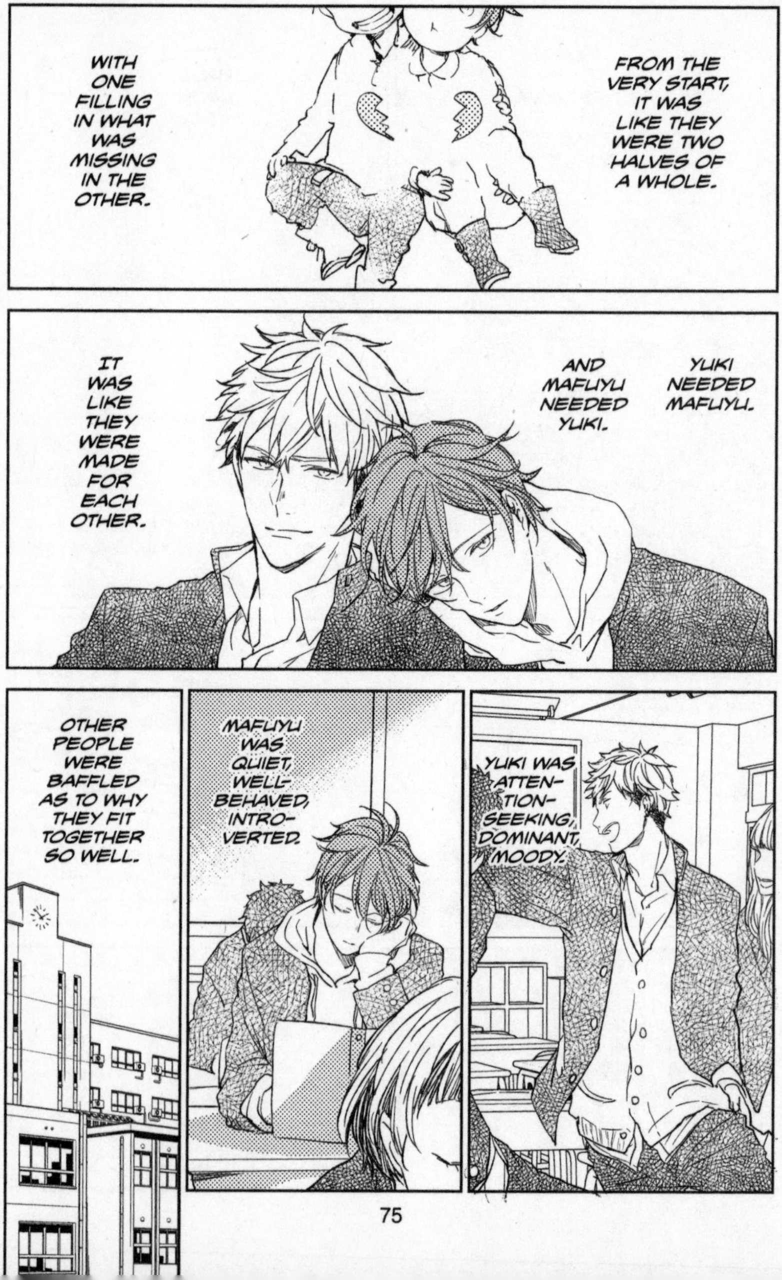
FROM THE VERY START, IT WAS LIKE THEY WERE TWO HALVES OF A WHOLE.
WITH ONE FILLING IN WHAT WAS MISSING IN THE OTHER.
YUKI NEEDED MAFUYU.
AND MAFUYU NEEDED YUKI.
IT WAS LIKE THEY WERE MADE FOR EACH OTHER.
YUKI WAS ATTEN-TION-SEEKING, DOMINANT, MOODY.
MAFUYU WAS QUIET, WELL-BEHAVED, INTRO-VERTED.
OTHER PEOPLE WERE BAFFLED AS TO WHY THEY FIT TOGETHER SO WELL.

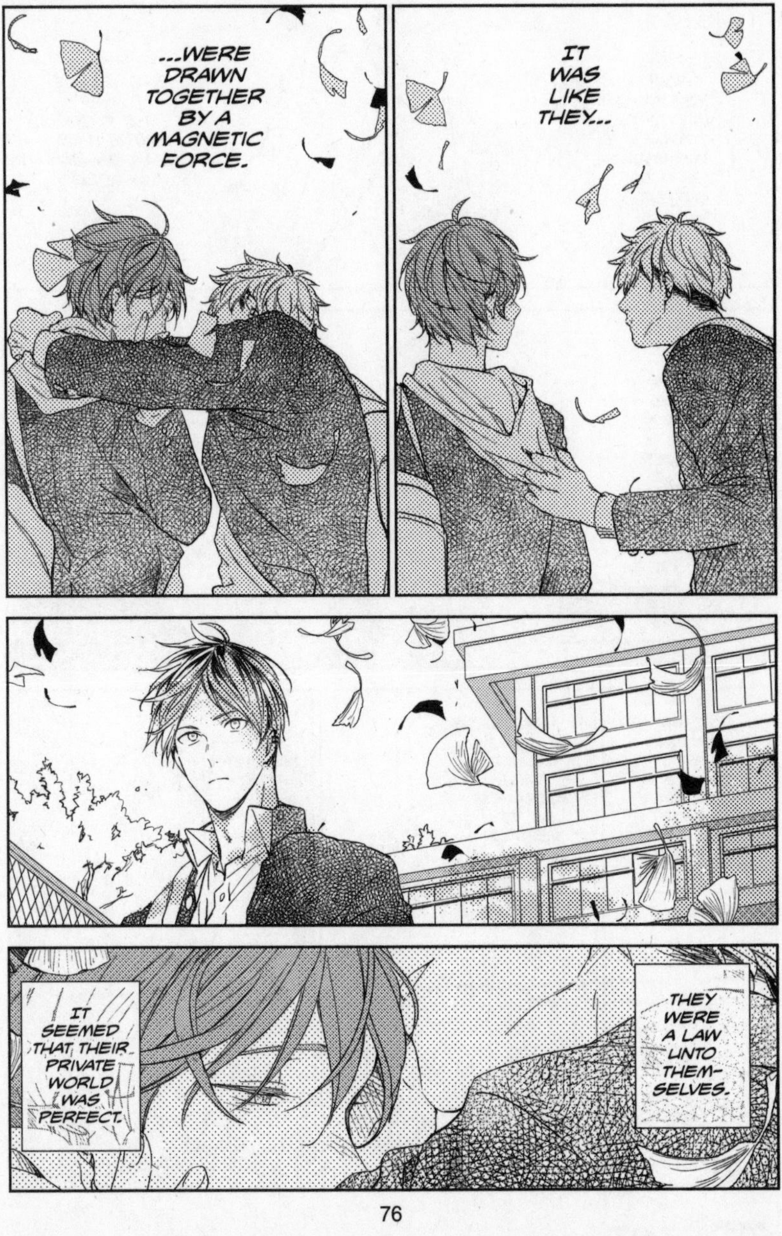
IT WAS LIKE THEY...
...WERE DRAWN TOGETHER BY A MAGNETIC FORCE.
THEY WERE A LAW UNTO THEM-SELVES.
IT SEEMED THAT THEIR PRIVATE WORLD WAS PERFECT.

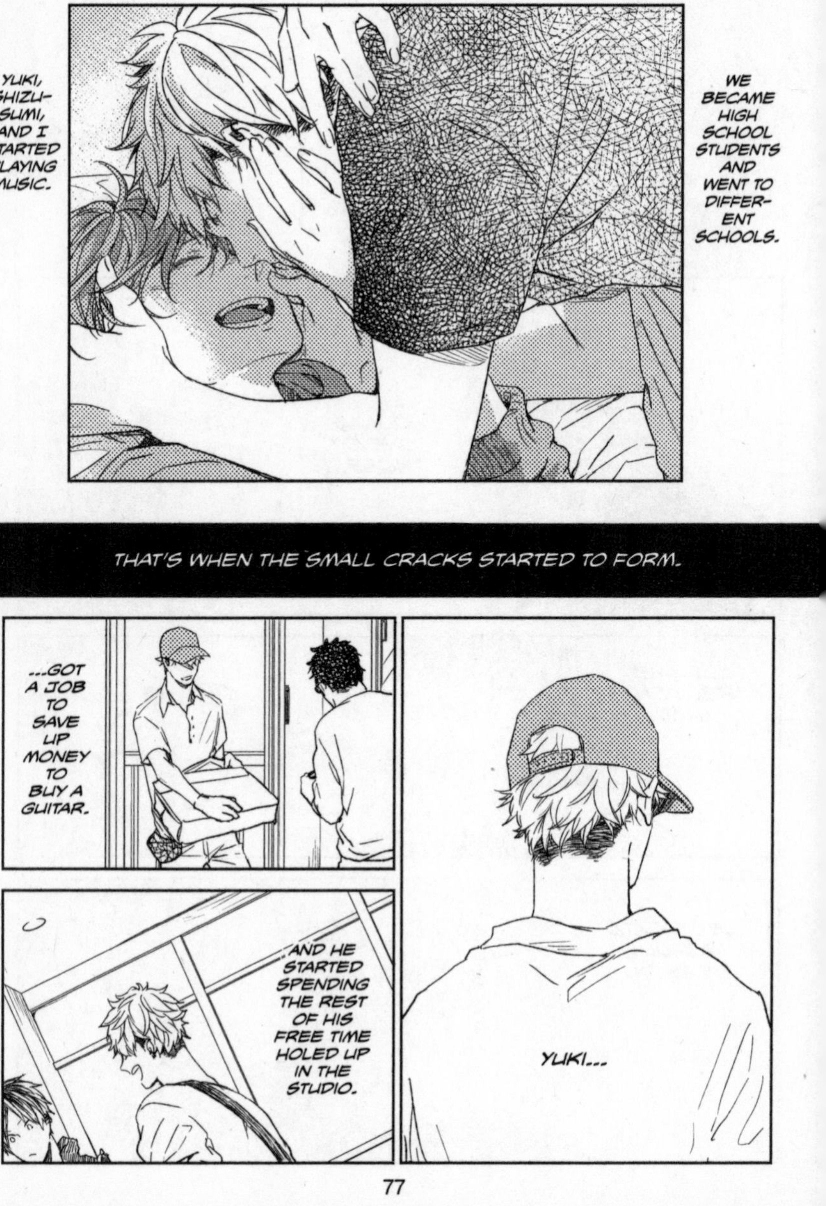
WE BECAME HIGH SCHOOL STUDENTS AND WENT TO DIFFER-ENT SCHOOLS.
YUKI, SHIZU-SUMI, AND I STARTED PLAYING MUSIC.
THAT'S WHEN THE SMALL CRACKS STARTED TO FORM.
YUKI...
...GOT A JOB TO SAVE UP MONEY TO BUY A GUITAR.
AND HE STARTED SPENDING THE REST OF HIS FREE TIME HOLED UP IN THE STUDIO.

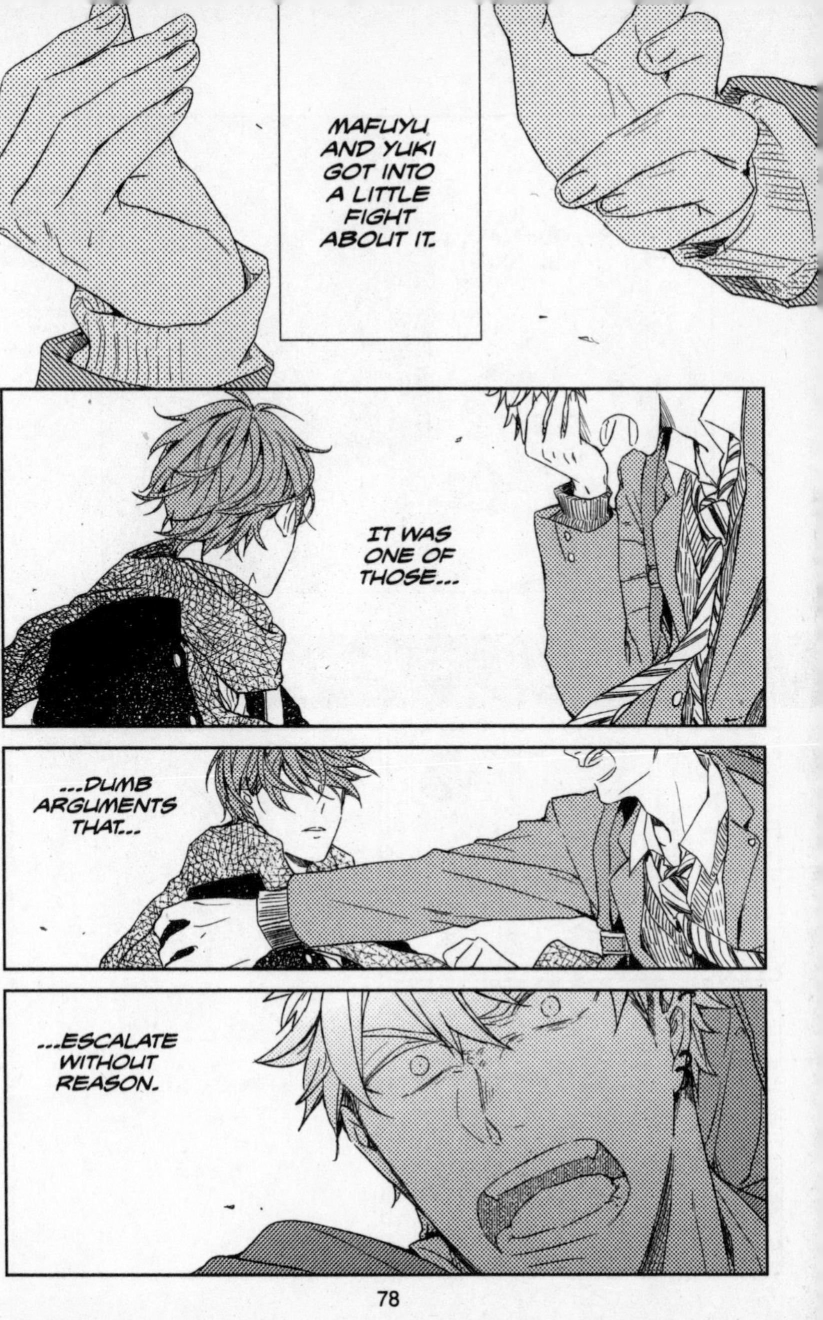
MAFUYU AND YUKI GOT INTO A LITTLE FIGHT ABOUT IT.
IT WAS ONE OF THOSE...
...DUMB ARGUMENTS THAT...
...ESCALATE WITHOUT REASON.

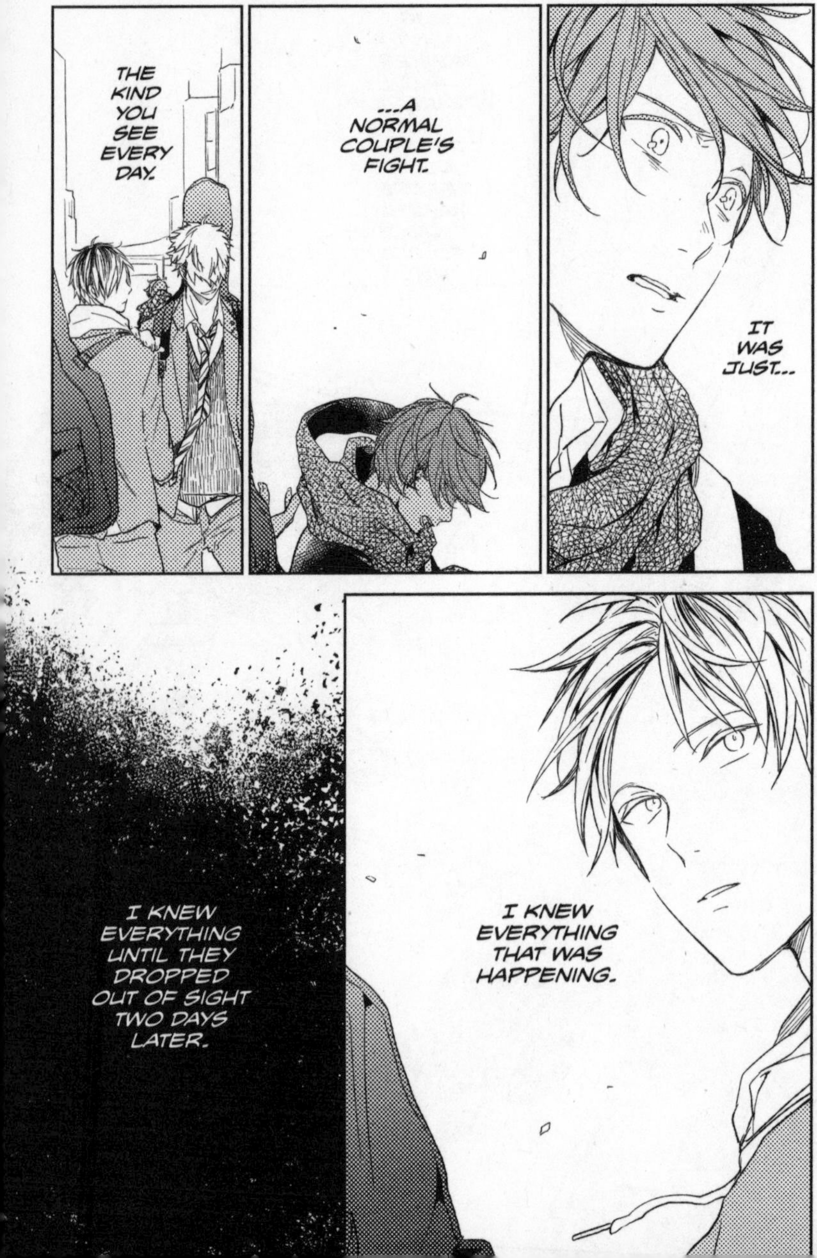
IT WAS JUST...
...A NORMAL COUPLE'S FIGHT.
THE KIND YOU SEE EVERY DAY.
I KNEW EVERYTHING THAT WAS HAPPENING.
I KNEW EVERYTHING UNTIL THEY DROPPED OUT OF SIGHT TWO DAYS LATER.

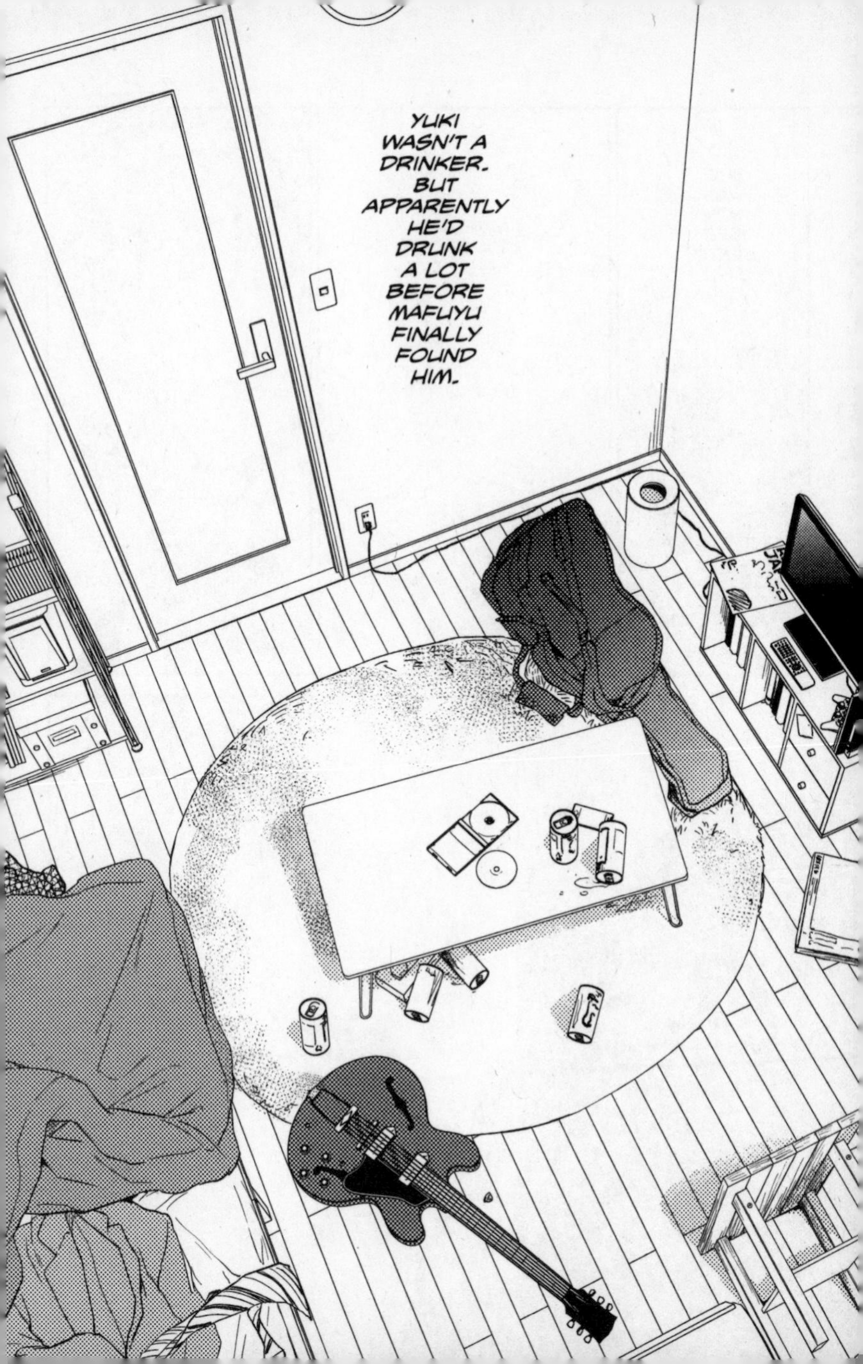
YUKI WASN'T A DRINKER. BUT APPARENTLY HE'D DRUNK A LOT BEFORE MAFUYU FINALLY FOUND HIM.

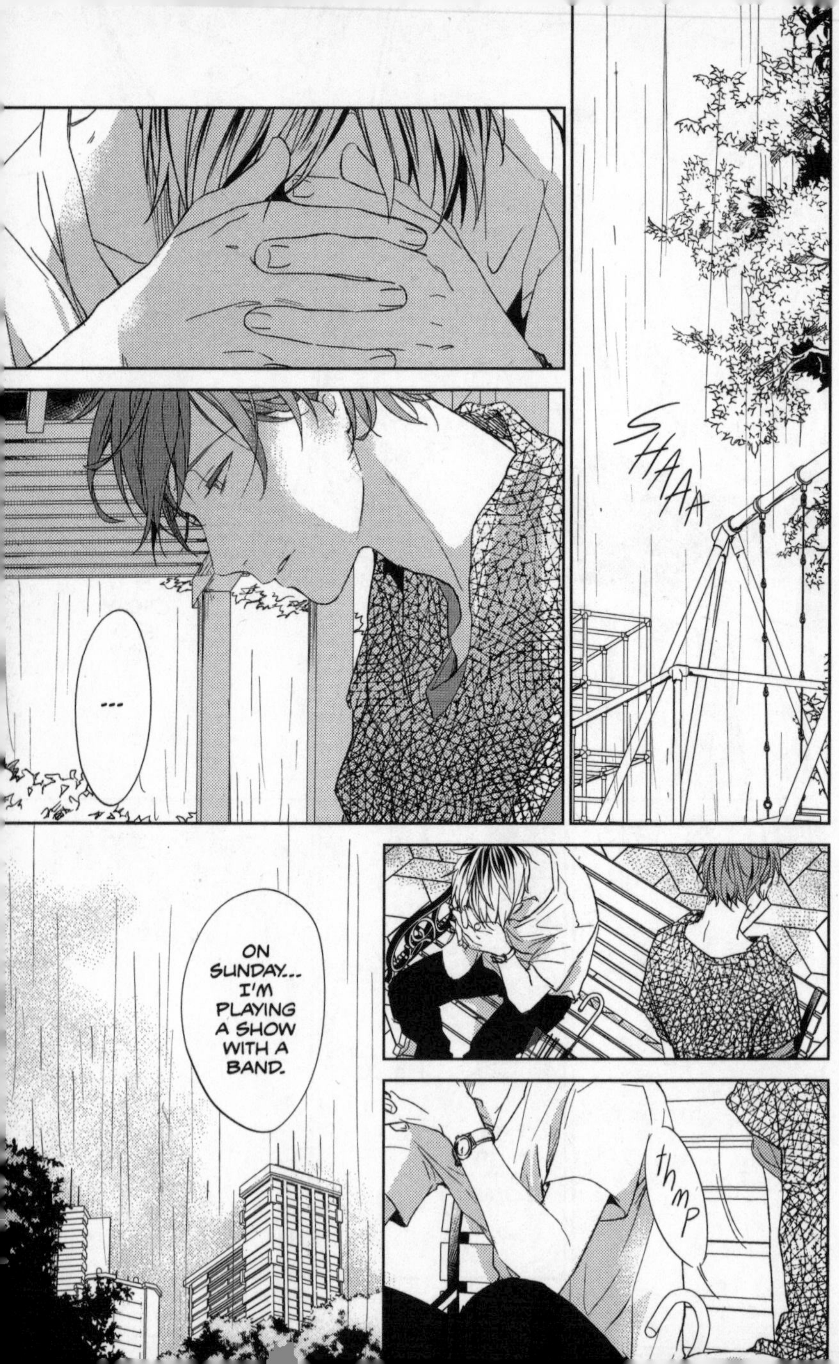
SHAAAA
...
thmp
ON SUNDAY... I'M PLAYING A SHOW WITH A BAND.

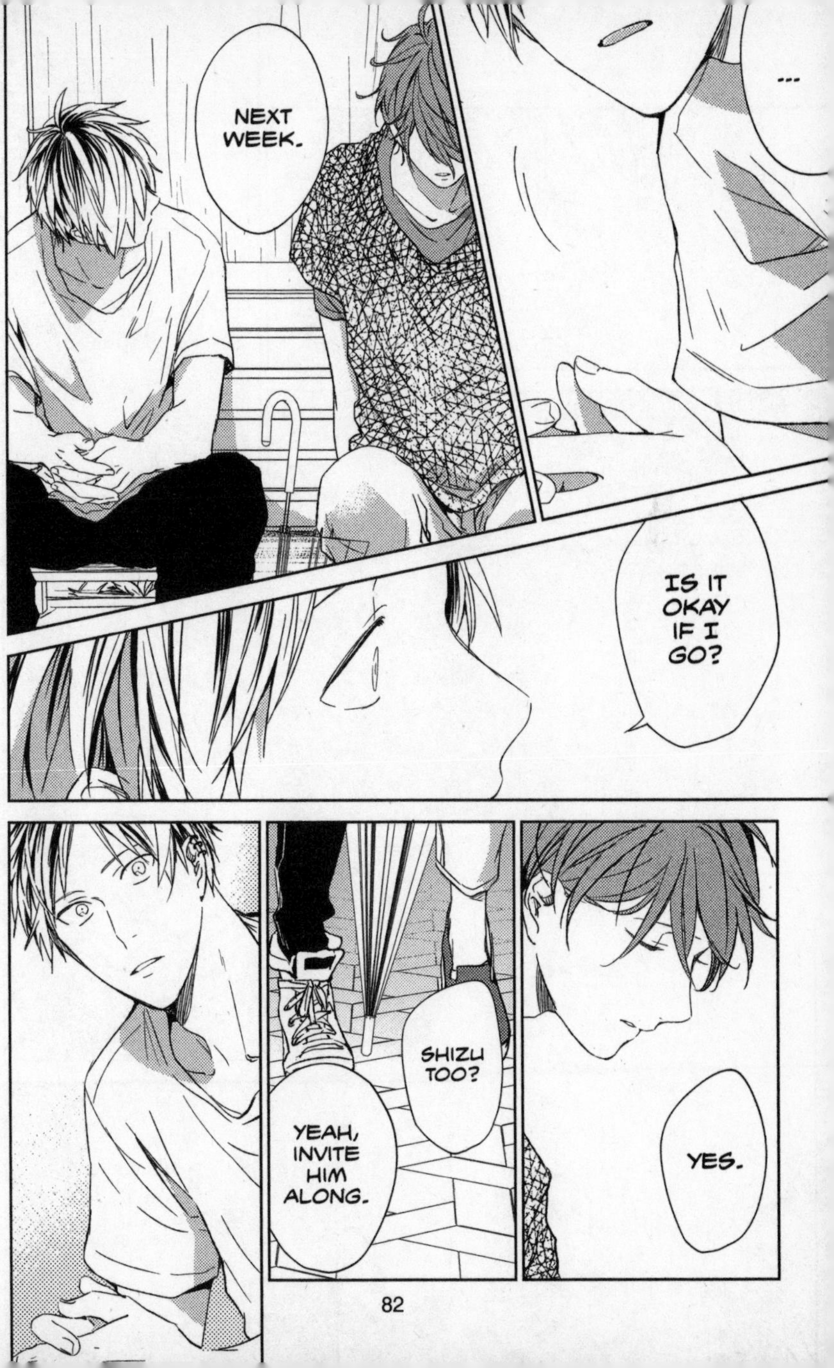
...
NEXT WEEK.
IS IT OKAY IF I GO?
YES.
SHIZU TOO?
YEAH, INVITE HIM ALONG.

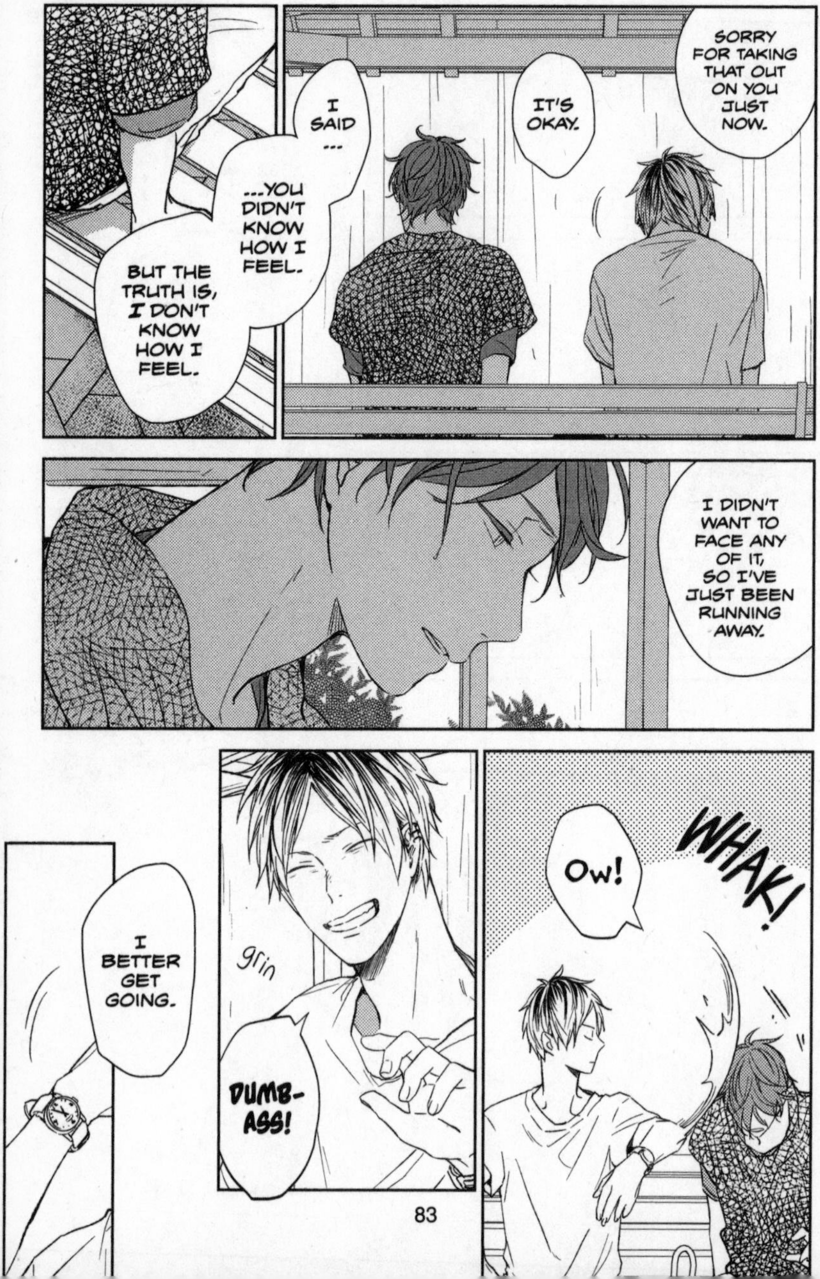
SORRY FOR TAKING THAT OUT ON YOU JUST NOW.
IT'S OKAY.
I SAID ...
...YOU DIDN'T KNOW HOW I FEEL.
BUT THE TRUTH IS, I DON'T KNOW HOW I FEEL.
I DIDN'T WANT TO FACE ANY OF IT, SO I'VE JUST BEEN RUNNING AWAY.
WHAK!
Ow!
grin
DUMB-ASS!
I BETTER GET GOING.

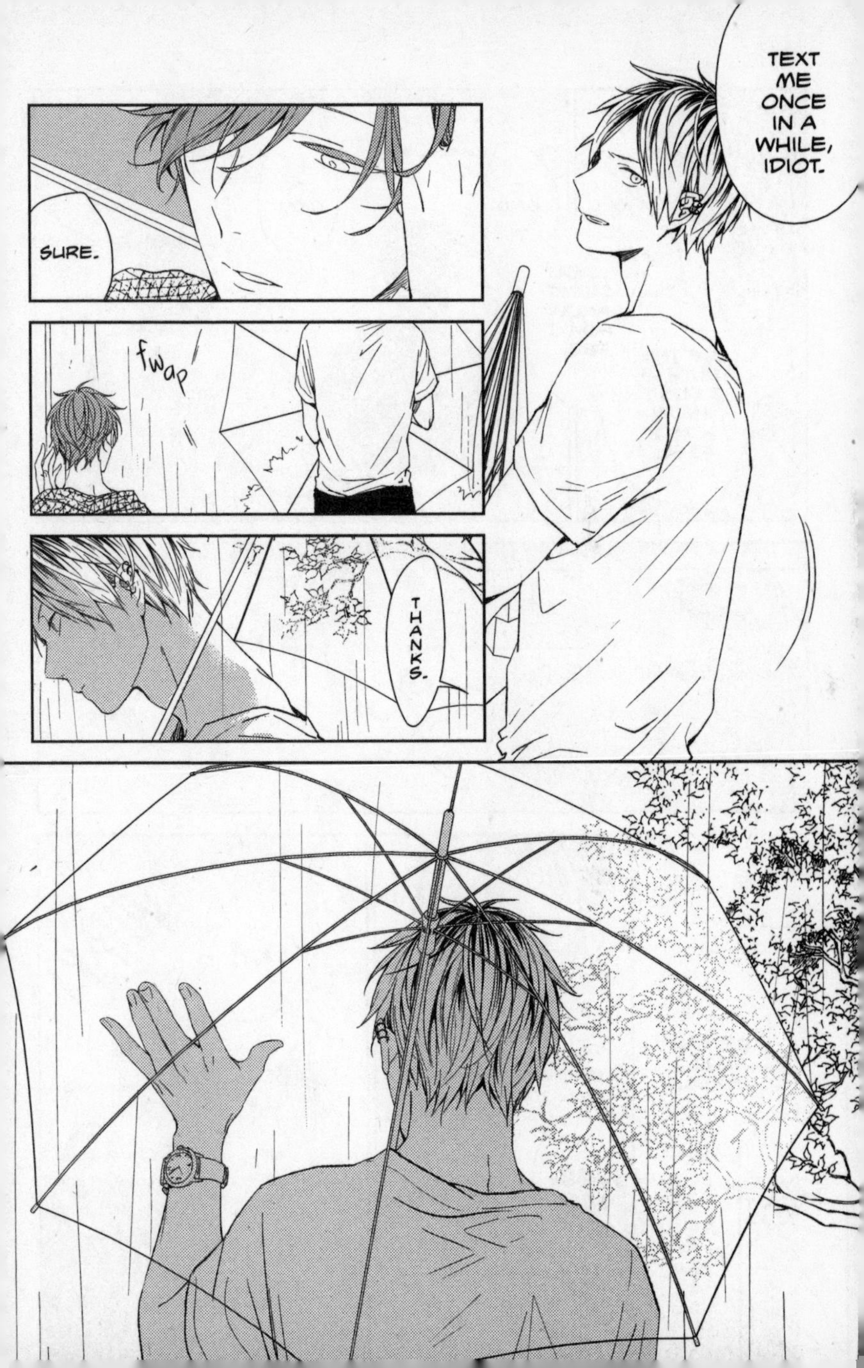
TEXT ME ONCE IN A WHILE, IDIOT.
SURE.
fwap
THANKS.

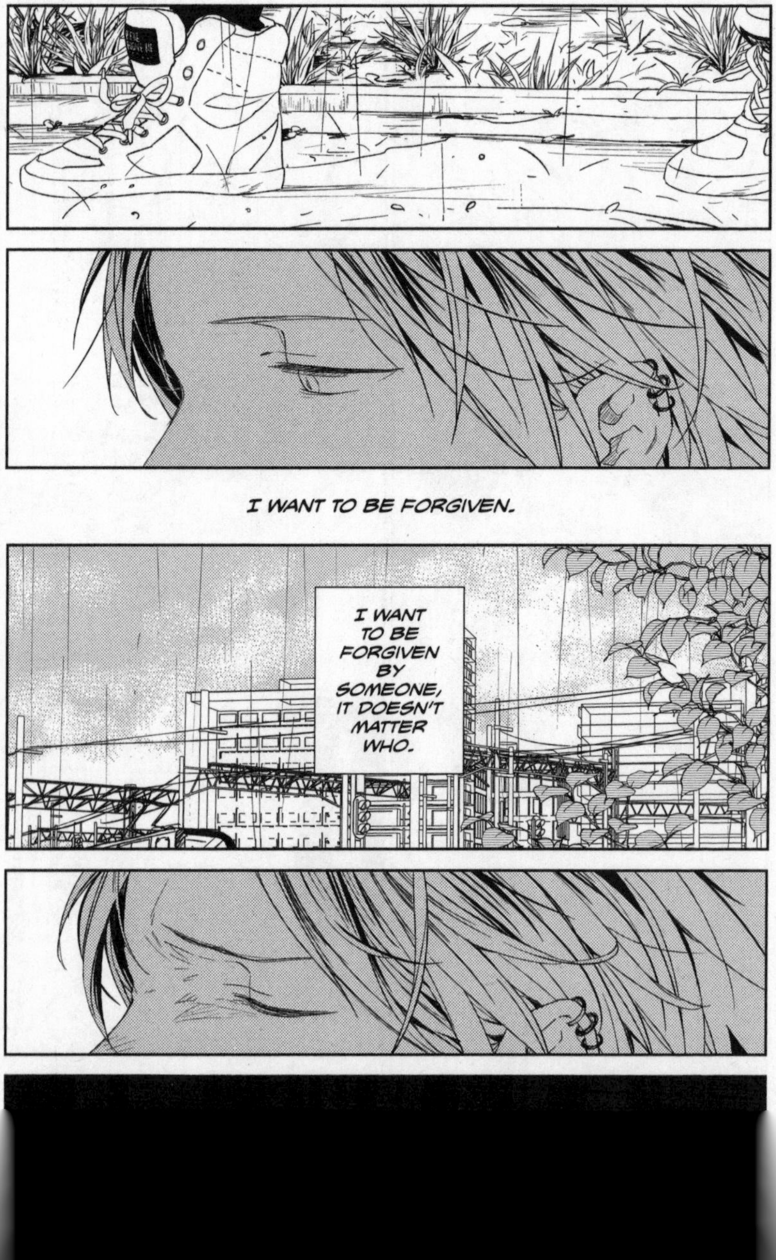
I WANT TO BE FORGIVEN.
I WANT TO BE FORGIVEN BY SOMEONE, IT DOESN'T MATTER WHO.

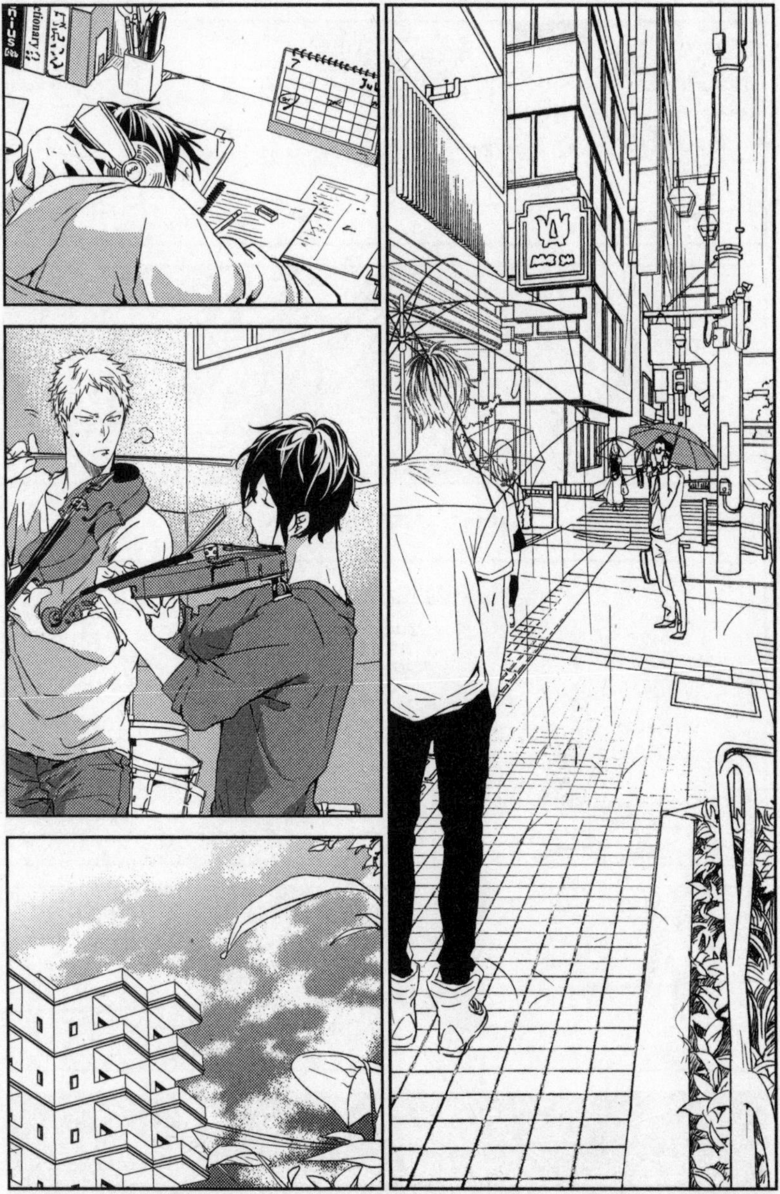

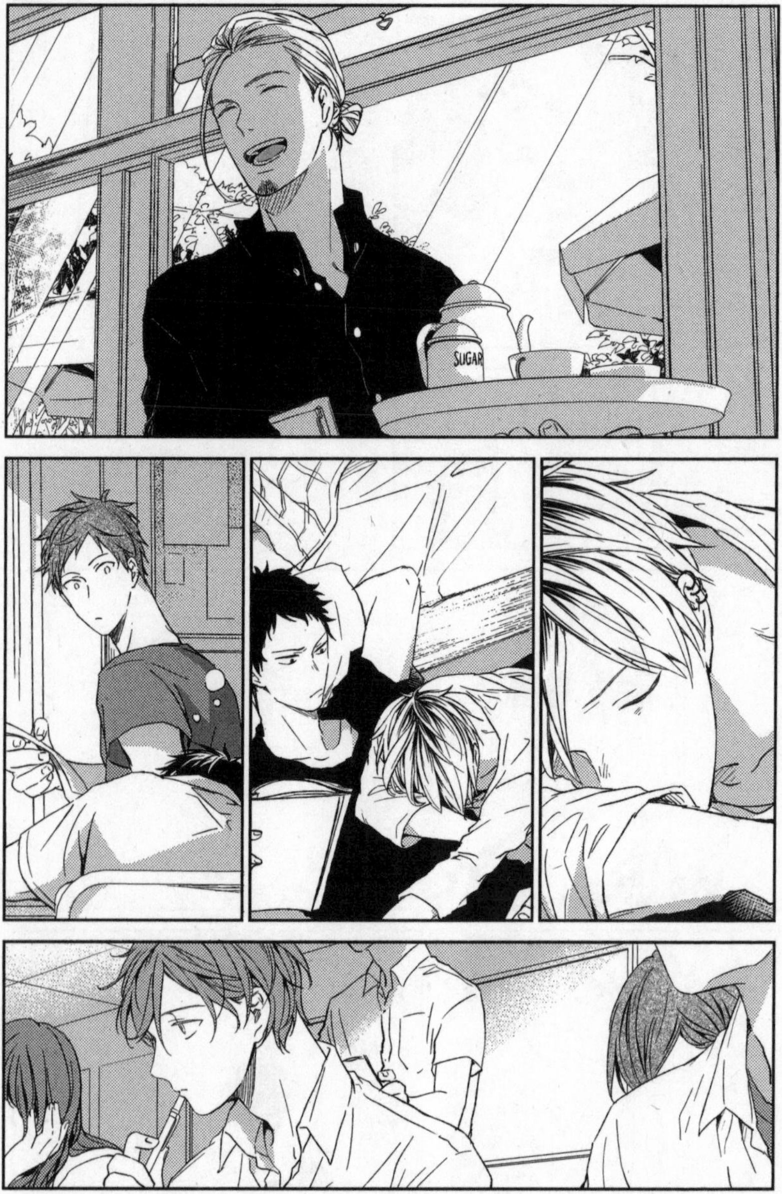
SUGAR

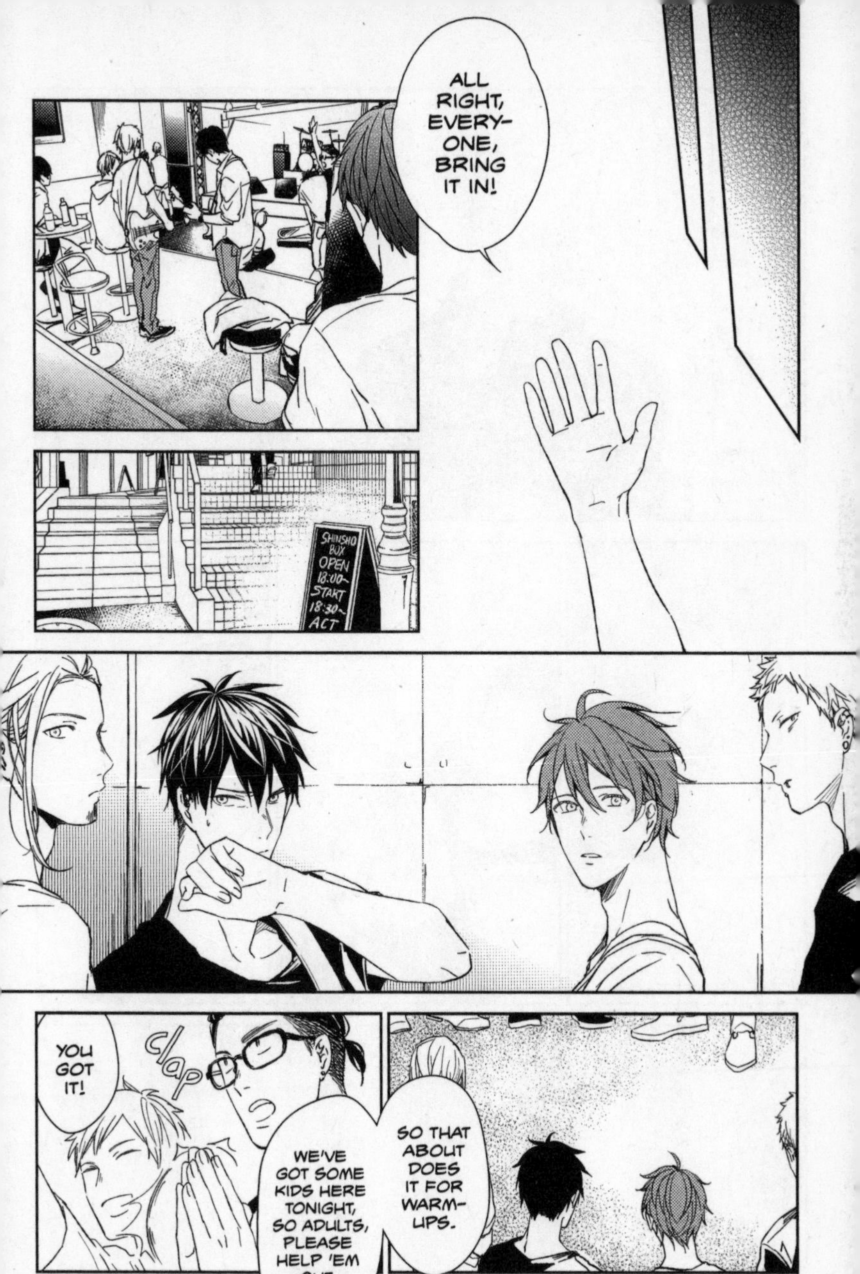
ALL RIGHT, EVERY-ONE, BRING IT IN!
SHINSHO BOX
OPEN 18:00~
START 18:30~
ACT
SO THAT ABOUT DOES IT FOR WARM-UPS.
WE'VE GOT SOME KIDS HERE TONIGHT, SO ADULTS, PLEASE HELP 'EM OUT.
YOU GOT IT!
clap

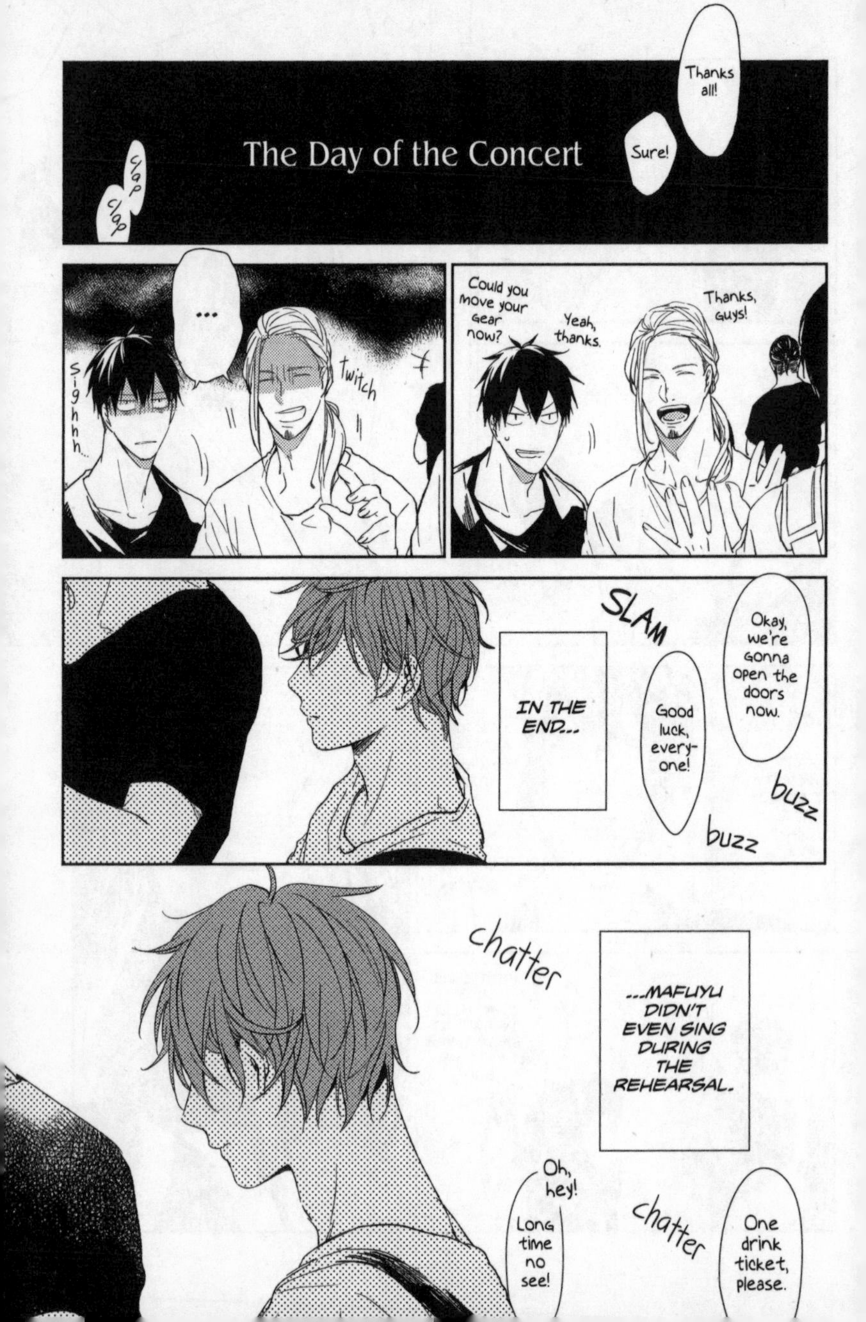
Thanks all!
Sure!
The Day of the Concert
clap clap
Thanks, Guys!
Yeah, thanks.
Could you move your Gear now?
twitch
...
Sighhh...
Okay, we're Gonna open the doors now.
SLAM
buzz
buzz
Good luck, every-one!
IN THE END...
...MAFUYU DIDN'T EVEN SING DURING THE REHEARSAL.
chatter
One drink ticket, please.
chatter
Oh, hey!
Long time no see!

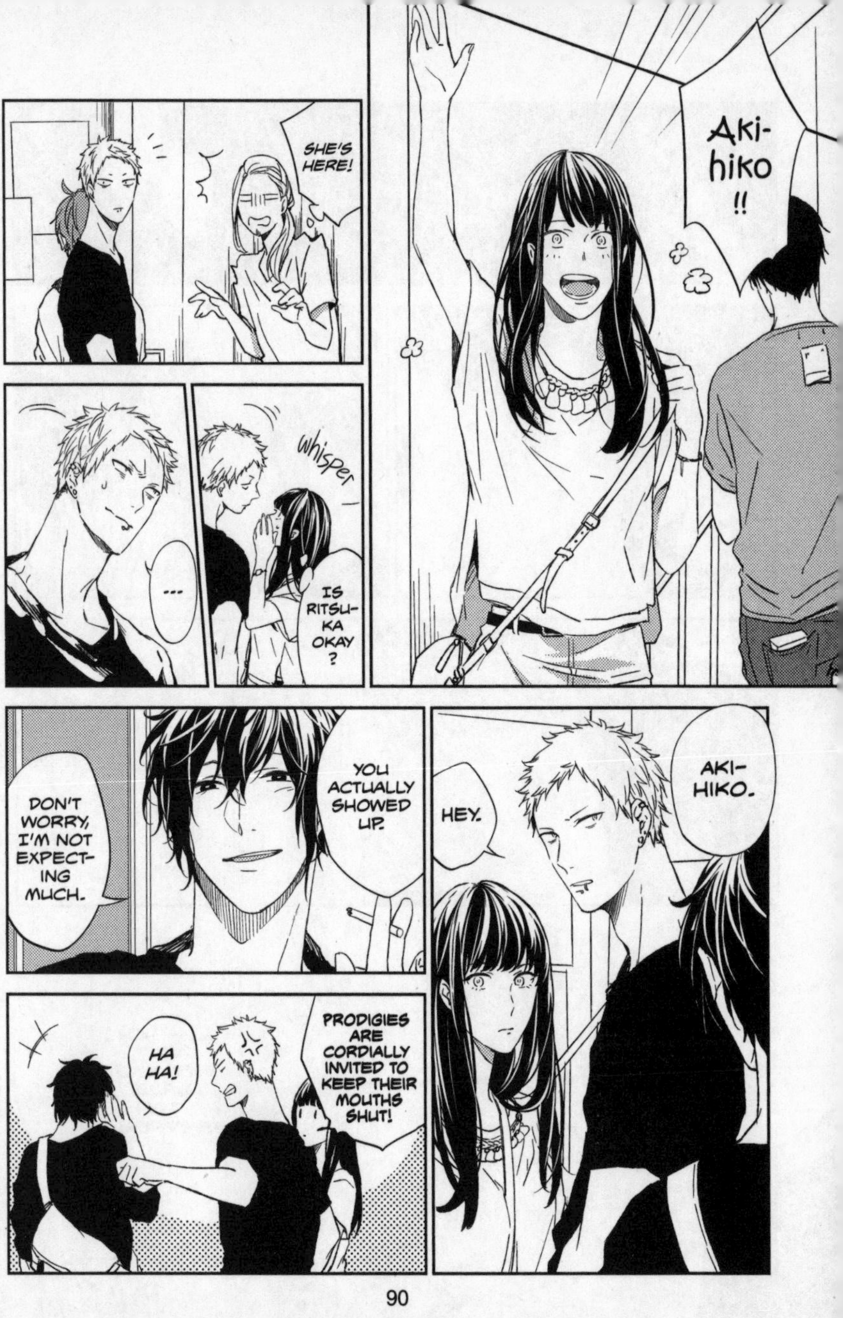
Aki-hiko !!
SHE'S HERE!
whisper
IS RITSU-KA OKAY ?
...
AKI-HIKO.
HEY.
YOU ACTUALLY SHOWED UP.
DON'T WORRY, I'M NOT EXPECT-ING MUCH.
PRODIGIES ARE CORDIALLY INVITED TO KEEP THEIR MOUTHS SHUT!
HA HA!

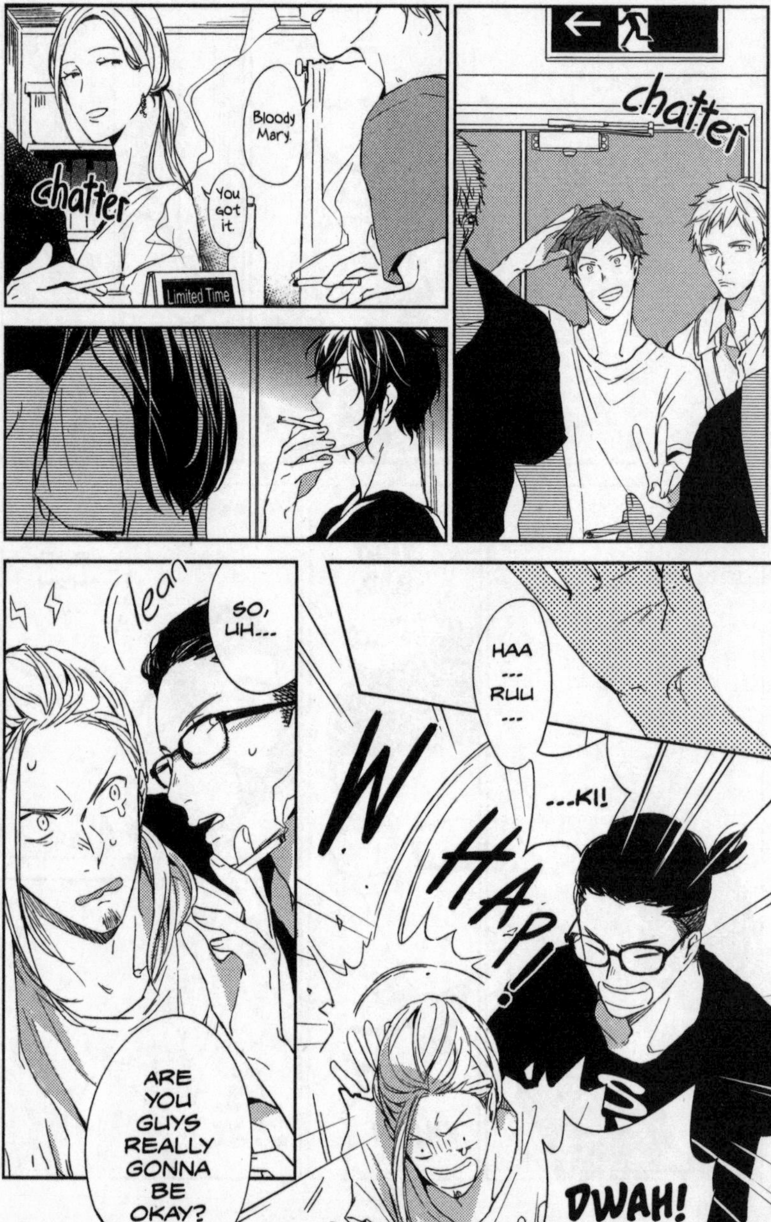
chatter
Bloody Mary.
You got it.
chatter
Limited Time
HAA---RUU---
---KI!
WHAP!
DWAH!
lean
SO, UH---
ARE YOU GUYS REALLY GONNA BE OKAY?

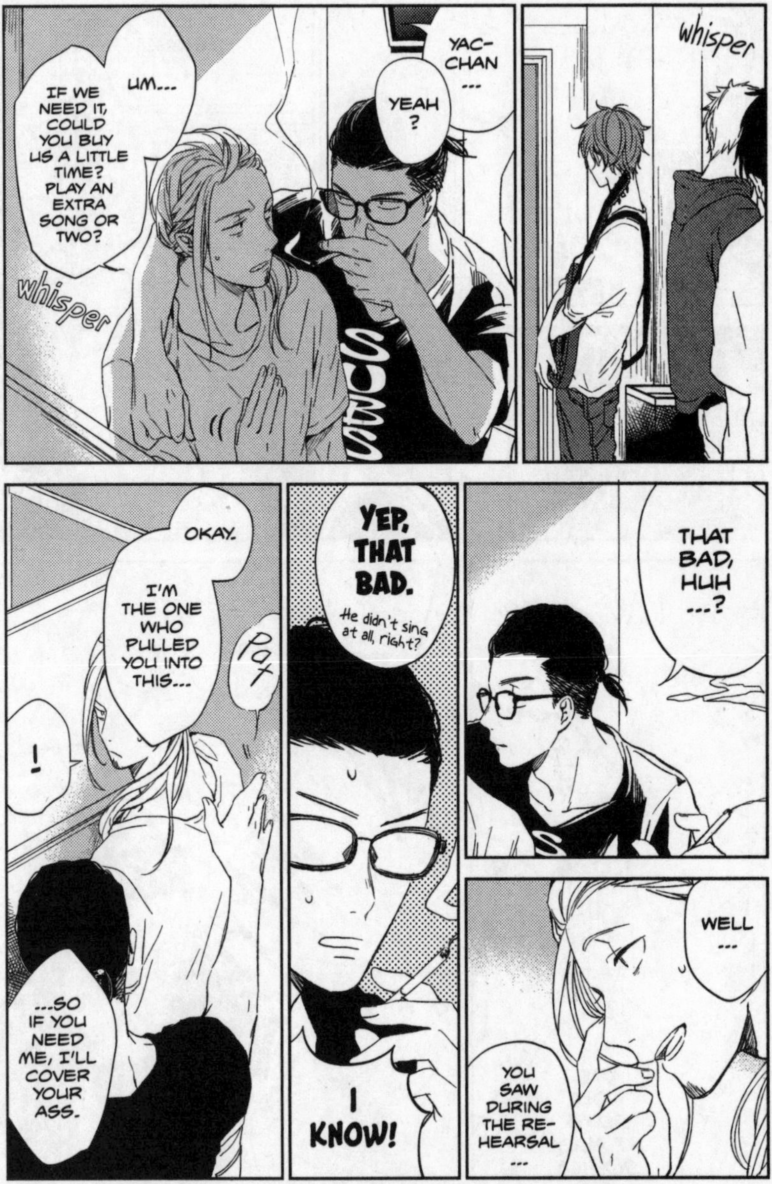
whisper
YAC-CHAN ...
YEAH ?
UM...
IF WE NEED IT, COULD YOU BUY US A LITTLE TIME? PLAY AN EXTRA SONG OR TWO?
whisper
THAT BAD, HUH ...?
WELL ...
YOU SAW DURING THE RE-HEARSAL ...
YEP, THAT BAD.
He didn't sing at all, right?
I KNOW!
OKAY.
I'M THE ONE WHO PULLED YOU INTO THIS...
pat
!
...SO IF YOU NEED ME, I'LL COVER YOUR ASS.

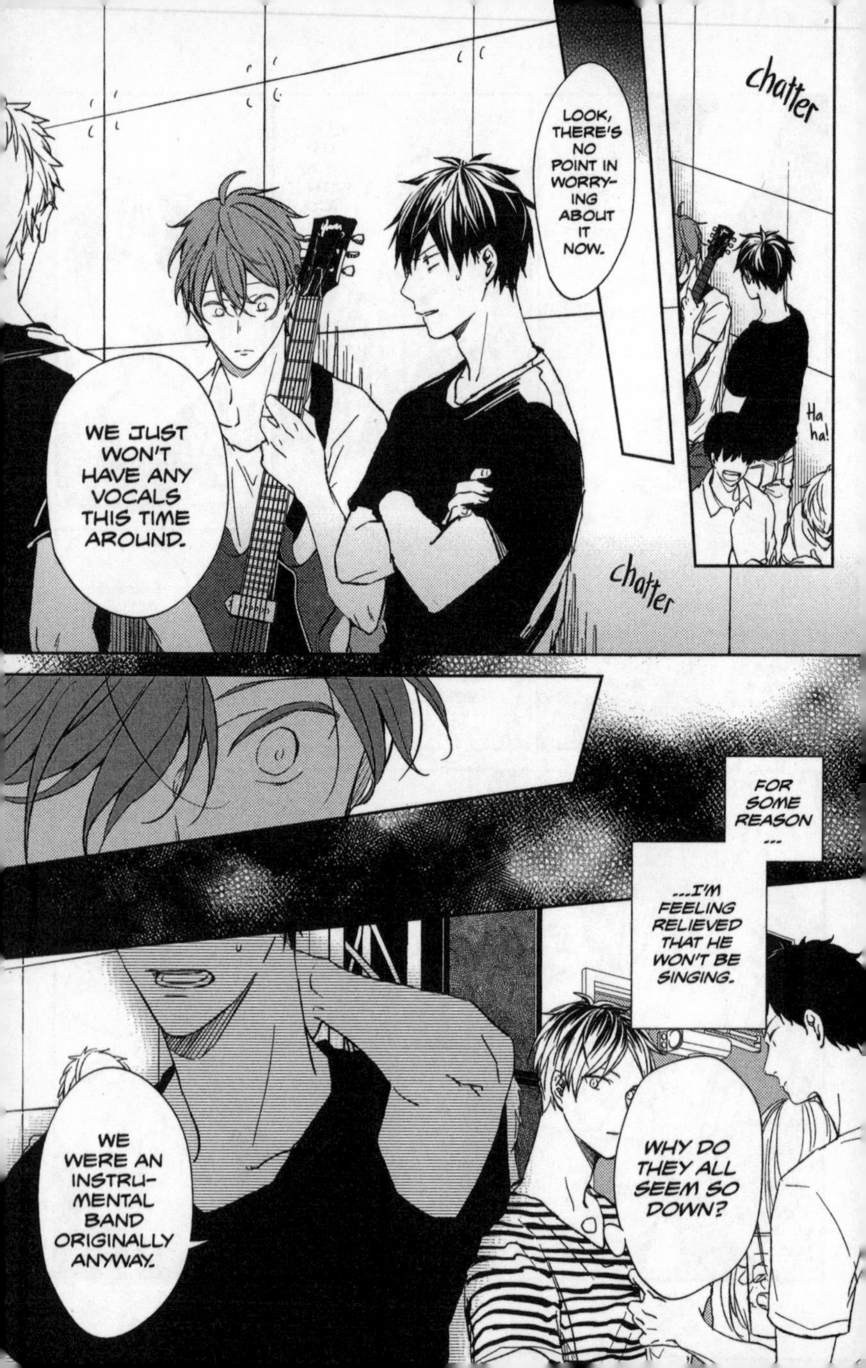
chatter
Ha ha!
LOOK, THERE'S NO POINT IN WORRYING ABOUT IT NOW.
WE JUST WON'T HAVE ANY VOCALS THIS TIME AROUND.
chatter
FOR SOME REASON...
...I'M FEELING RELIEVED THAT HE WON'T BE SINGING.
WHY DO THEY ALL SEEM SO DOWN?
WE WERE AN INSTRUMENTAL BAND ORIGINALLY ANYWAY.

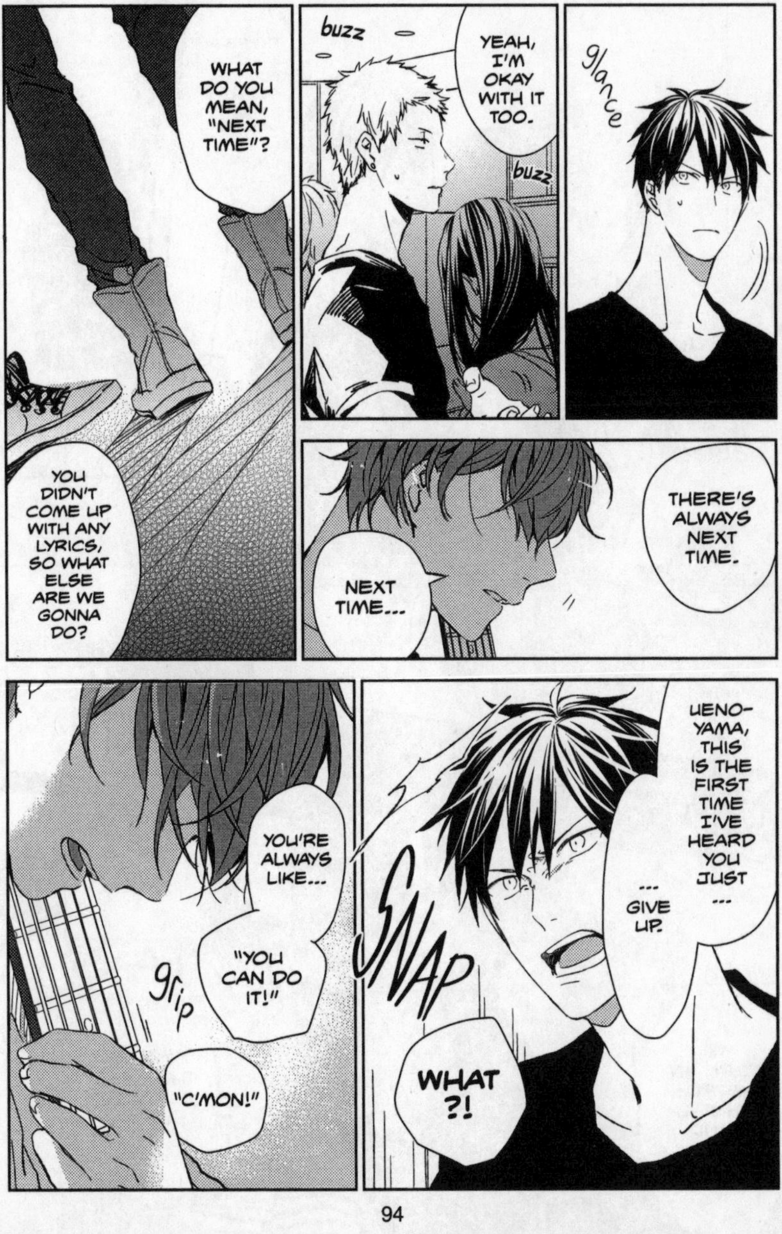
glance
buzz
YEAH, I'M OKAY WITH IT TOO.
buzz
THERE'S ALWAYS NEXT TIME.
NEXT TIME...
WHAT DO YOU MEAN, "NEXT TIME"?
YOU DIDN'T COME UP WITH ANY LYRICS, SO WHAT ELSE ARE WE GONNA DO?
UENO-YAMA, THIS IS THE FIRST TIME I'VE HEARD YOU JUST ...
... GIVE UP.
SNAP
WHAT ?!
YOU'RE ALWAYS LIKE...
"YOU CAN DO IT!"
grip
"C'MON!"

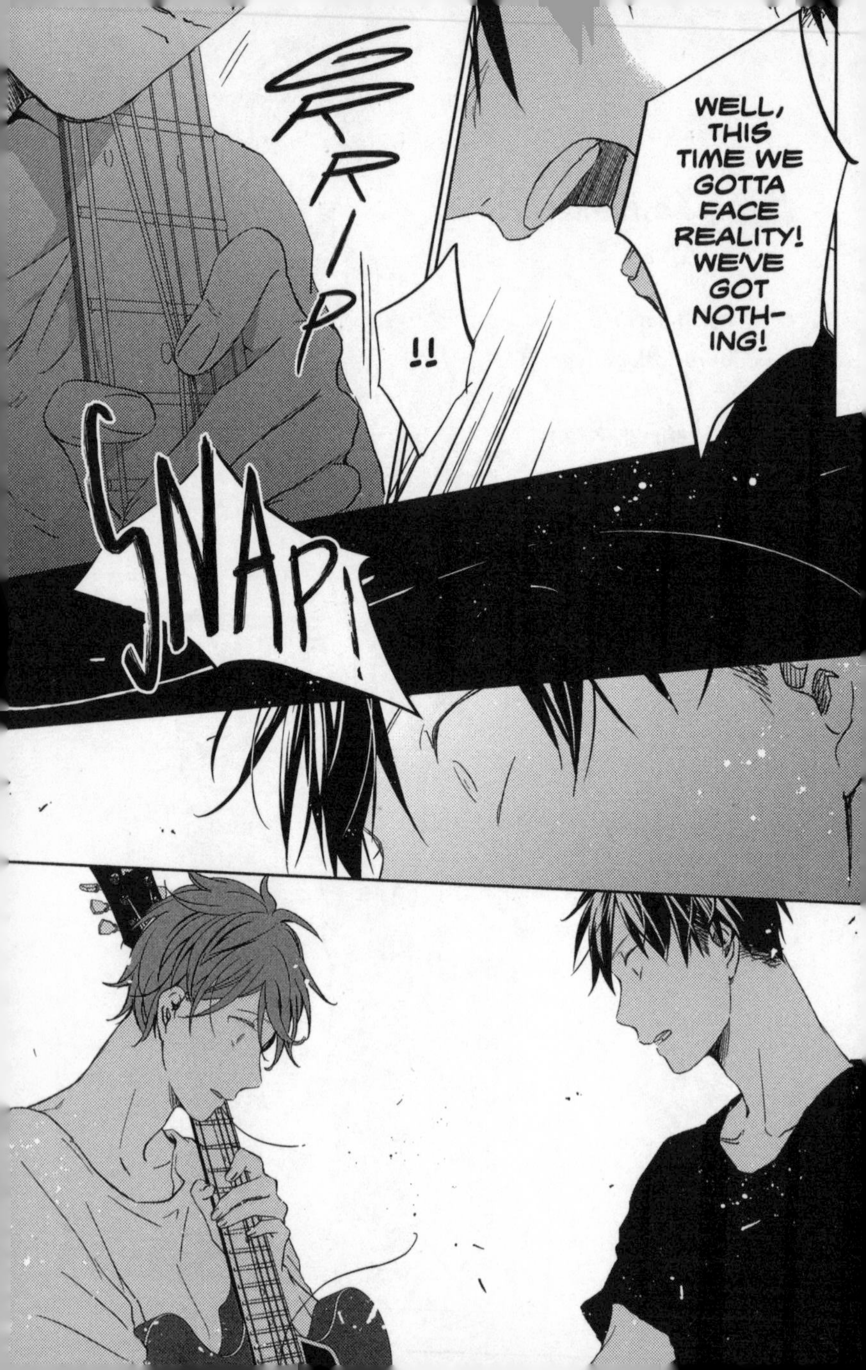
WELL, THIS TIME WE GOTTA FACE REALITY! WE'VE GOT NOTH-ING!
!!
GRRIP
SNAP!

Hiragi Kashima (17)

175 cm

Birthday: 5/8

Sign: Taurus Blood Type: A

Plays bass, supposedly.

Dyes his hair.
Goes to the same high school
as Yuki and Shizusumi.

Ever Since We Were Kids

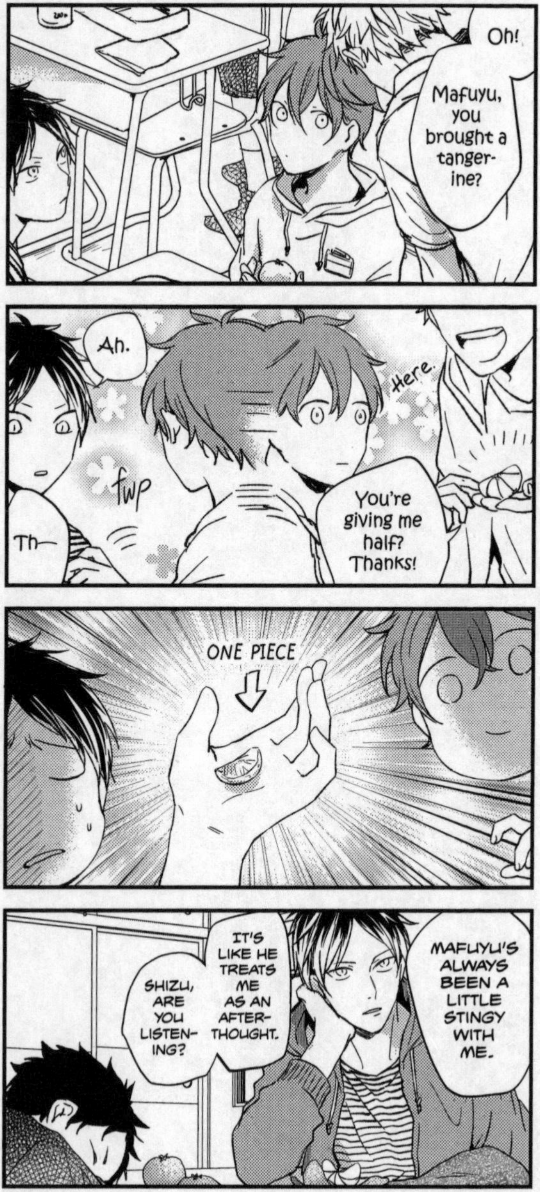
Oh!
Mafuyu, you brought a tanger-ine?
Here.
You're giving me half? Thanks!
Ah.
fwp
Th—
ONE PIECE
MAFUYU'S ALWAYS BEEN A LITTLE STINGY WITH ME.
IT'S LIKE HE TREATS ME AS AN AFTER-THOUGHT.
SHIZU, ARE YOU LISTEN-ING?

given

by Natsuki Kizu

chapter 10

given

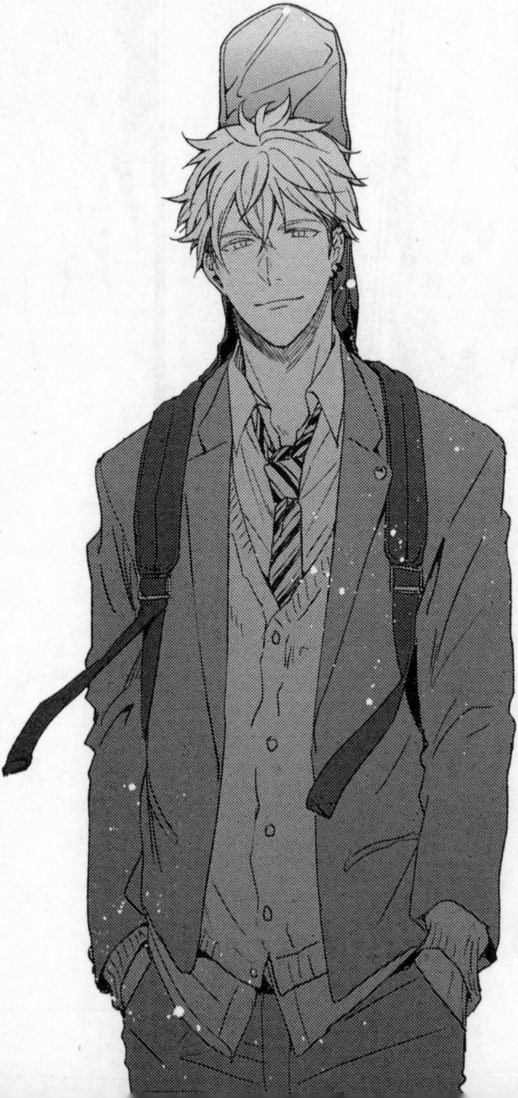

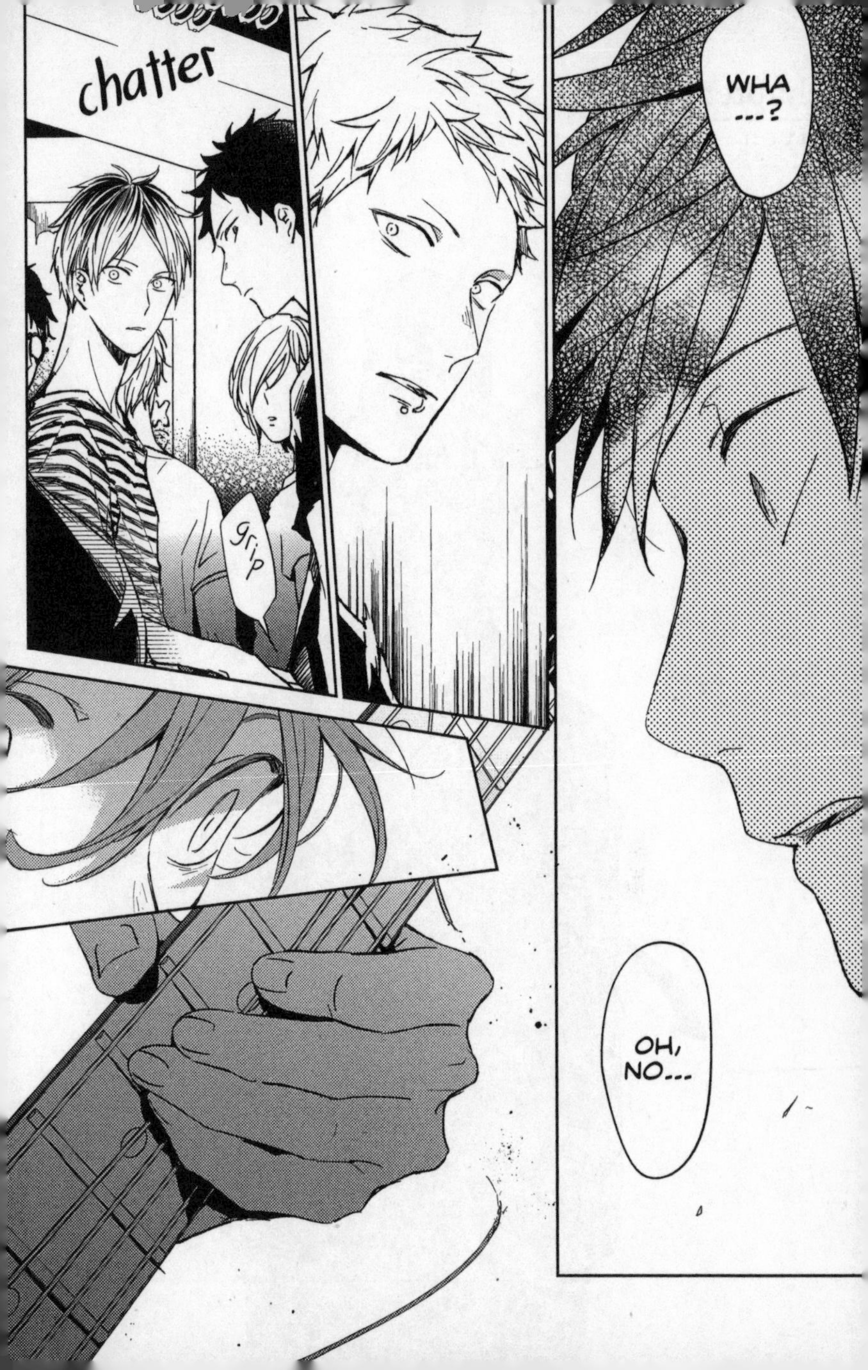
WHA ---?
OH, NO...
chatter
grip

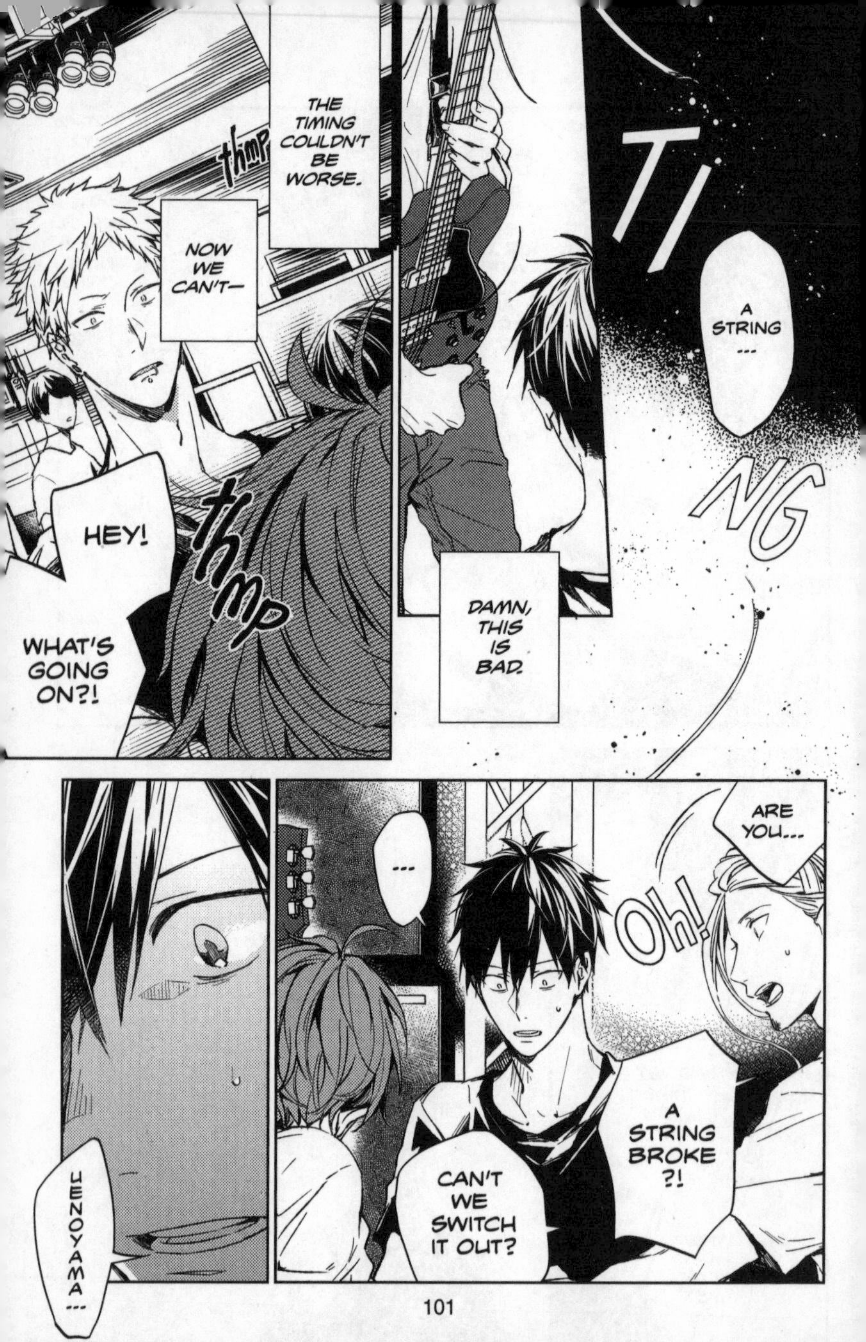
TI
A STRING ...
NG
THE TIMING COULDN'T BE WORSE.
DAMN, THIS IS BAD.
thmp
NOW WE CAN'T—
HEY!
thmp
WHAT'S GOING ON?!
ARE YOU...
Oh!
A STRING BROKE?!
...
CAN'T WE SWITCH IT OUT?
UENOYAMA ...

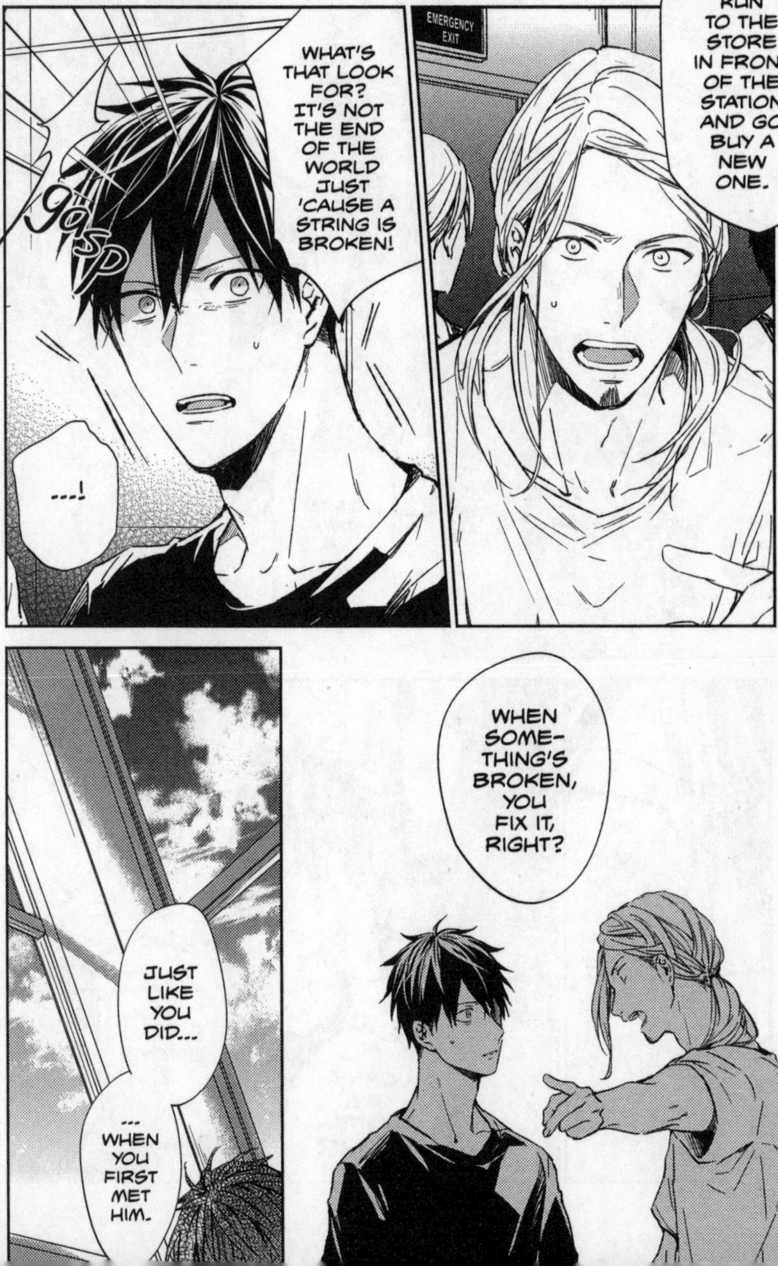
EMERGENCY EXIT
RUN TO THE STORE IN FRONT OF THE STATION AND GO BUY A NEW ONE.
WHAT'S THAT LOOK FOR? IT'S NOT THE END OF THE WORLD JUST 'CAUSE A STRING IS BROKEN!
gasp
...!
WHEN SOME-THING'S BROKEN, YOU FIX IT, RIGHT?
JUST LIKE YOU DID...
...WHEN YOU FIRST MET HIM.

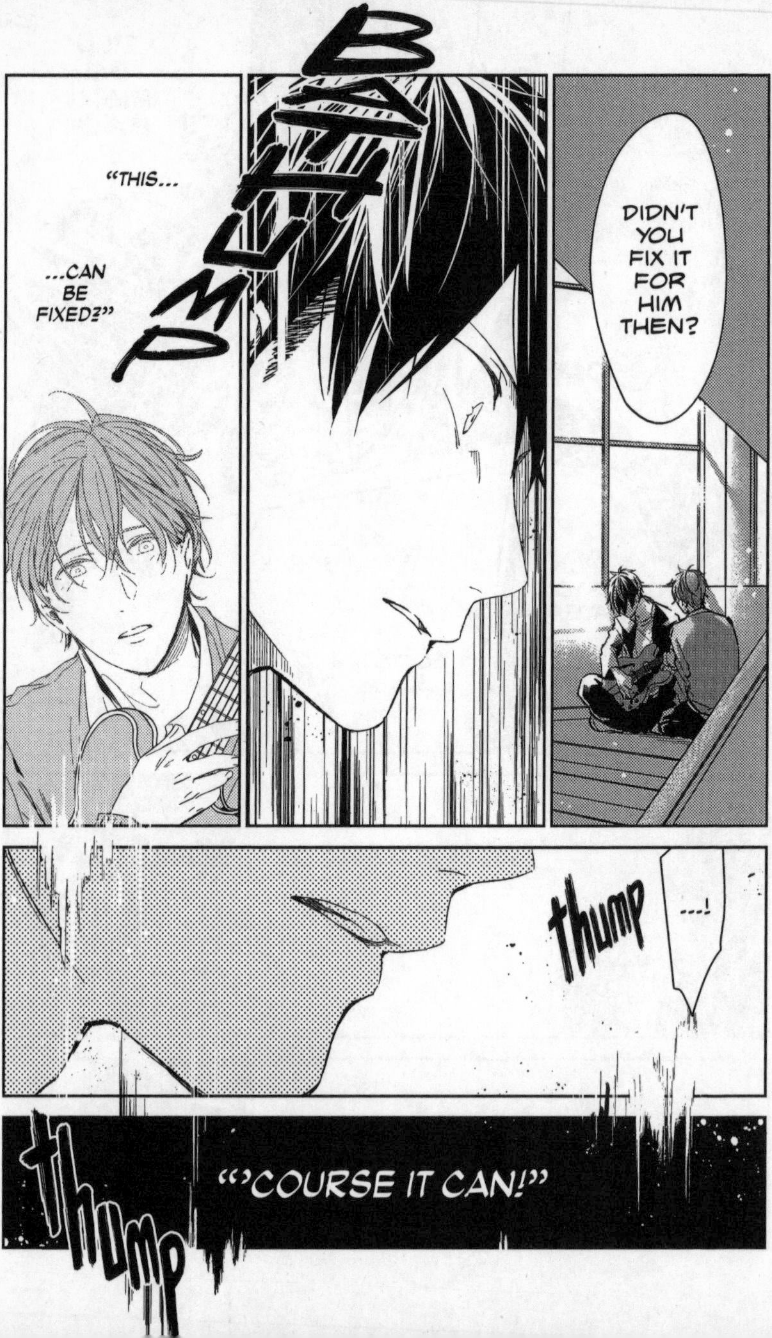
DIDN'T YOU FIX IT FOR HIM THEN?
BA-THUMP
"THIS...
...CAN BE FIXED?"
...!
thump
thump
"'COURSE IT CAN!"

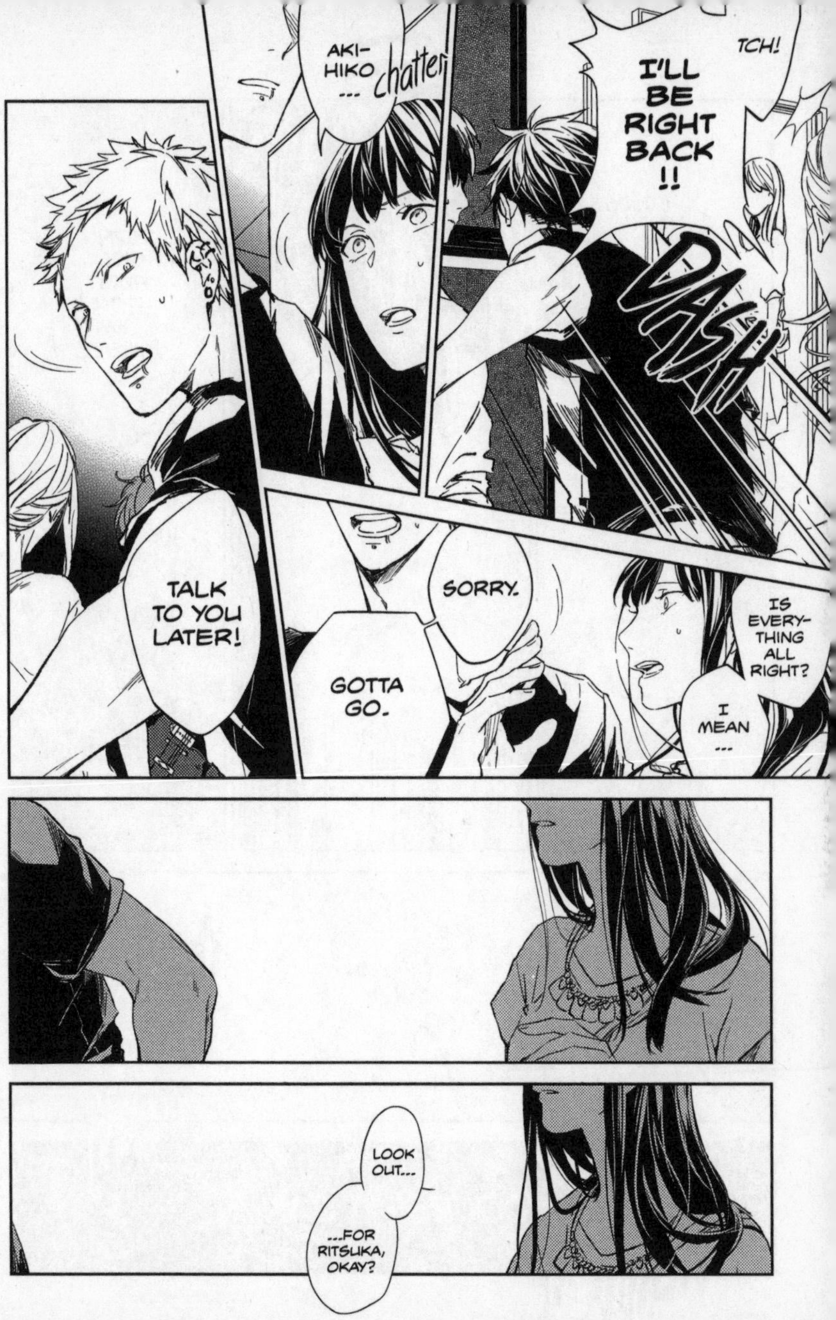
TCH!
I'LL BE RIGHT BACK!!
DASH
AKI-HIKO...
chatter
IS EVERYTHING ALL RIGHT?
I MEAN...
SORRY.
GOTTA GO.
TALK TO YOU LATER!
LOOK OUT...
...FOR RITSUKA, OKAY?

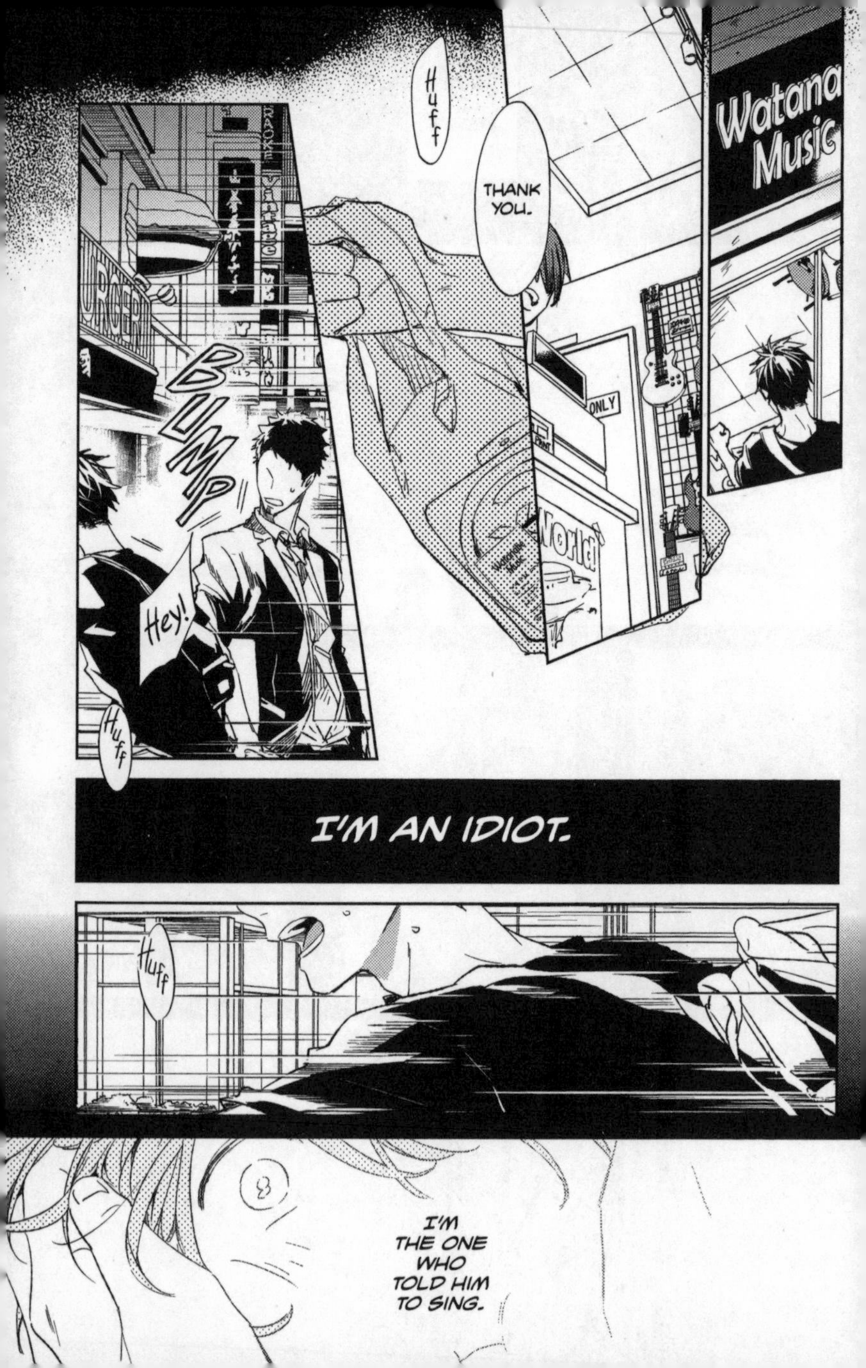
Watana
Music
Huff
THANK YOU.
BUMP
Hey!
Huff
I'M AN IDIOT.
Huff
I'M THE ONE WHO TOLD HIM TO SING.

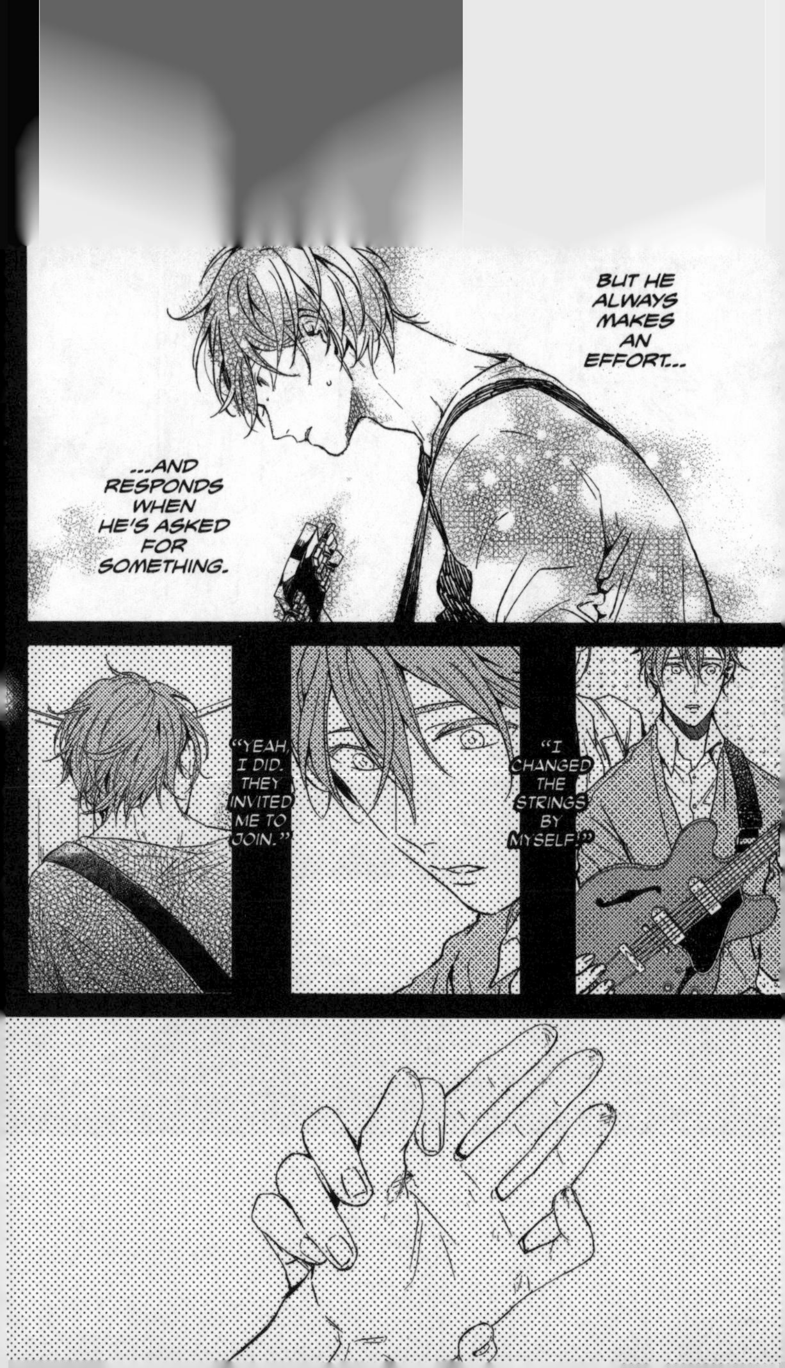
BUT HE ALWAYS MAKES AN EFFORT...
...AND RESPONDS WHEN HE'S ASKED FOR SOMETHING.
"I CHANGED THE STRINGS BY MYSELF!"
"YEAH, I DID. THEY INVITED ME TO JOIN."

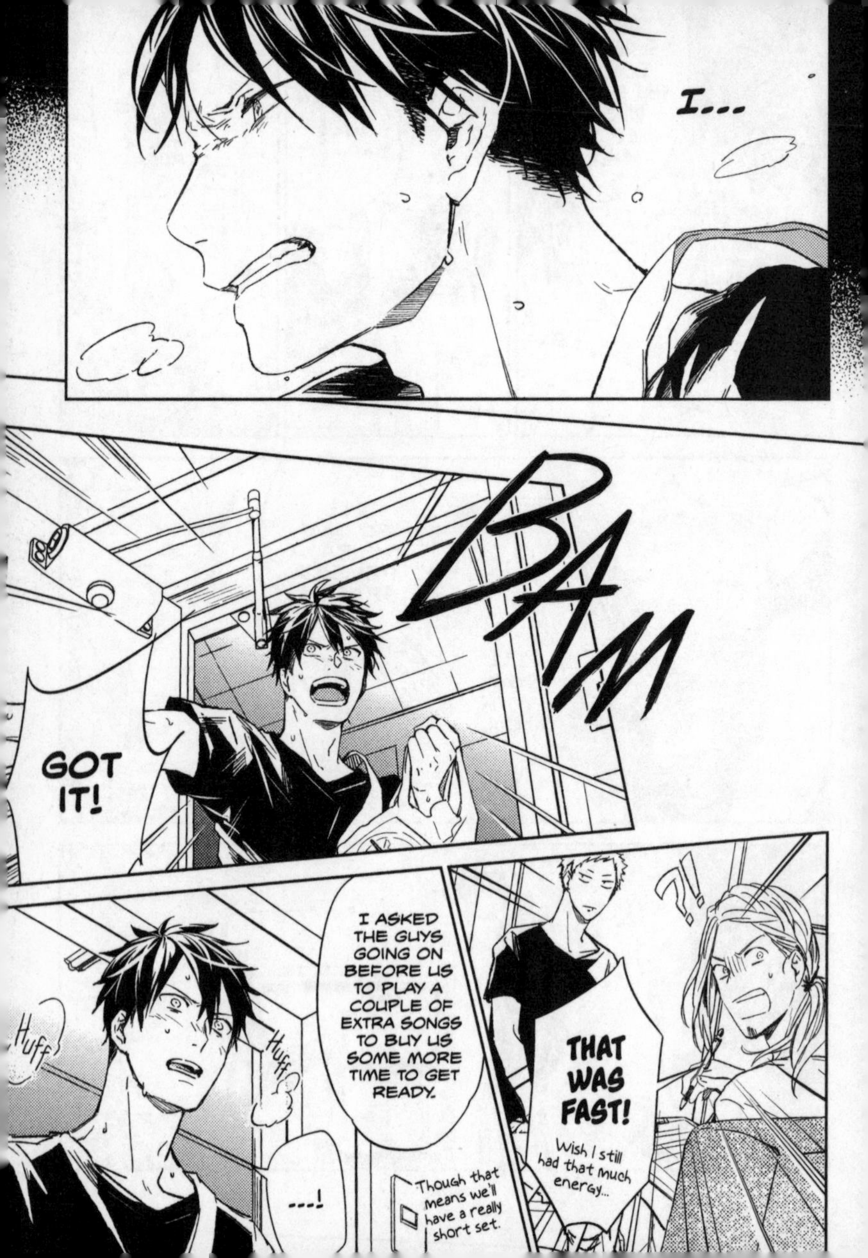
I...
BAM
GOT IT!
?!
THAT WAS FAST!
Wish I still had that much energy...
Huff
Huff
I ASKED THE GUYS GOING ON BEFORE US TO PLAY A COUPLE OF EXTRA SONGS TO BUY US SOME MORE TIME TO GET READY.
Though that means we'll have a really short set.
...!

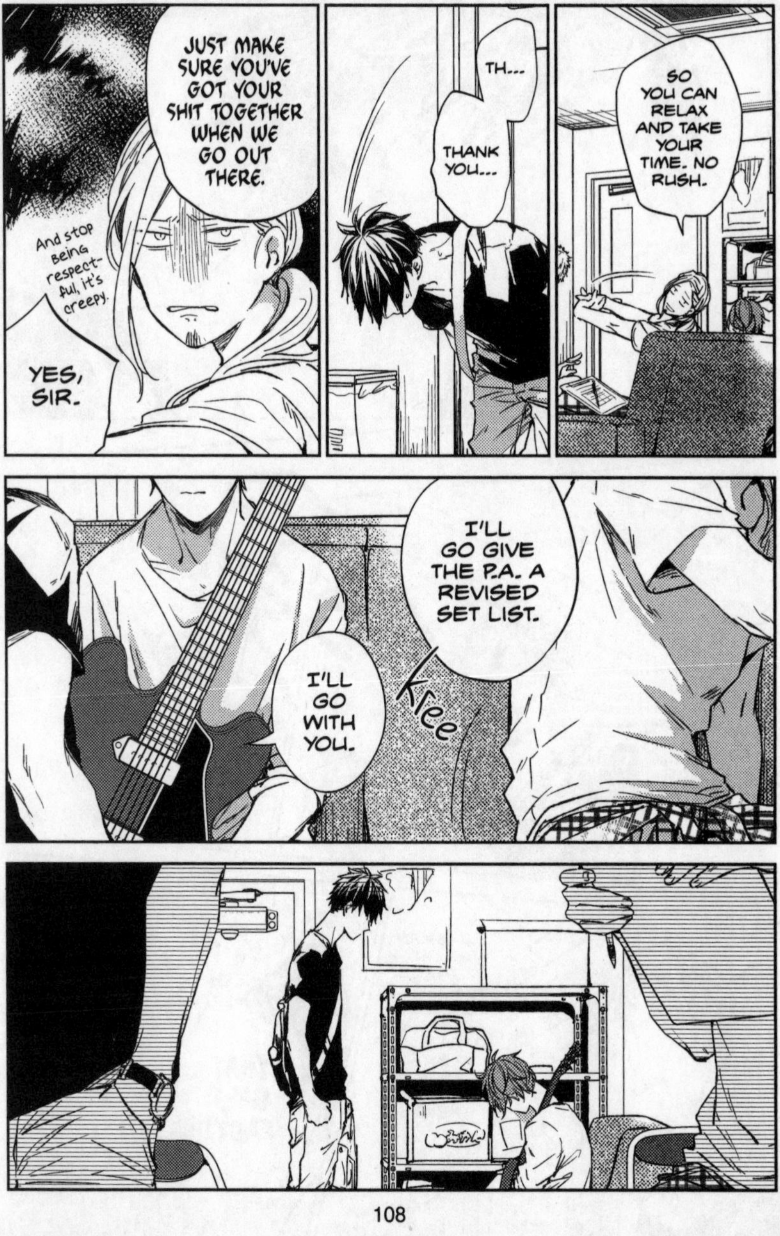
SO YOU CAN RELAX AND TAKE YOUR TIME. NO RUSH.
TH...
THANK YOU...
JUST MAKE SURE YOU'VE GOT YOUR SHIT TOGETHER WHEN WE GO OUT THERE.
And stop being respect-ful, it's creepy.
YES, SIR.
I'LL GO GIVE THE P.A. A REVISED SET LIST.
kree
I'LL GO WITH YOU.

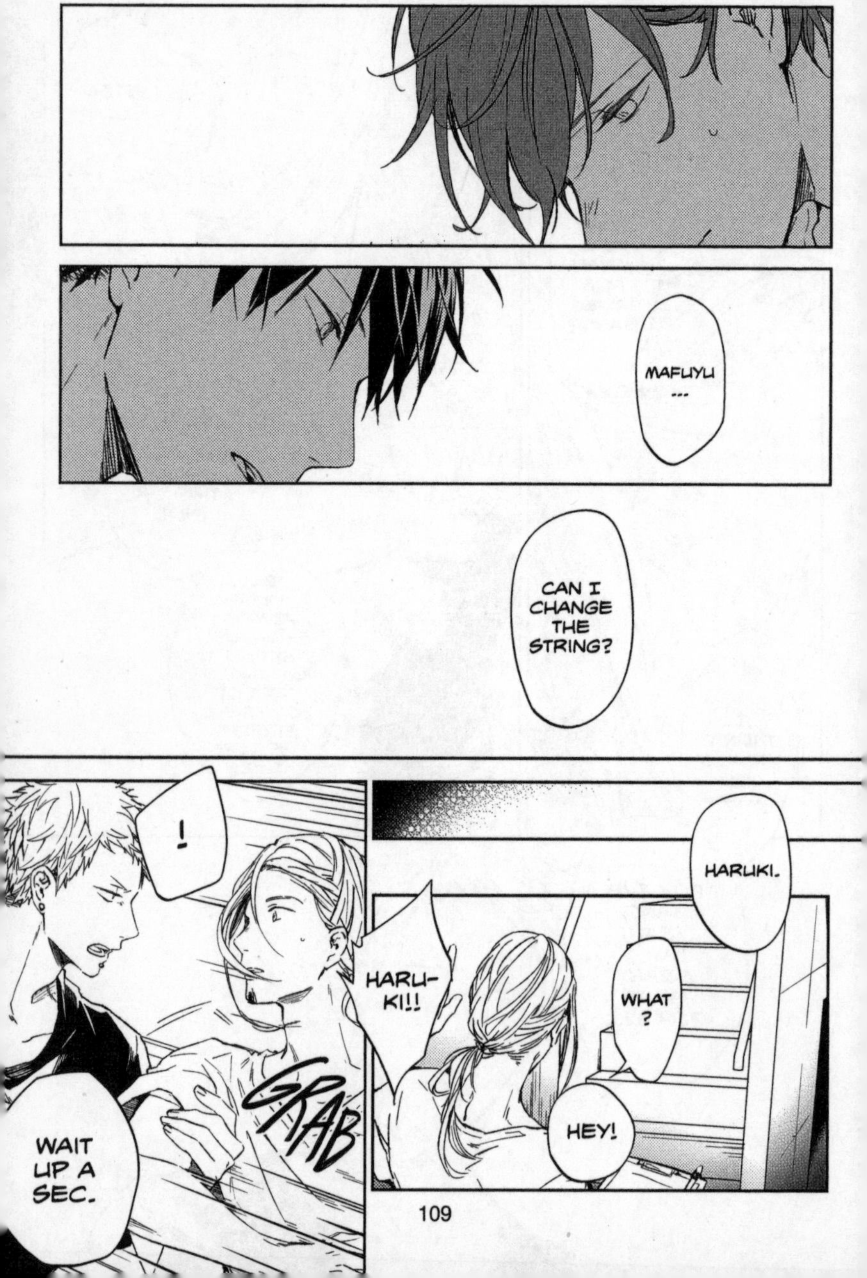
MAFUYU ...
CAN I CHANGE THE STRING?
HARUKI.
WHAT?
HEY!
HARU-KI!!
!
GRAB
WAIT UP A SEC.

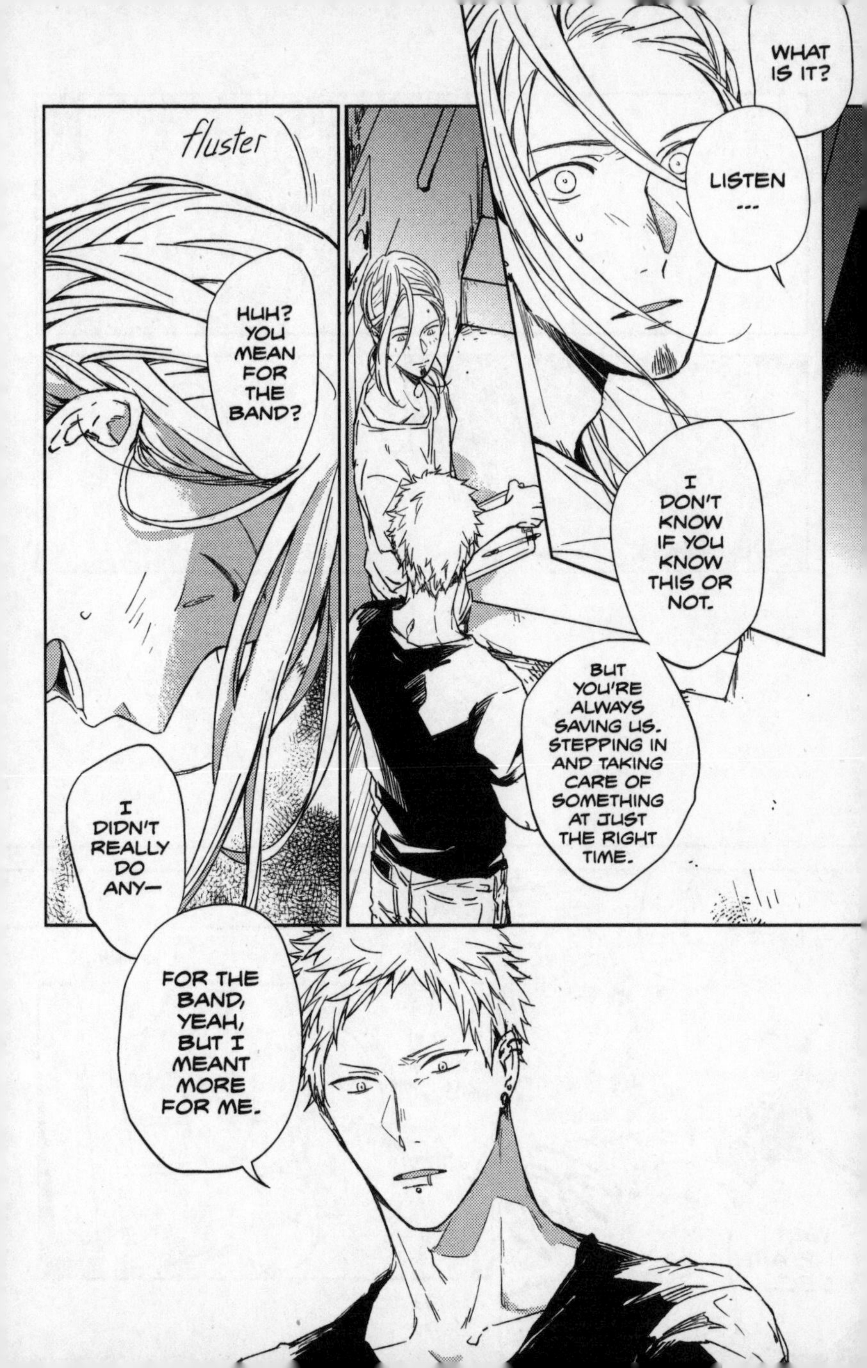
WHAT IS IT?
LISTEN ---
I DON'T KNOW IF YOU KNOW THIS OR NOT.
BUT YOU'RE ALWAYS SAVING US. STEPPING IN AND TAKING CARE OF SOMETHING AT JUST THE RIGHT TIME.
fluster
HUH? YOU MEAN FOR THE BAND?
I DIDN'T REALLY DO ANY—
FOR THE BAND, YEAH, BUT I MEANT MORE FOR ME.

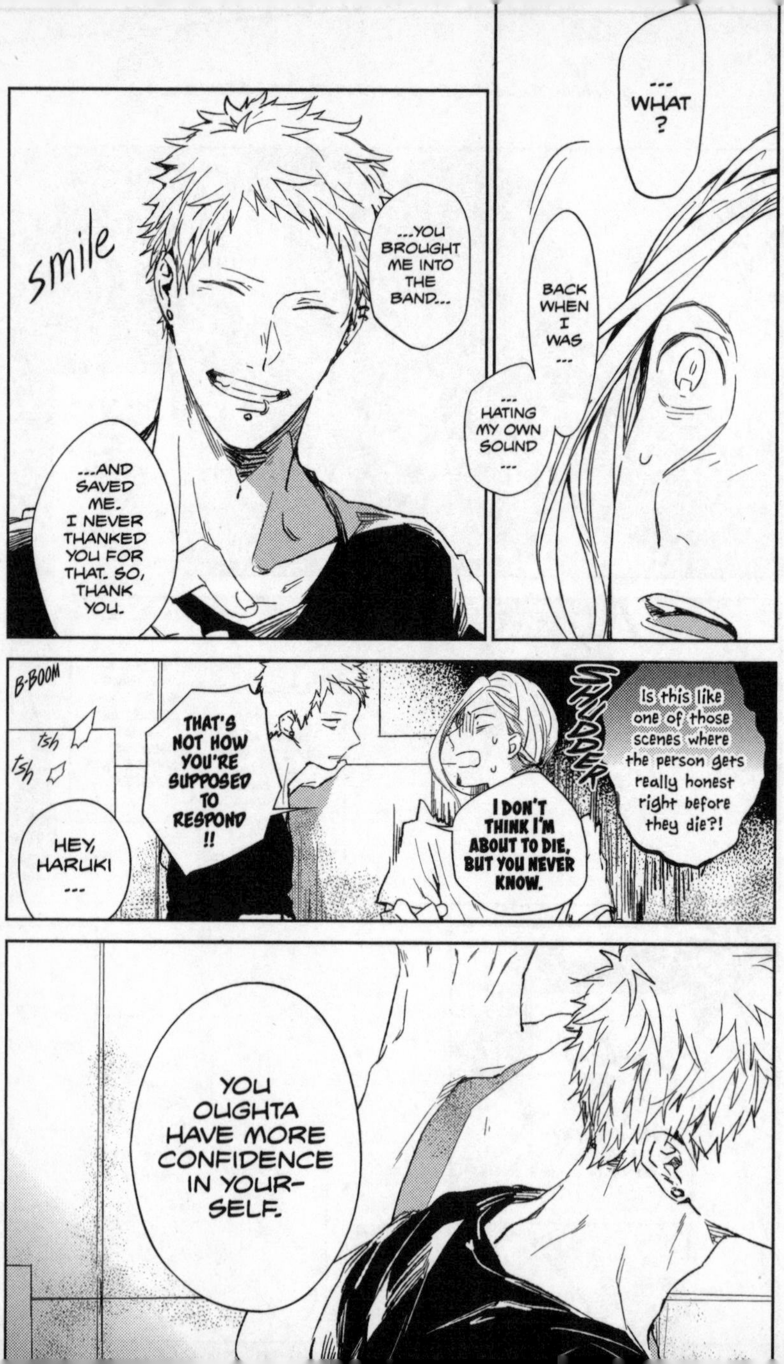
...WHAT?
BACK WHEN I WAS...
...HATING MY OWN SOUND...
smile
...YOU BROUGHT ME INTO THE BAND...
...AND SAVED ME. I NEVER THANKED YOU FOR THAT. SO, THANK YOU.
SHUDDER
Is this like one of those scenes where the person gets really honest right before they die?!
I DON'T THINK I'M ABOUT TO DIE, BUT YOU NEVER KNOW.
THAT'S NOT HOW YOU'RE SUPPOSED TO RESPOND!!
B-BOOM
tsh
tsh
HEY, HARUKI...
YOU OUGHTA HAVE MORE CONFIDENCE IN YOUR-SELF.

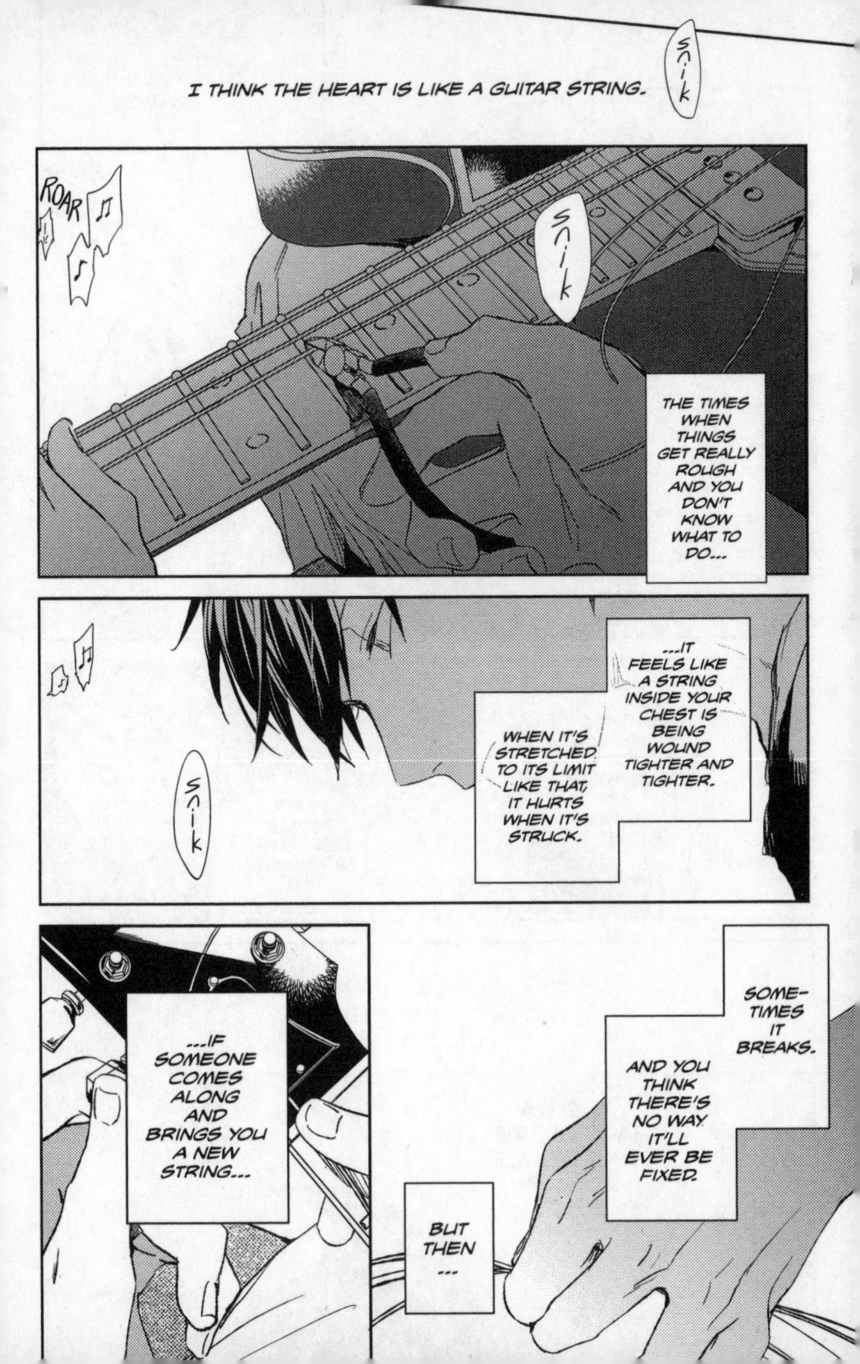
I THINK THE HEART IS LIKE A GUITAR STRING.
snik
snik
ROAR
THE TIMES WHEN THINGS GET REALLY ROUGH AND YOU DON'T KNOW WHAT TO DO...
...IT FEELS LIKE A STRING INSIDE YOUR CHEST IS BEING WOUND TIGHTER AND TIGHTER.
WHEN IT'S STRETCHED TO ITS LIMIT LIKE THAT, IT HURTS WHEN IT'S STRUCK.
snik
SOME-TIMES IT BREAKS.
AND YOU THINK THERE'S NO WAY IT'LL EVER BE FIXED.
BUT THEN...
...IF SOMEONE COMES ALONG AND BRINGS YOU A NEW STRING...

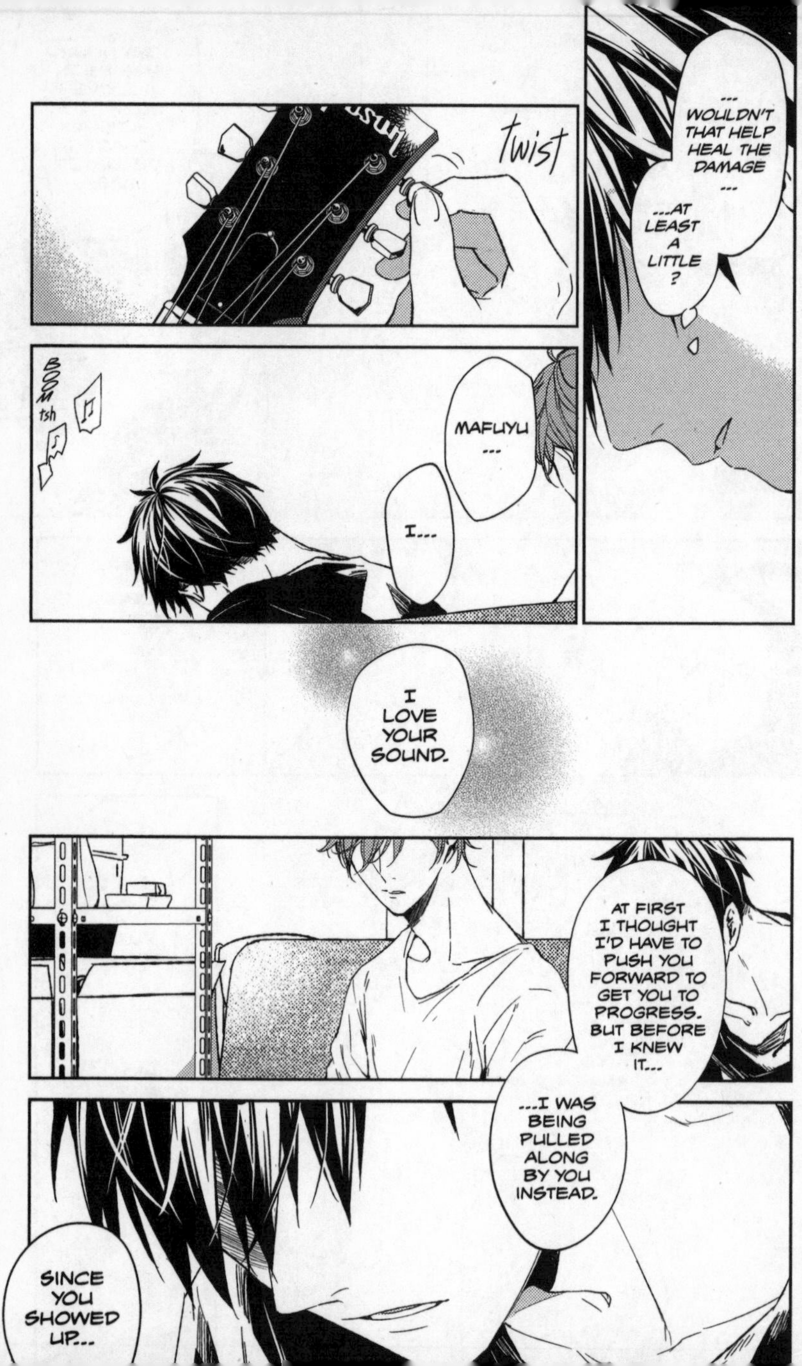
...WOULDN'T THAT HELP HEAL THE DAMAGE...
...AT LEAST A LITTLE?
twist
MAFUYU...
I...
BOOM tsh
I LOVE YOUR SOUND.
AT FIRST I THOUGHT I'D HAVE TO PUSH YOU FORWARD TO GET YOU TO PROGRESS. BUT BEFORE I KNEW IT...
...I WAS BEING PULLED ALONG BY YOU INSTEAD.
SINCE YOU SHOWED UP...

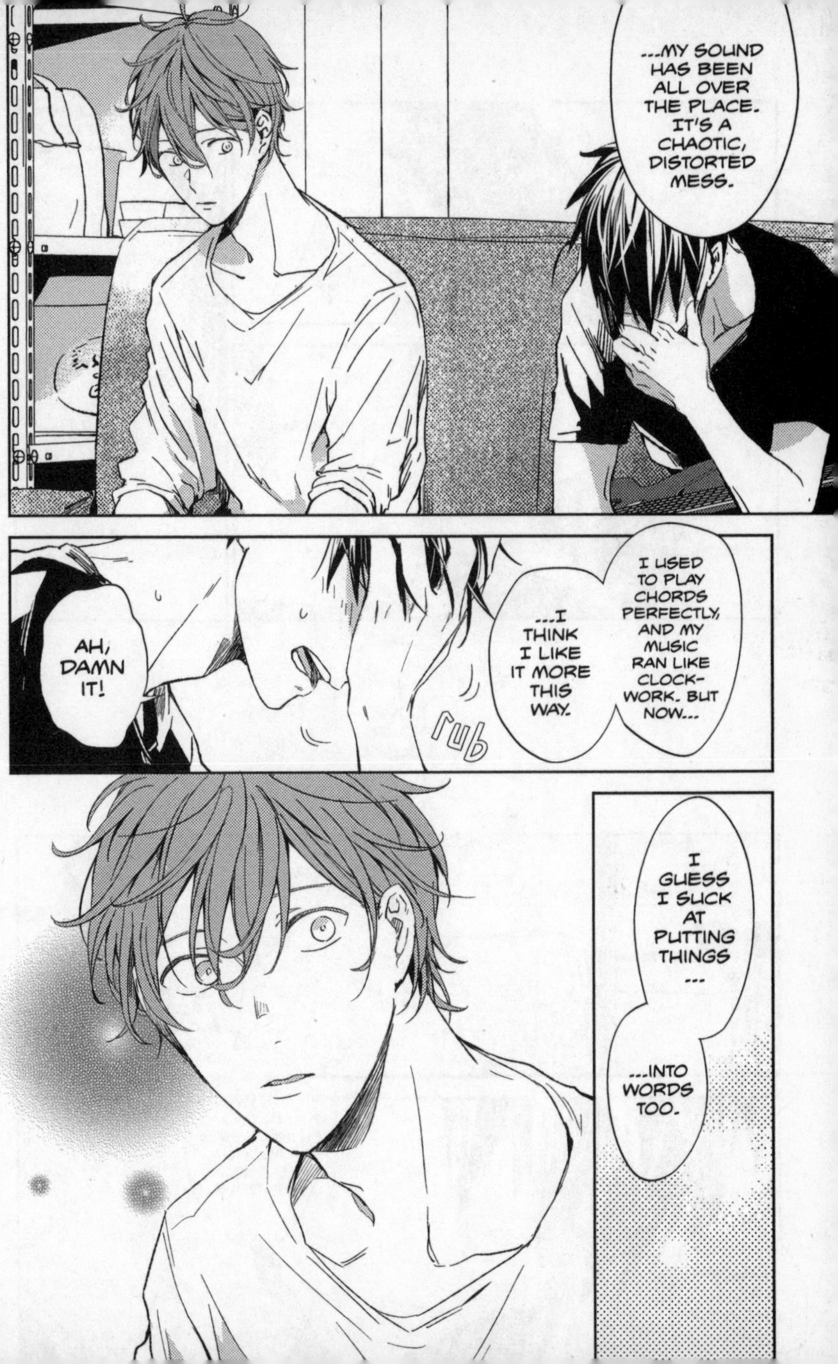
...MY SOUND HAS BEEN ALL OVER THE PLACE. IT'S A CHAOTIC, DISTORTED MESS.
I USED TO PLAY CHORDS PERFECTLY, AND MY MUSIC RAN LIKE CLOCK-WORK. BUT NOW...
...I THINK I LIKE IT MORE THIS WAY.
rub
AH, DAMN IT!
I GUESS I SUCK AT PUTTING THINGS ...
...INTO WORDS TOO.

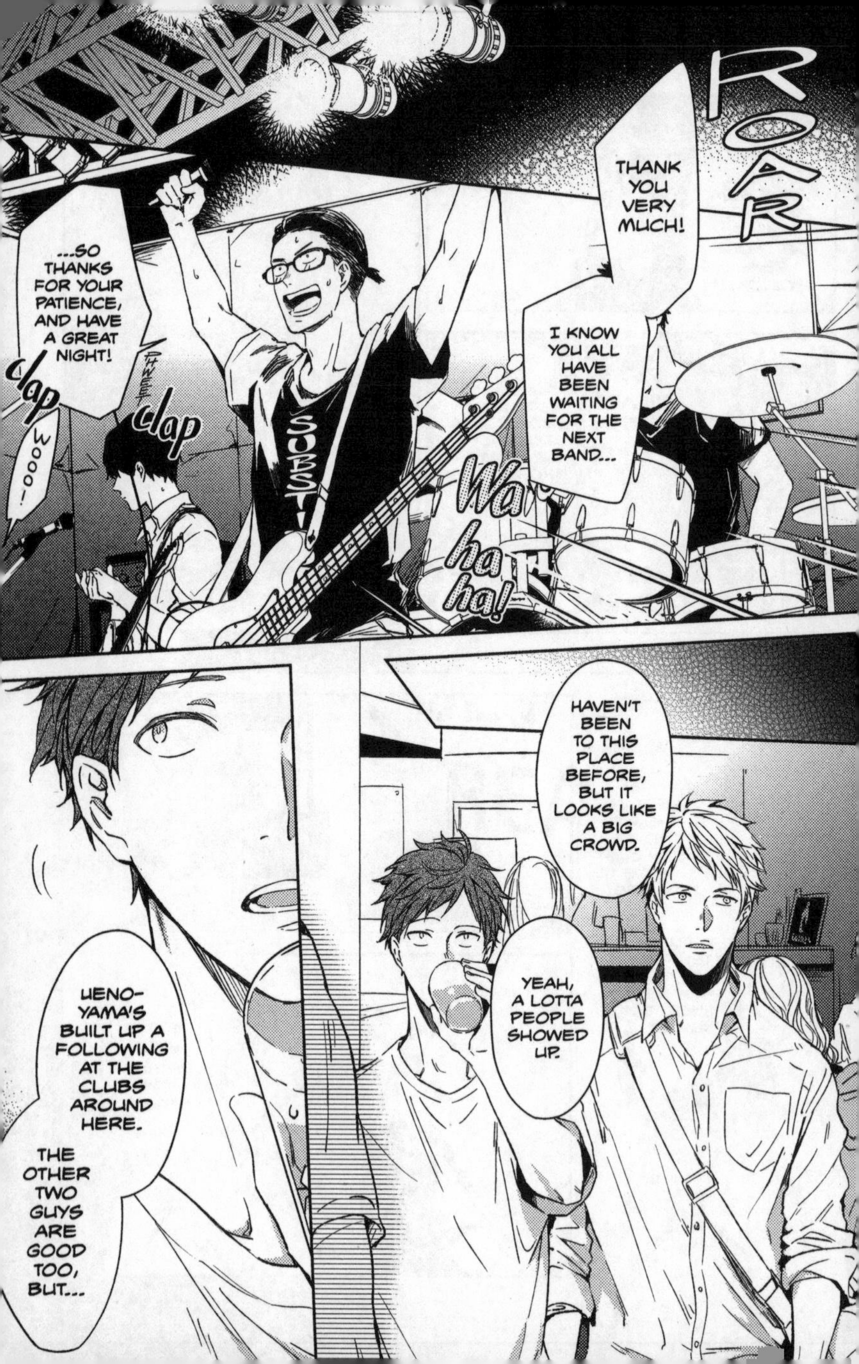
ROAR
THANK YOU VERY MUCH!
I KNOW YOU ALL HAVE BEEN WAITING FOR THE NEXT BAND...
Wa ha ha!
...SO THANKS FOR YOUR PATIENCE, AND HAVE A GREAT NIGHT!
PHWEE
clap
clap
WOOO!
HAVEN'T BEEN TO THIS PLACE BEFORE, BUT IT LOOKS LIKE A BIG CROWD.
YEAH, A LOTTA PEOPLE SHOWED UP.
UENO-YAMA'S BUILT UP A FOLLOWING AT THE CLUBS AROUND HERE.
THE OTHER TWO GUYS ARE GOOD TOO, BUT...

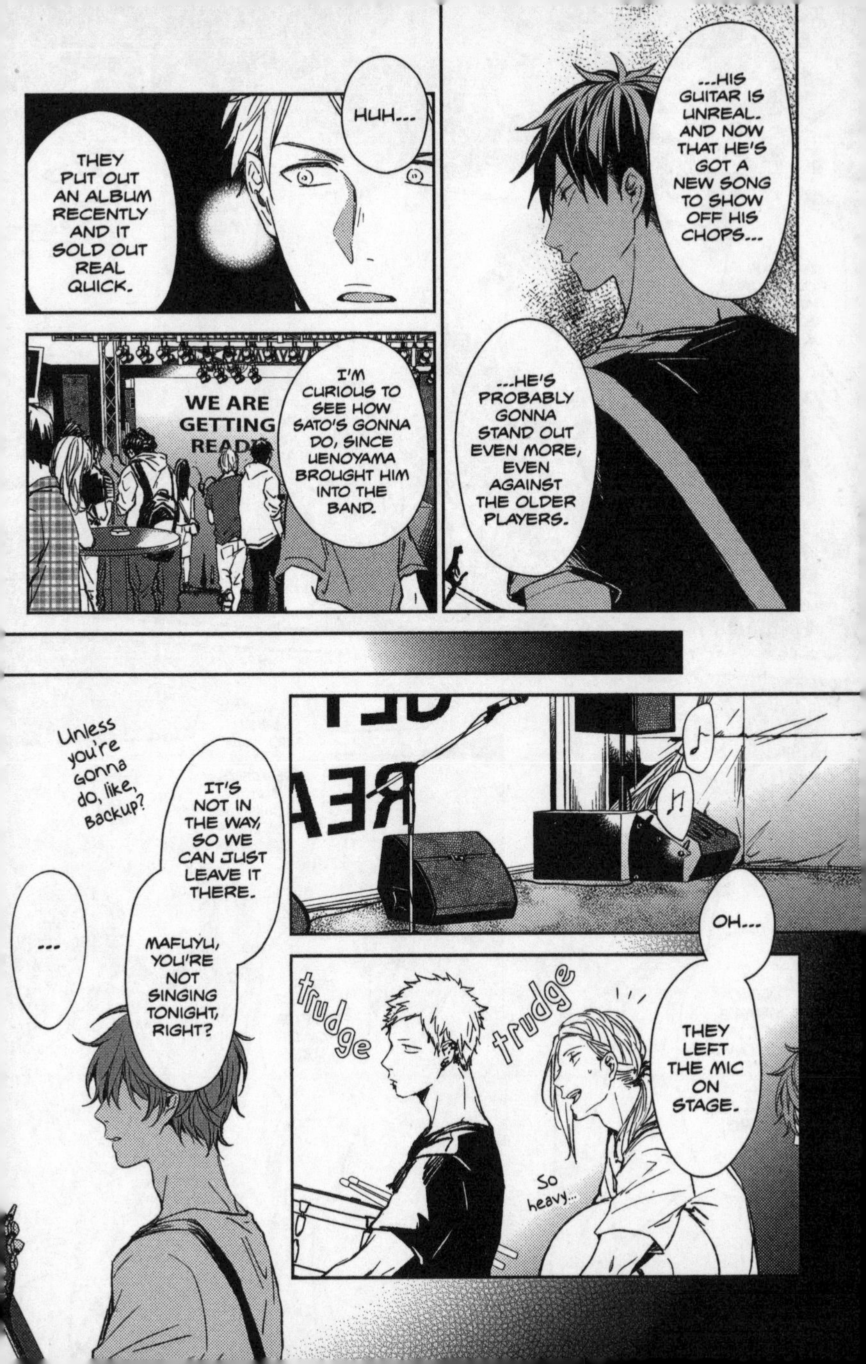
...HIS GUITAR IS UNREAL. AND NOW THAT HE'S GOT A NEW SONG TO SHOW OFF HIS CHOPS...
...HE'S PROBABLY GONNA STAND OUT EVEN MORE, EVEN AGAINST THE OLDER PLAYERS.
HUH...
THEY PUT OUT AN ALBUM RECENTLY AND IT SOLD OUT REAL QUICK.
I'M CURIOUS TO SEE HOW SATO'S GONNA DO, SINCE UENOYAMA BROUGHT HIM INTO THE BAND.
WE ARE GETTING READ
OH...
THEY LEFT THE MIC ON STAGE.
trudge
trudge
So heavy...
IT'S NOT IN THE WAY, SO WE CAN JUST LEAVE IT THERE.
MAFUYU, YOU'RE NOT SINGING TONIGHT, RIGHT?
...
Unless you're gonna do, like, backup?

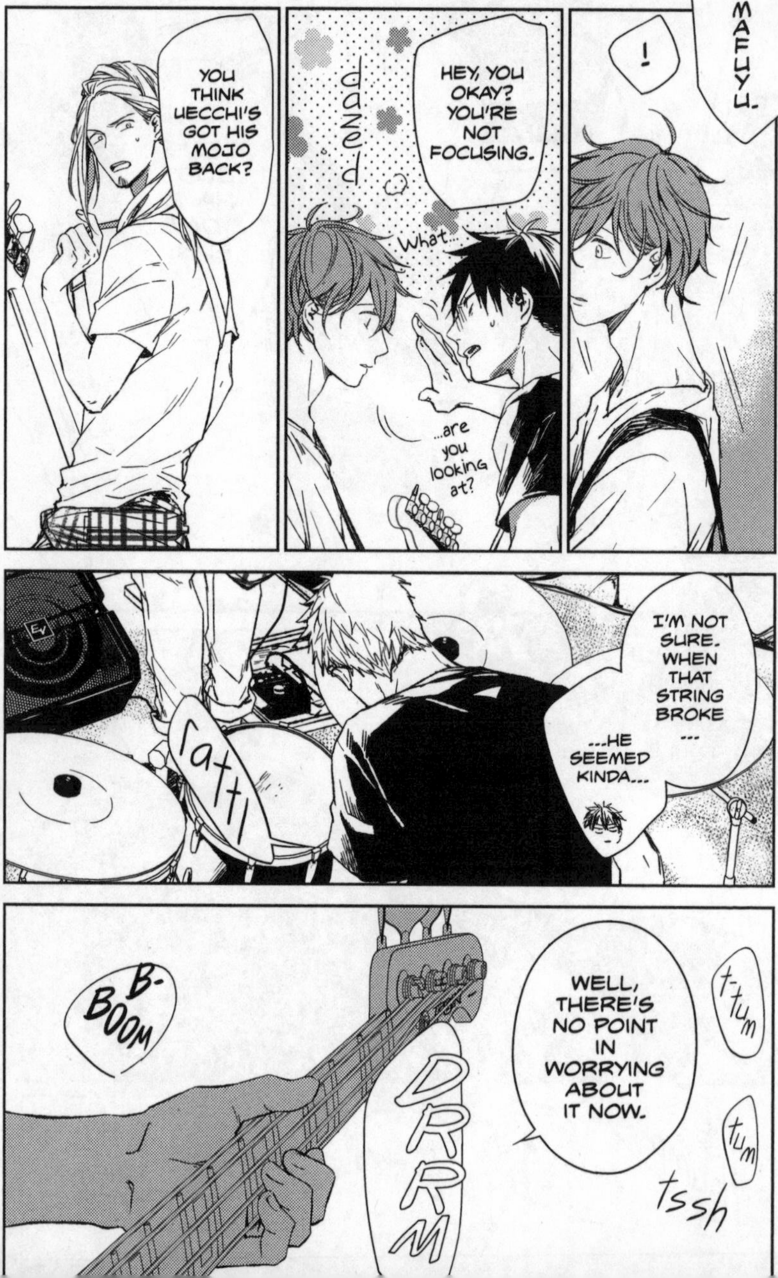
MAFUYU.
!
HEY, YOU OKAY? YOU'RE NOT FOCUSING.
dazed
What...
...are you looking at?
YOU THINK UECCHI'S GOT HIS MOJO BACK?
I'M NOT SURE. WHEN THAT STRING BROKE ...
...HE SEEMED KINDA...
rattl
t-tum
tum
tssh
WELL, THERE'S NO POINT IN WORRYING ABOUT IT NOW.
DRRM
B-BOOM

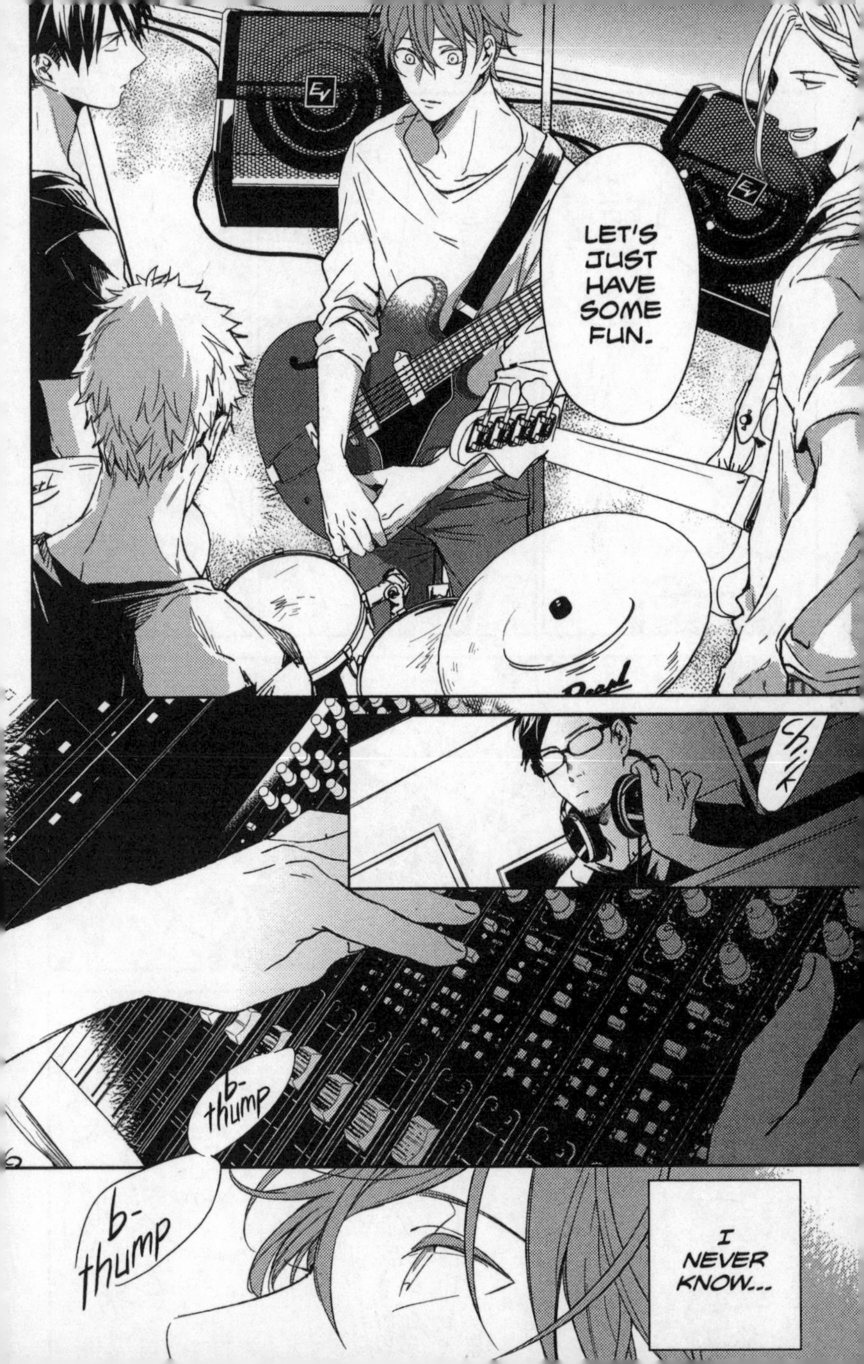
LET'S JUST HAVE SOME FUN.
chik
b-thump
I NEVER KNOW...
b-thump

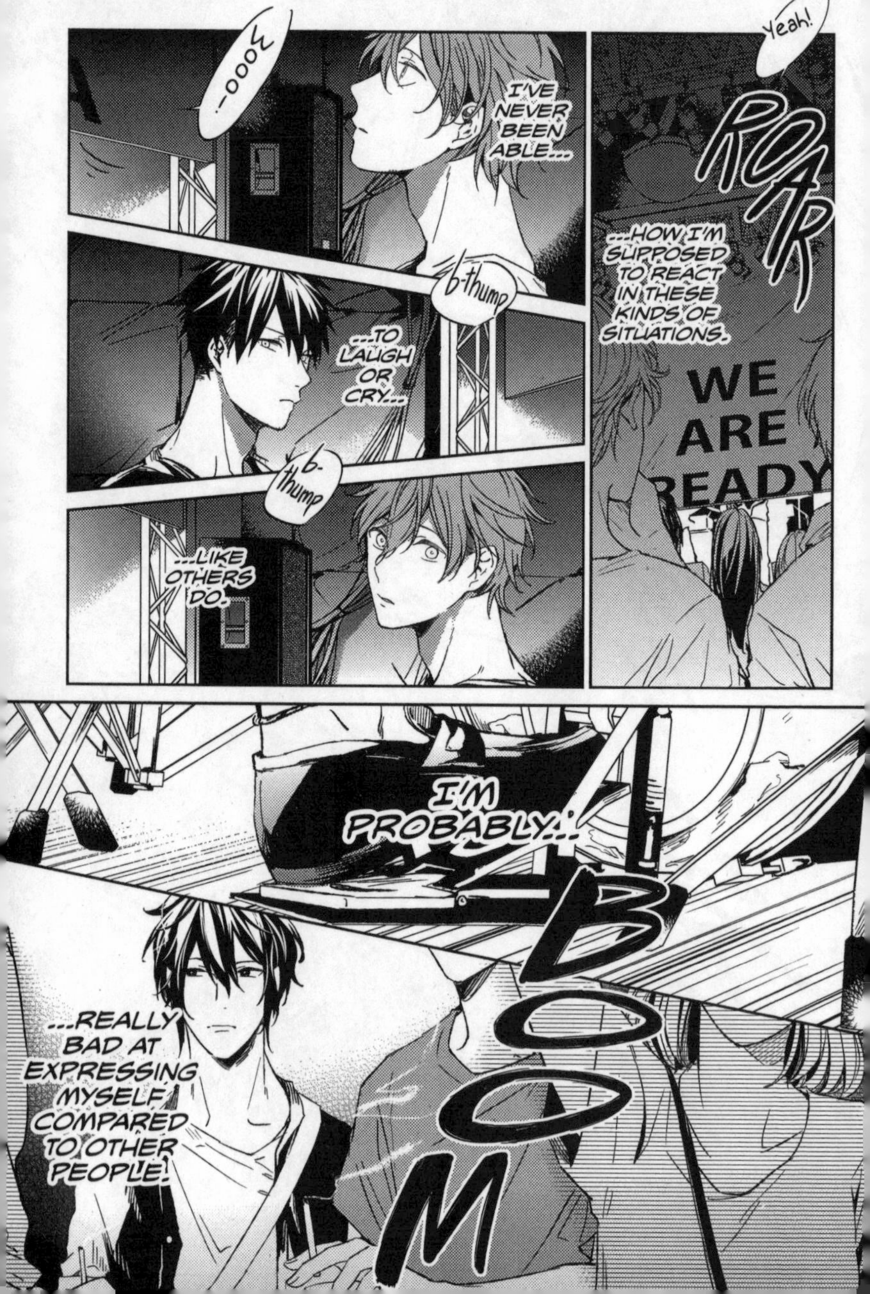
Yeah!
ROAR
...HOW I'M SUPPOSED TO REACT IN THESE KINDS OF SITUATIONS.
WE ARE READY
Wooo-!
I'VE NEVER BEEN ABLE...
b-thump
...TO LAUGH OR CRY...
b-thump
...LIKE OTHERS DO.
I'M PROBABLY...
BOOM
...REALLY BAD AT EXPRESSING MYSELF COMPARED TO OTHER PEOPLE.

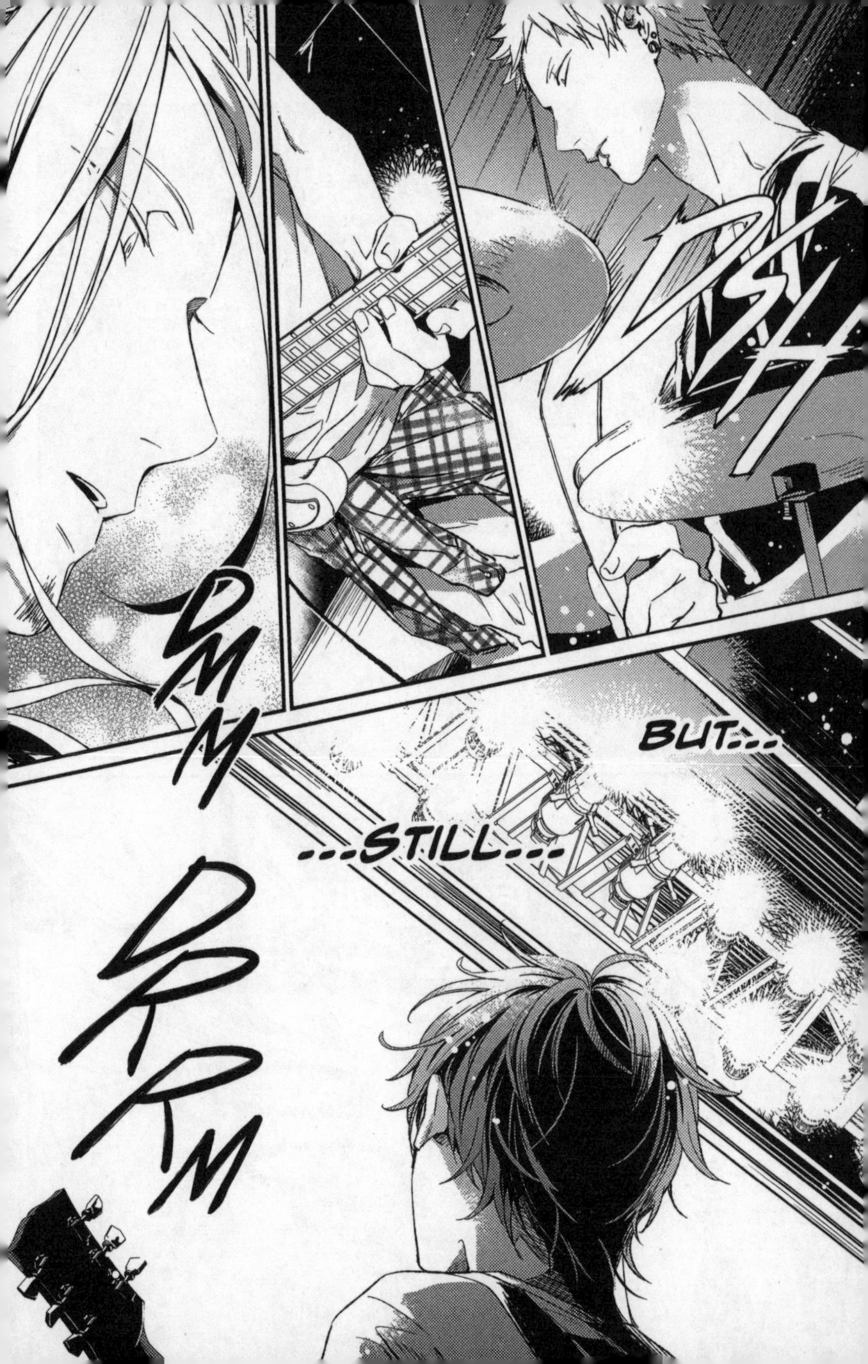
DSH
DMM
BUT...
...STILL...
DRRM

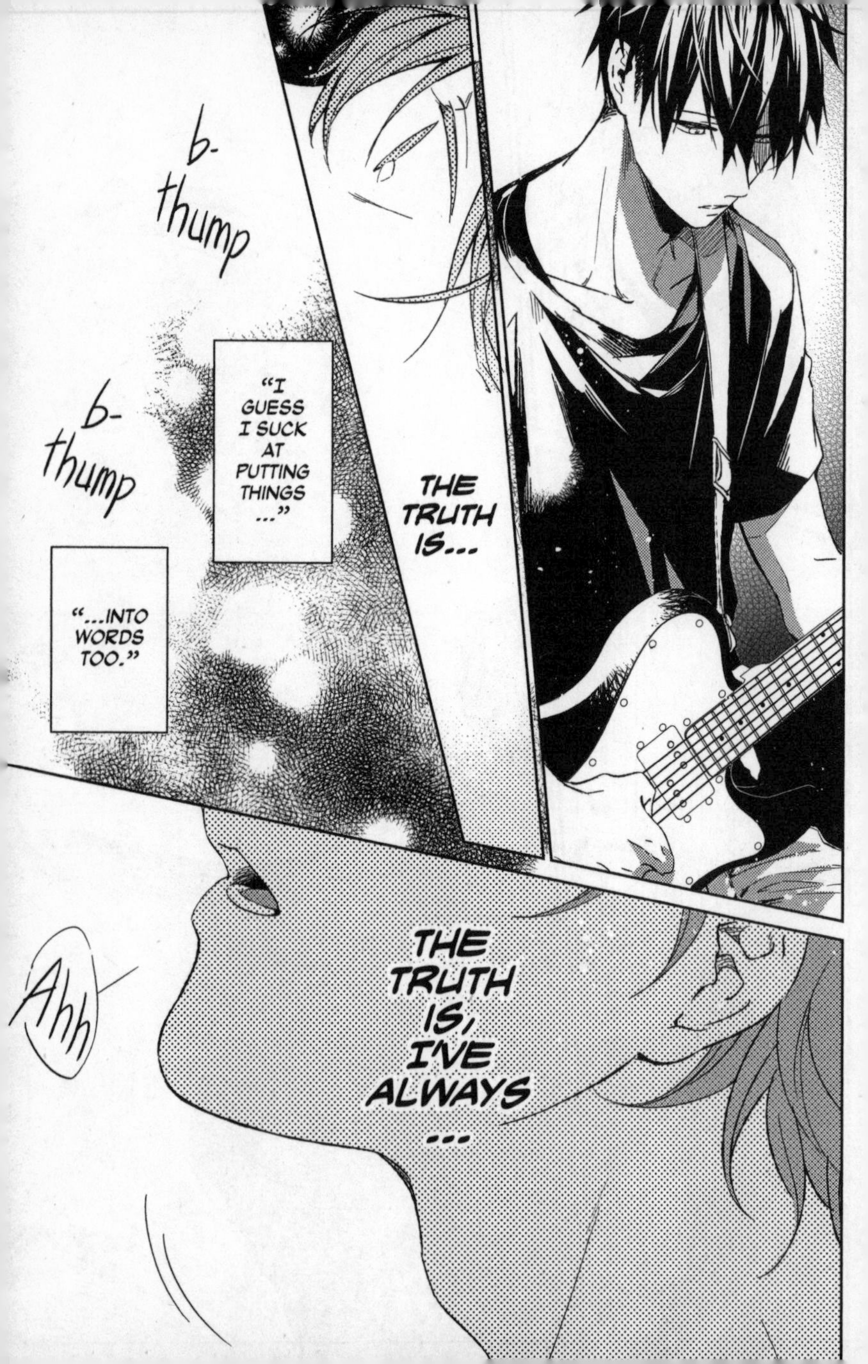
THE TRUTH IS...
b-thump
"I GUESS I SUCK AT PUTTING THINGS..."
b-thump
"...INTO WORDS TOO."
THE TRUTH IS, I'VE ALWAYS...
Ahh

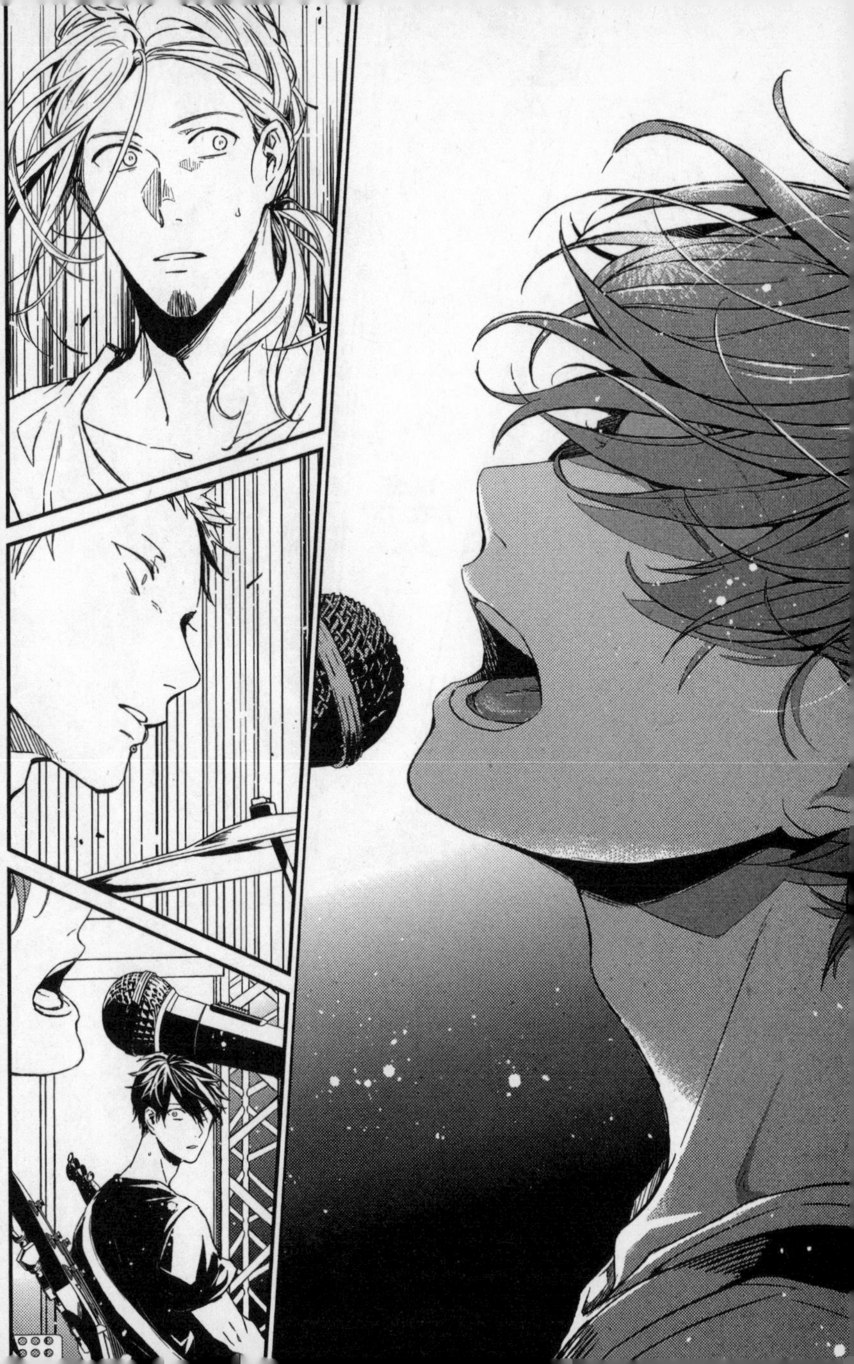

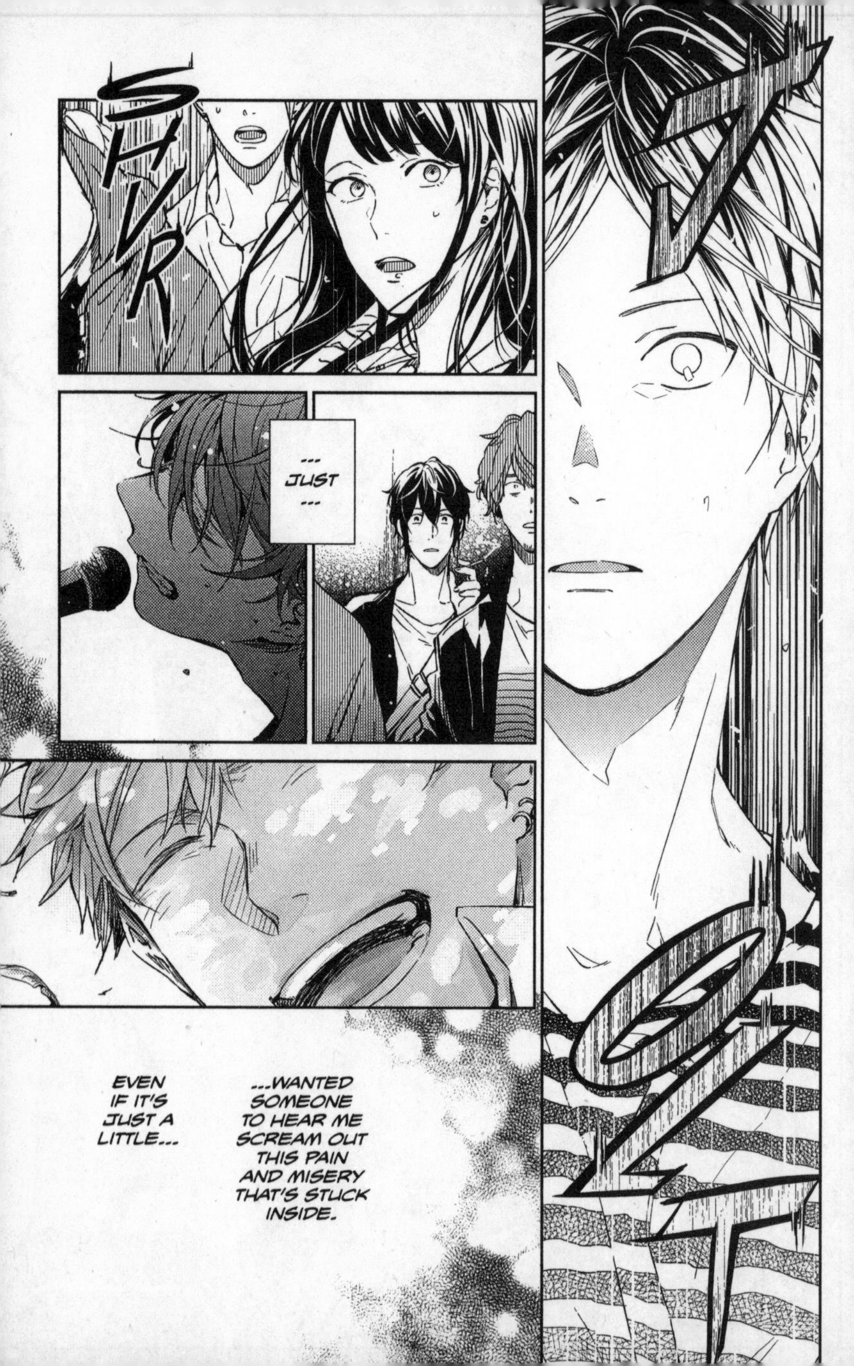
SHVR

JUST

EVEN IF IT'S JUST A LITTLE...
...WANTED SOMEONE TO HEAR ME SCREAM OUT THIS PAIN AND MISERY THAT'S STUCK INSIDE.

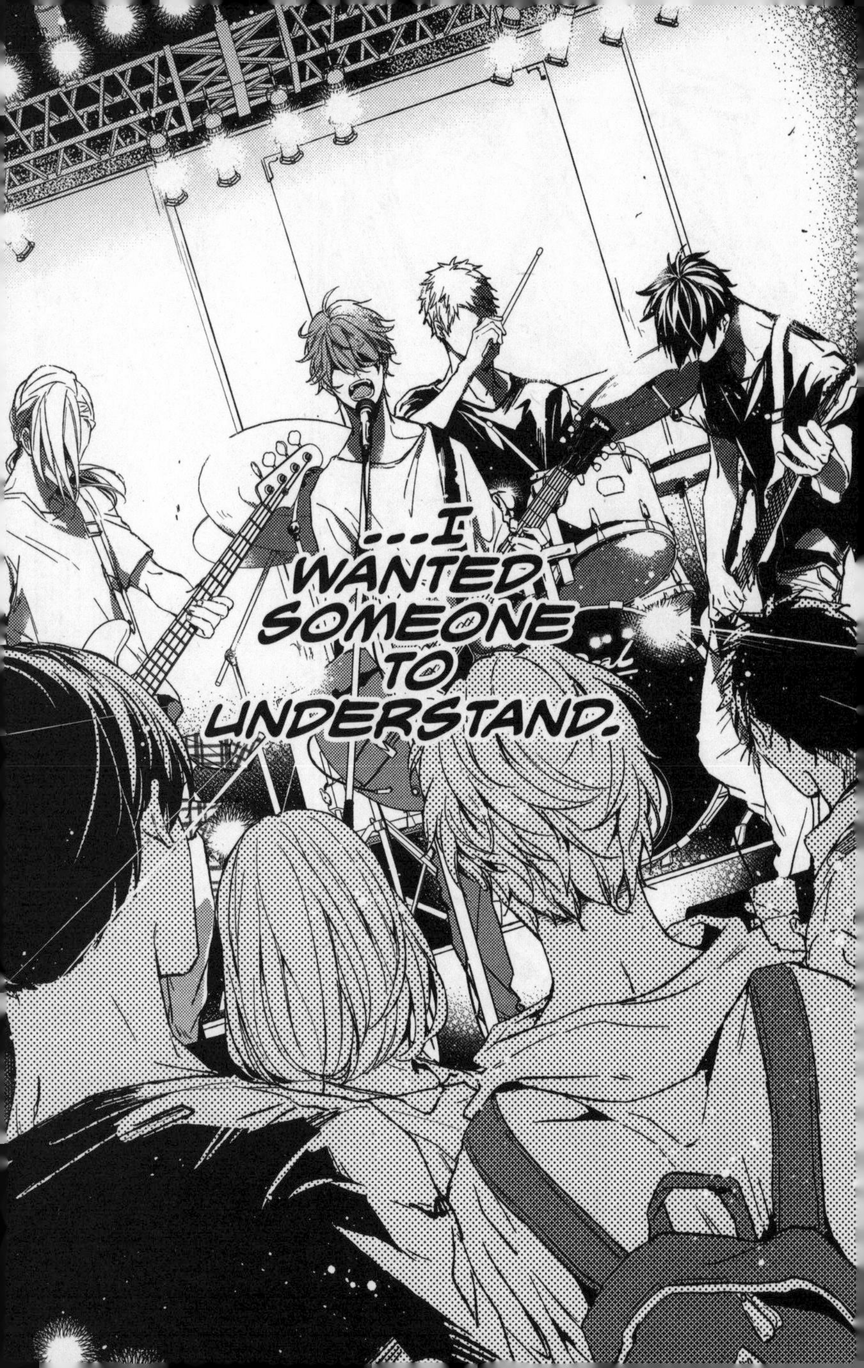
...I WANTED SOMEONE TO UNDERSTAND.

given

by Natsuki Kizu

chapter 11

given

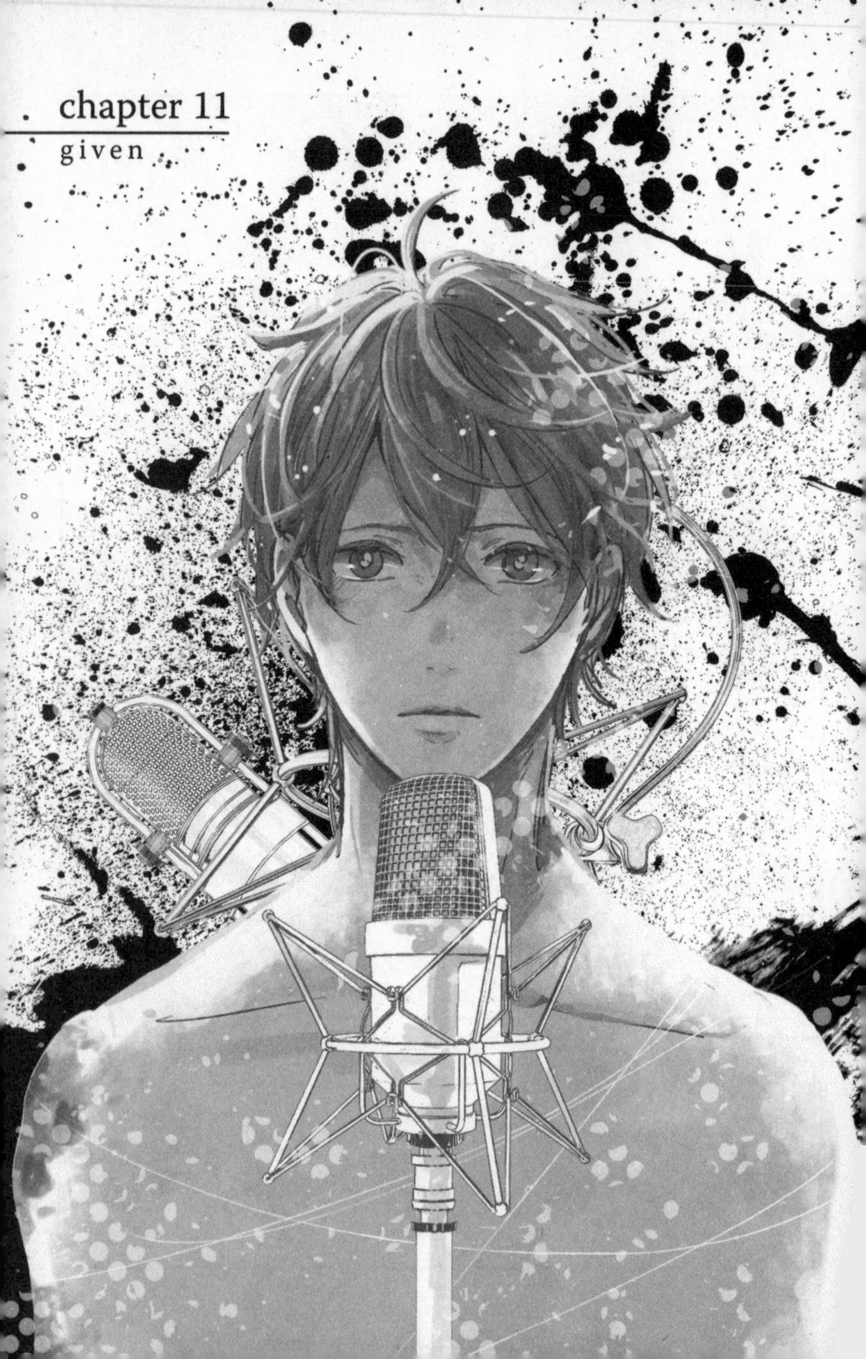

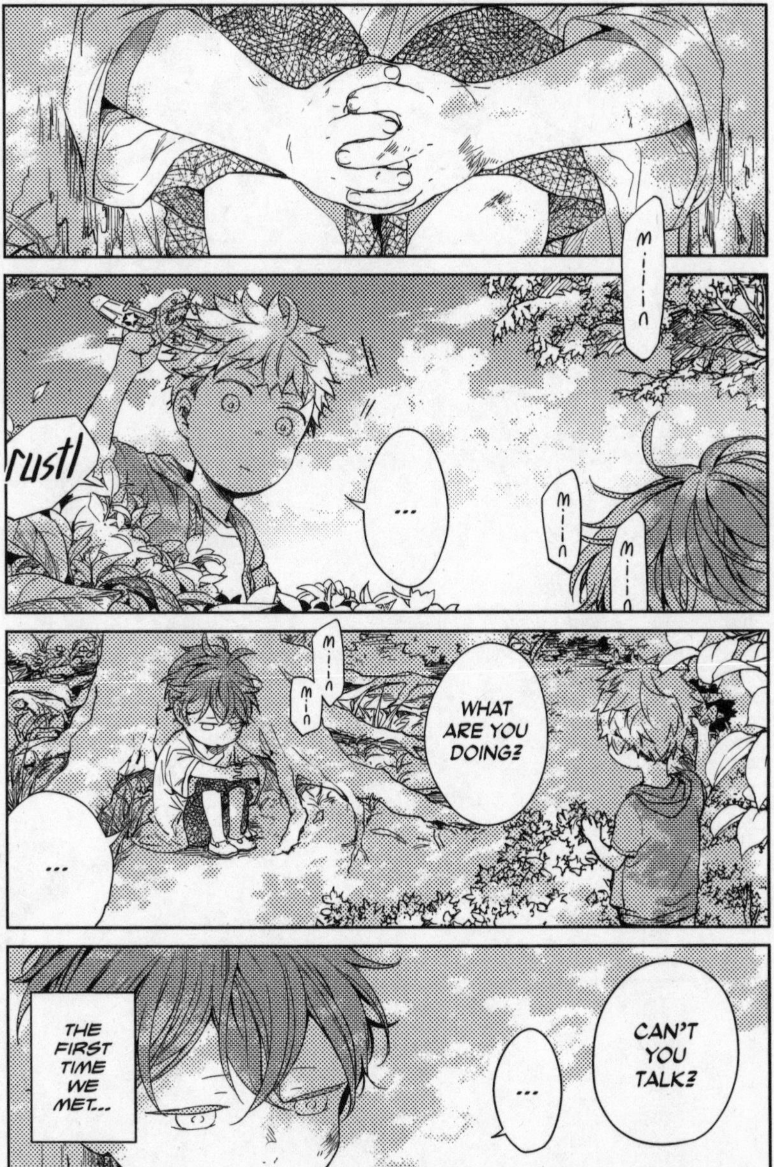
m...n
m...n
m...n
...
rustl
WHAT ARE YOU DOING?
m...n
m..n
...
CAN'T YOU TALK?
...
THE FIRST TIME WE MET...

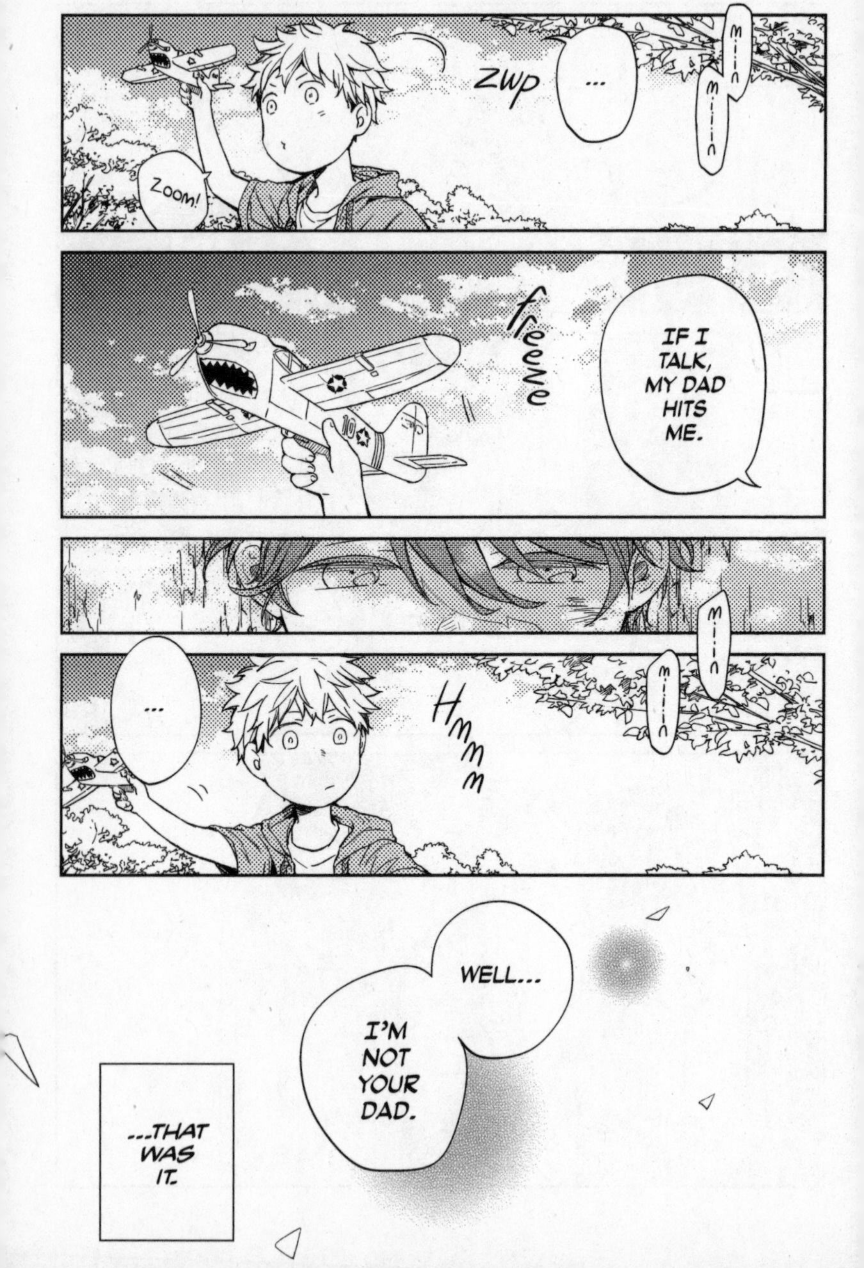
M-i-n
M-i-n
...
ZWP
ZOOM!
IF I TALK, MY DAD HITS ME.
FREEZE
M-i-n
M-i-n
HMMM
...
WELL...
I'M NOT YOUR DAD.
...THAT WAS IT.

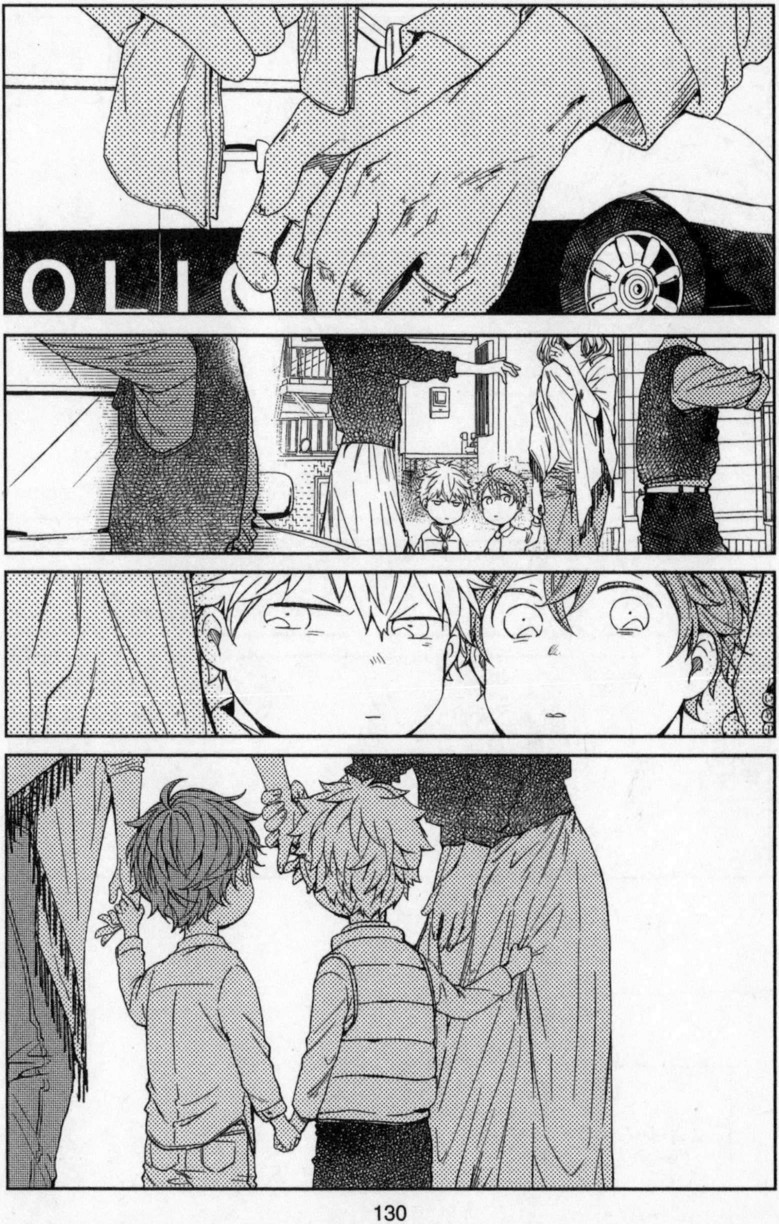
OLIC

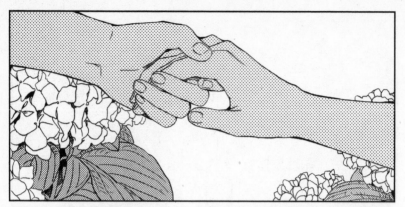

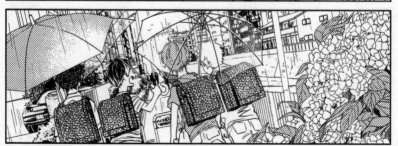

131

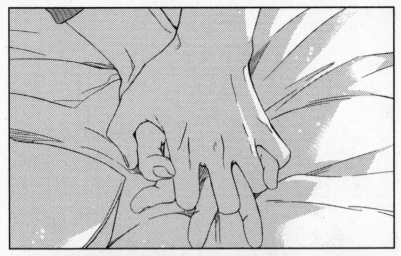

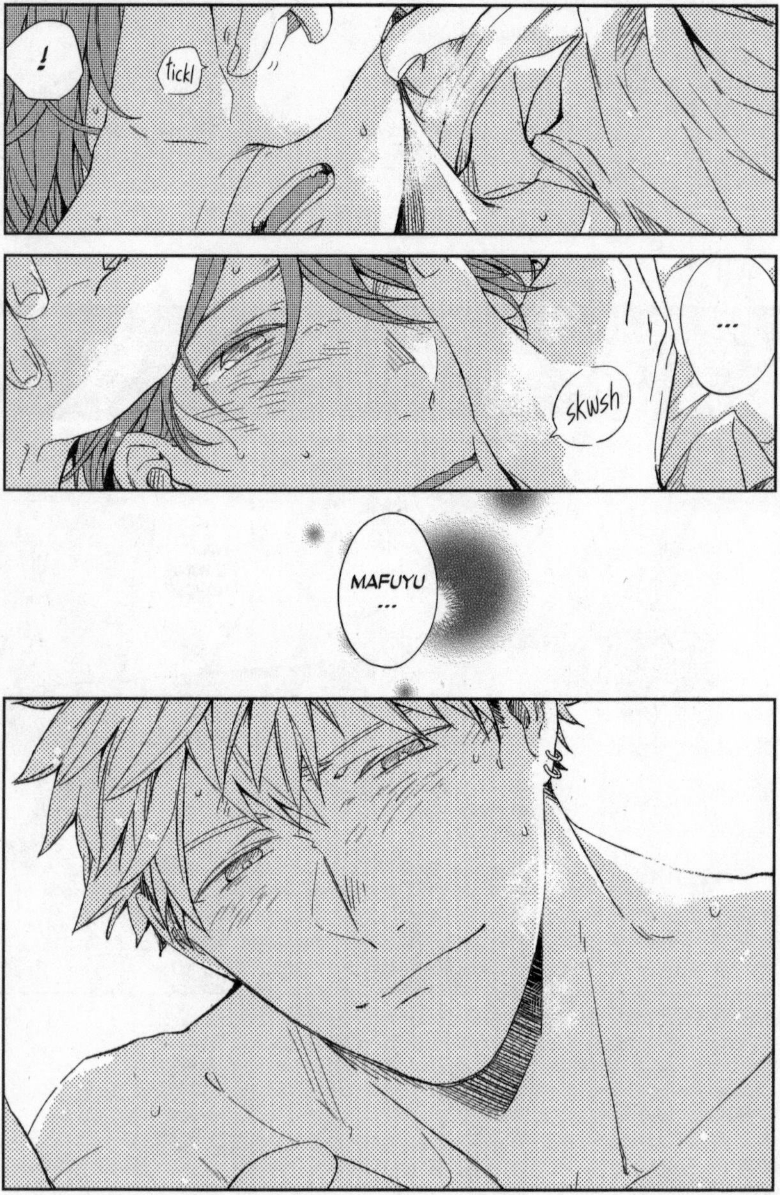
tickl
!
...
skwsh
MAFUYU ...

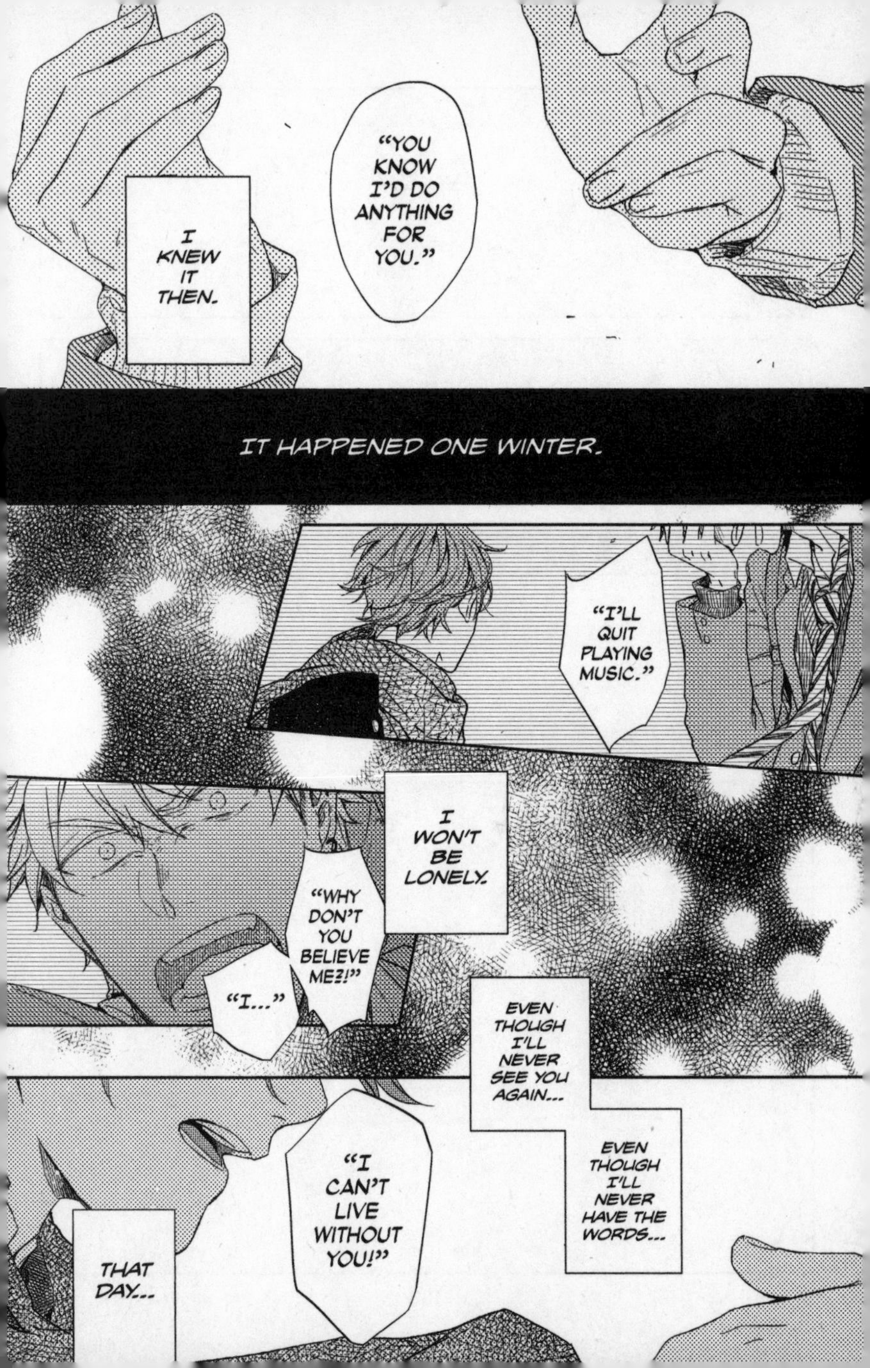
"YOU KNOW I'D DO ANYTHING FOR YOU."
I KNEW IT THEN.
IT HAPPENED ONE WINTER.
"I'LL QUIT PLAYING MUSIC."
I WON'T BE LONELY.
"WHY DON'T YOU BELIEVE ME?!"
"I..."
EVEN THOUGH I'LL NEVER SEE YOU AGAIN...
EVEN THOUGH I'LL NEVER HAVE THE WORDS...
"I CAN'T LIVE WITHOUT YOU!"
THAT DAY...

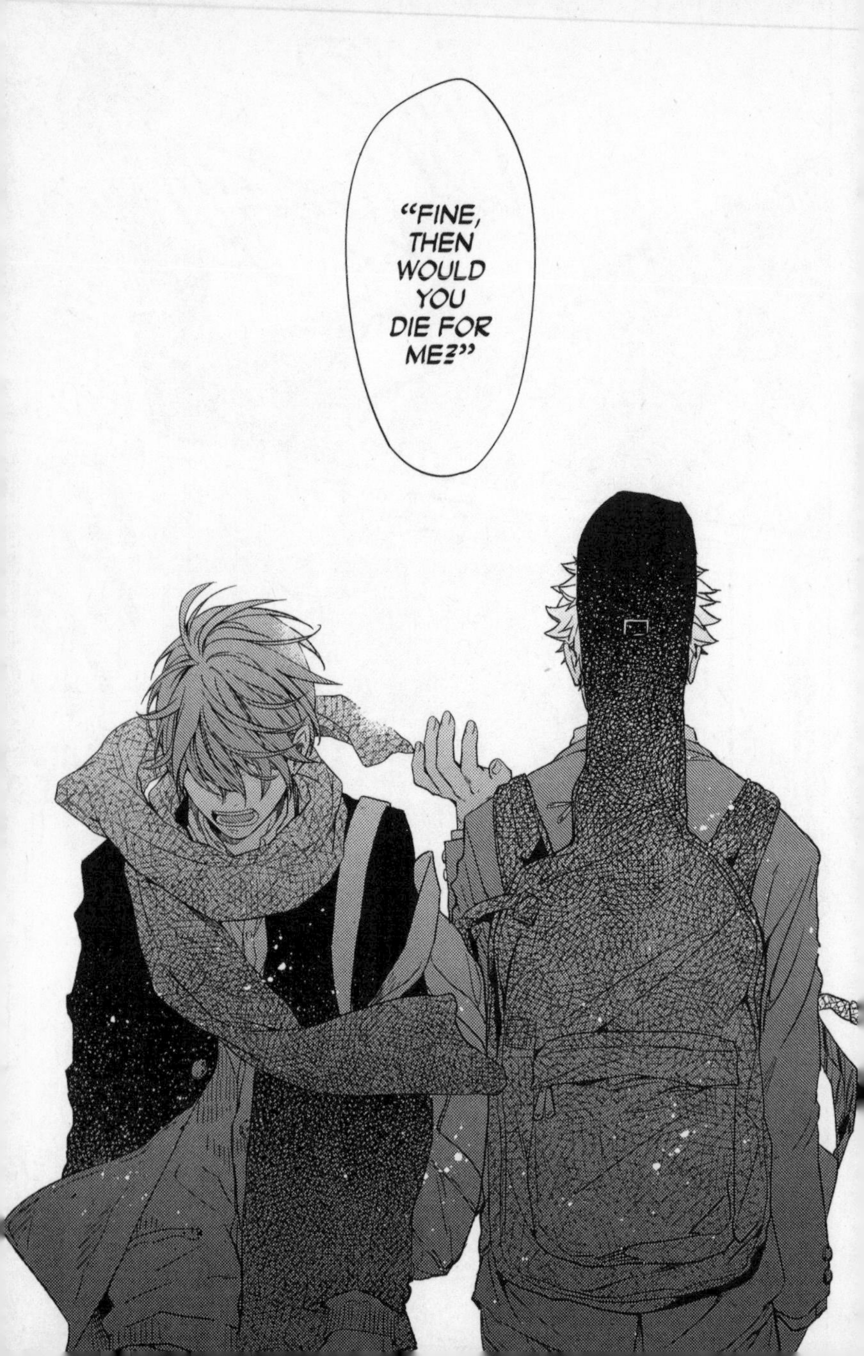
"FINE, THEN WOULD YOU DIE FOR ME?"

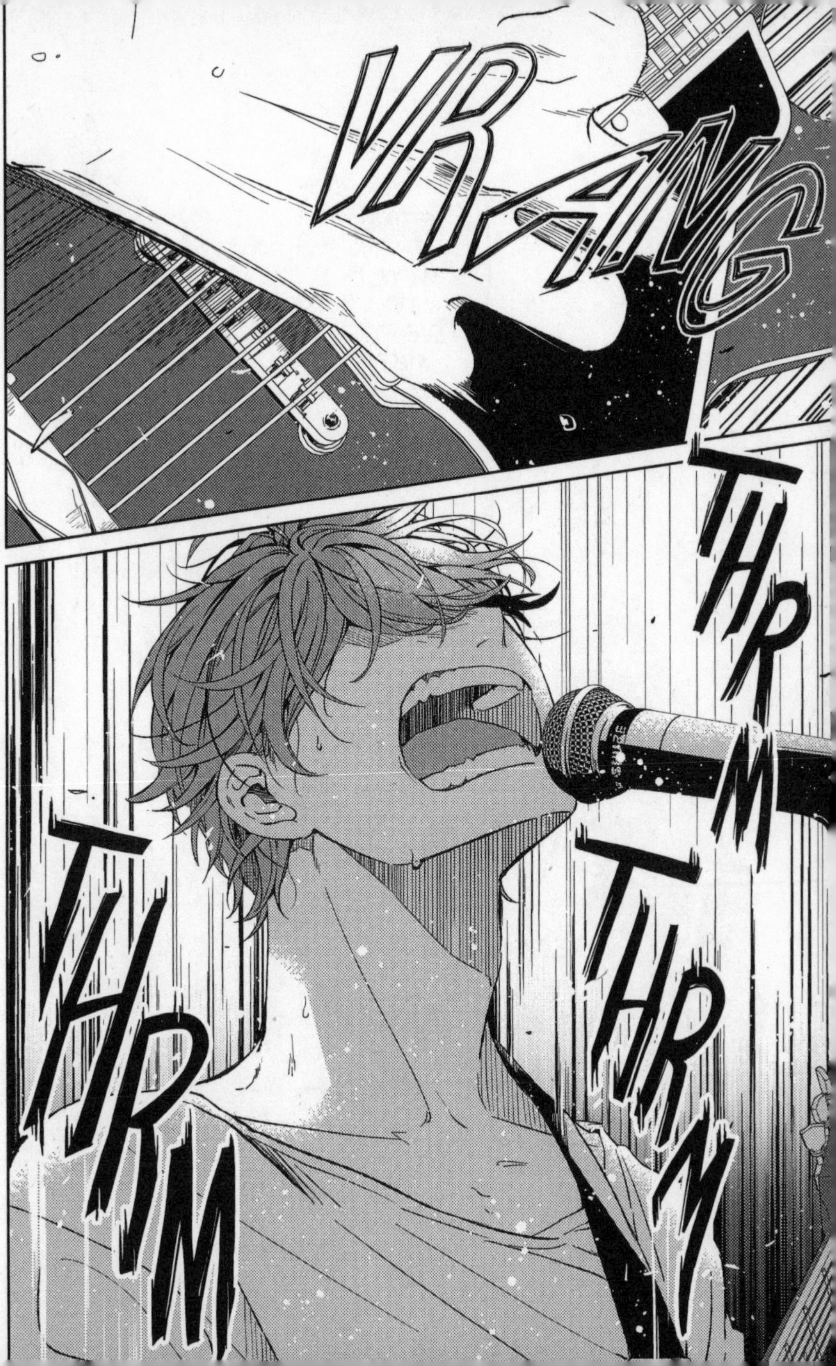
VRANG
THRM THRM
THRM

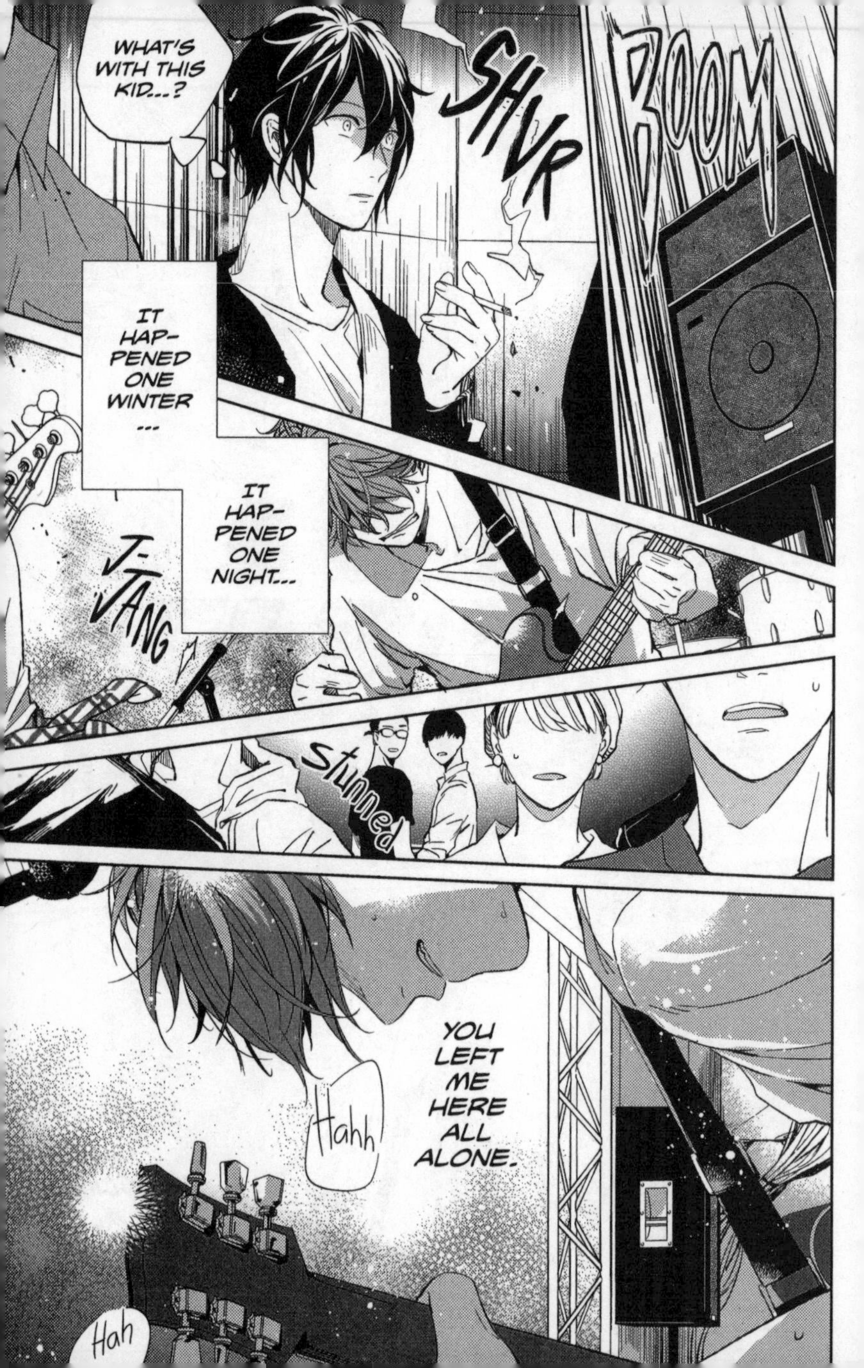
BOOM
SHVR
WHAT'S WITH THIS KID...?
IT HAP-PENED ONE WINTER ...
IT HAP-PENED ONE NIGHT...
J-JANG
Stunned
YOU LEFT ME HERE ALL ALONE.
Hahh
Hah

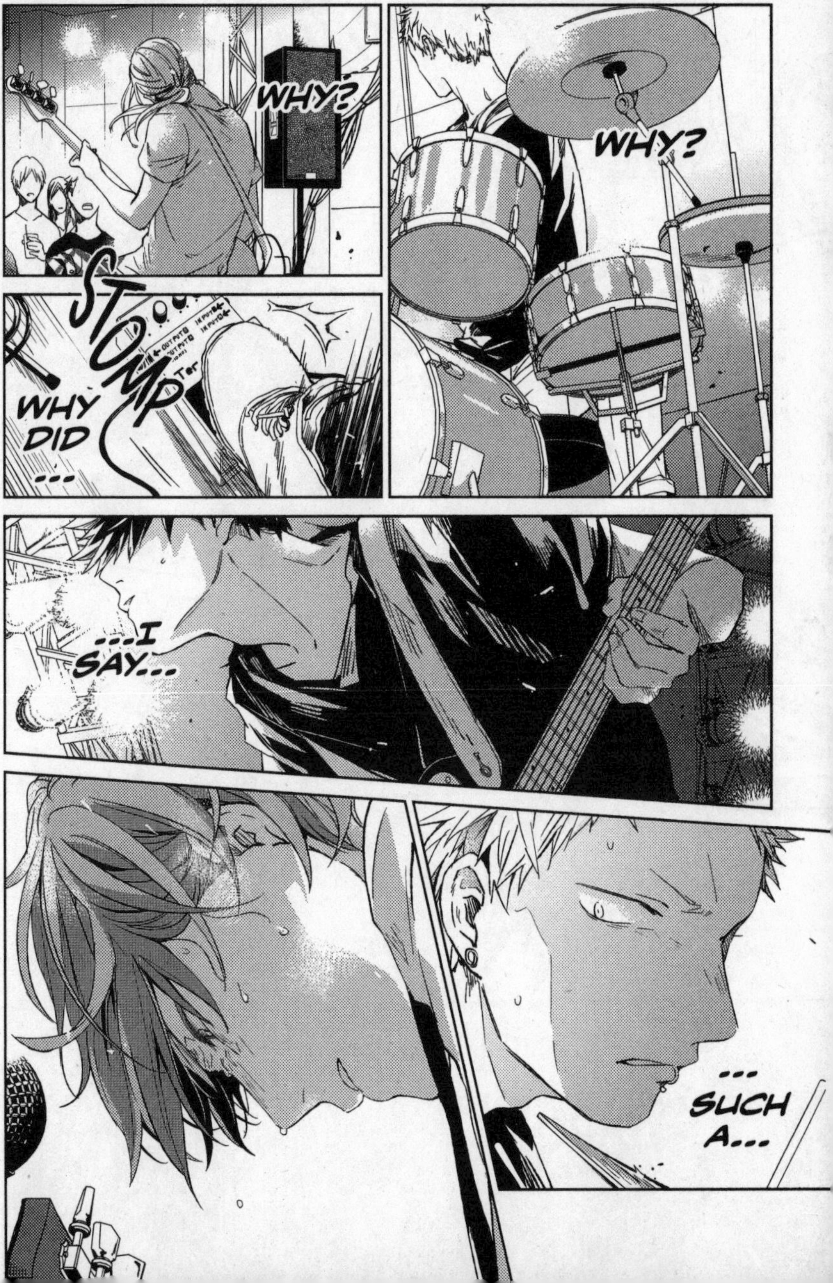
WHY?
WHY?
STOMP
WHY DID ...
...I SAY...
...SUCH A...

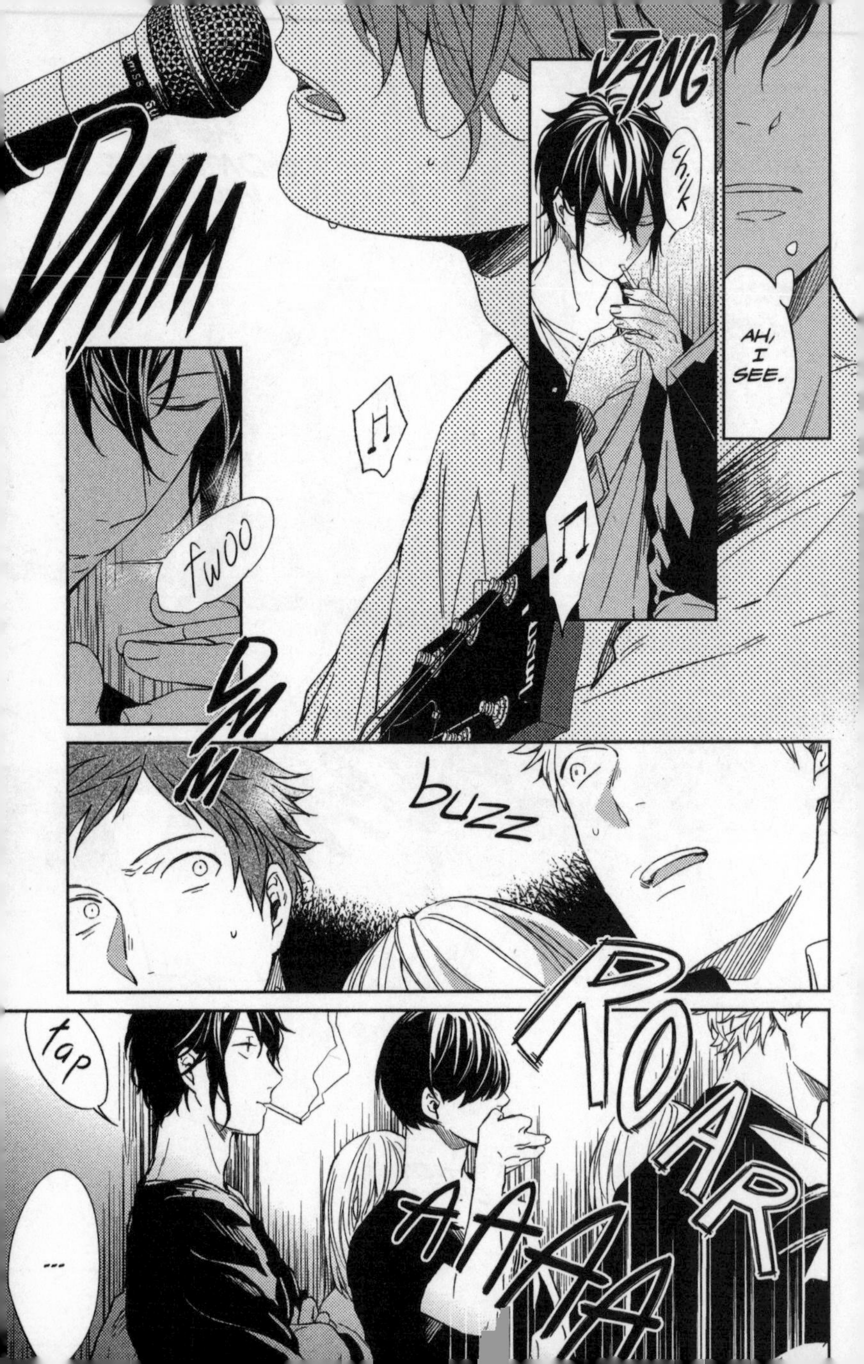
AH, I SEE.
JANG
chik
DMM
fwoo
DMM
buzz
ROAR
AAAA
tap
...

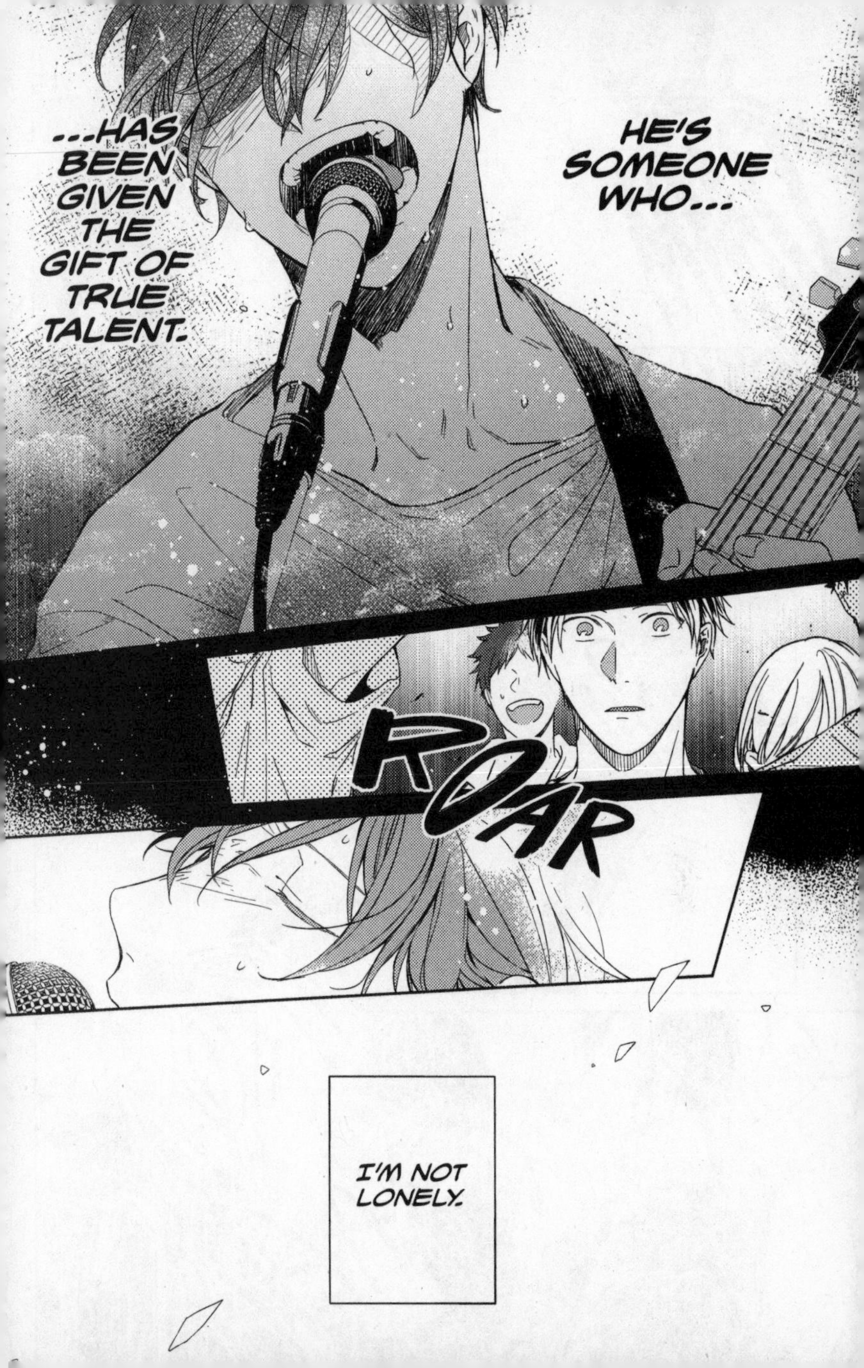
HE'S SOMEONE WHO...
...HAS BEEN GIVEN THE GIFT OF TRUE TALENT.
ROAR
I'M NOT LONELY.

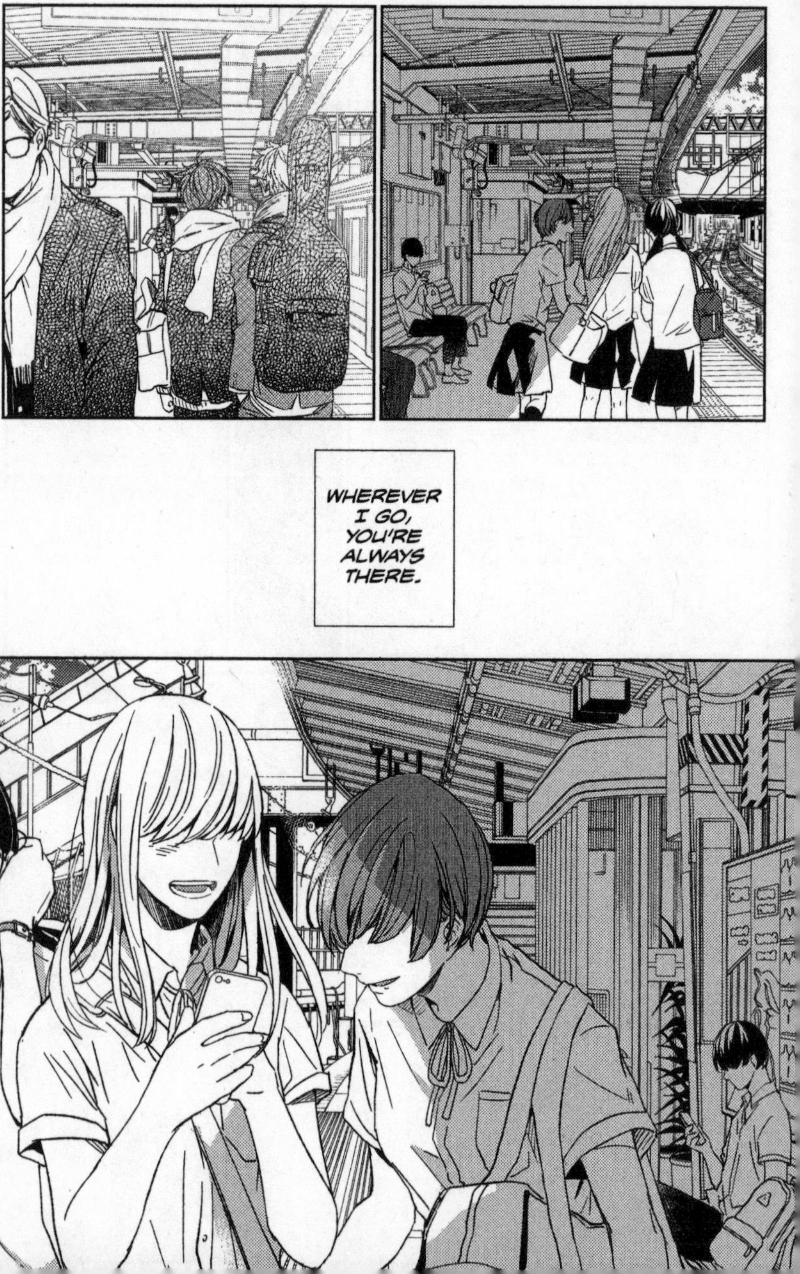
WHEREVER I GO, YOU'RE ALWAYS THERE.

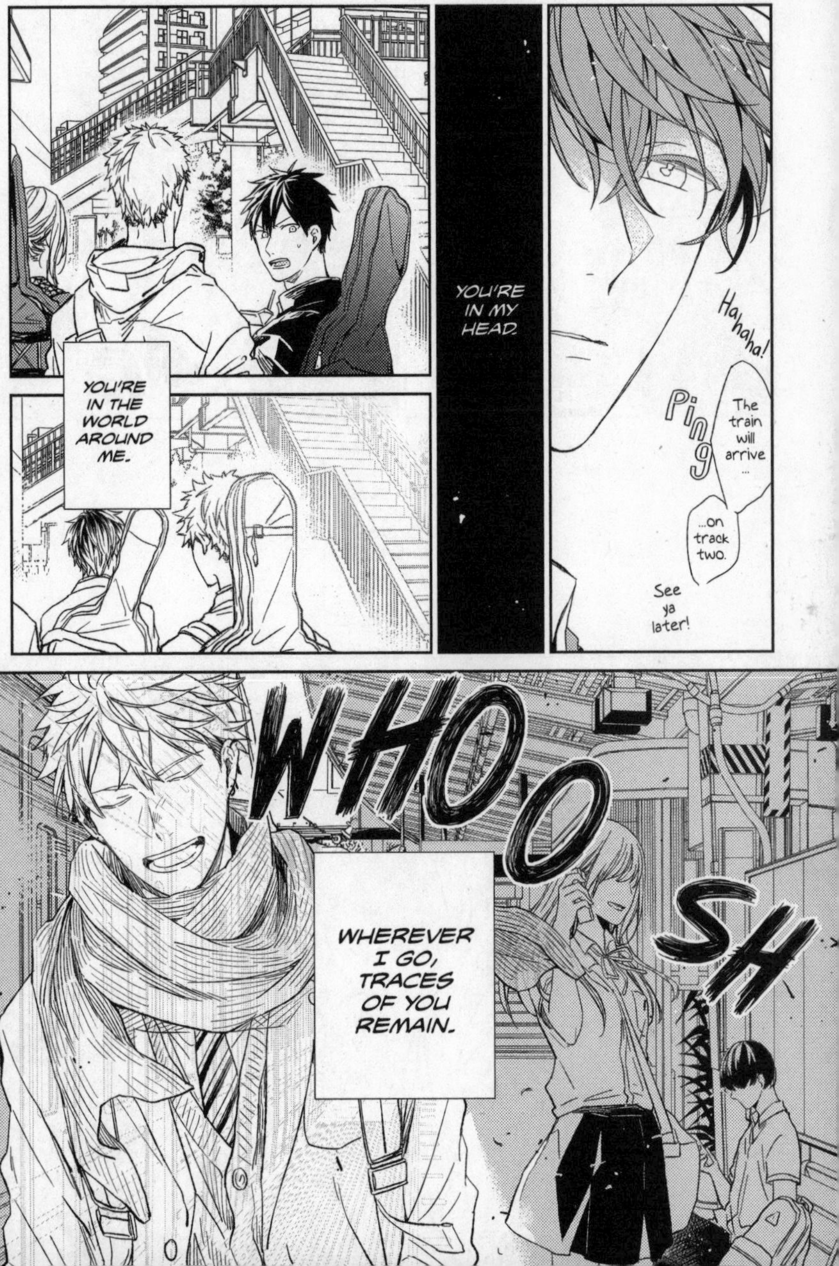

Hahaha!
Ping
The train will arrive...
...on track two.
See ya later!
YOU'RE IN MY HEAD.
YOU'RE IN THE WORLD AROUND ME.
WHOOOSH
WHEREVER I GO, TRACES OF YOU REMAIN.

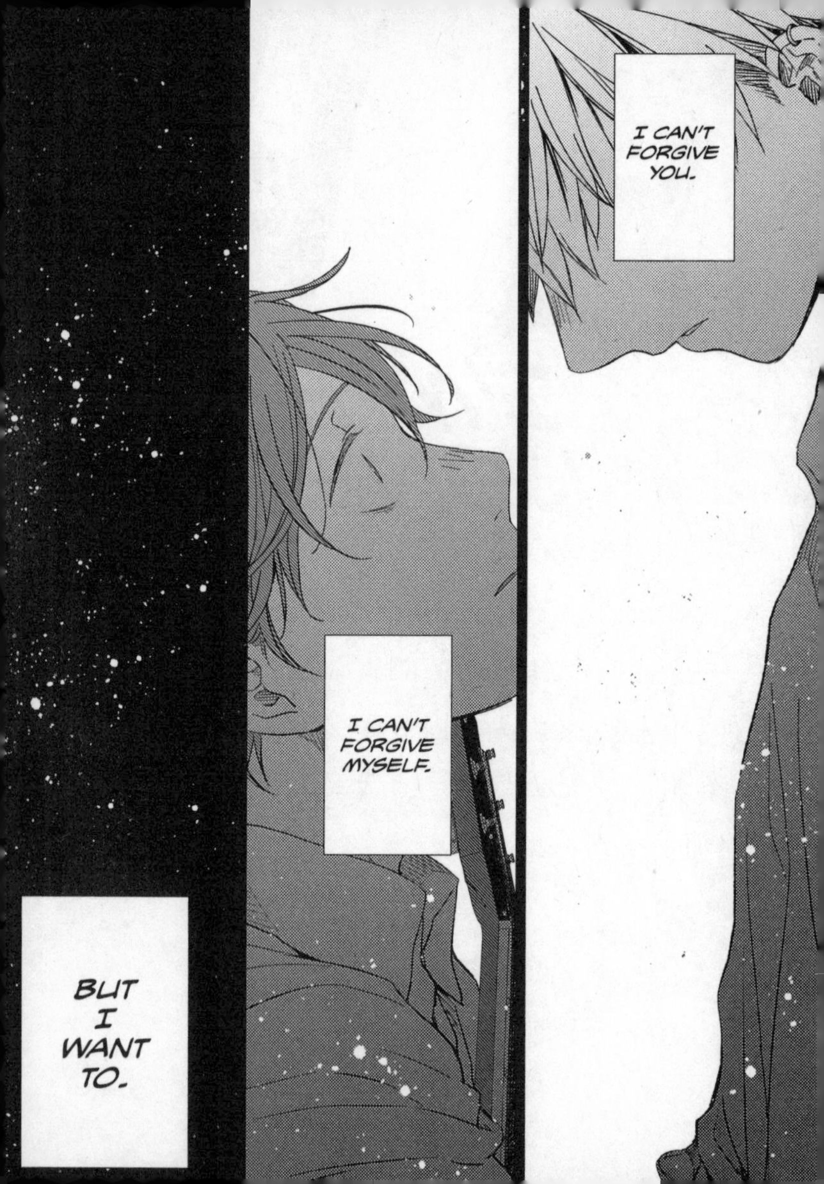
I CAN'T FORGIVE YOU.
I CAN'T FORGIVE MYSELF.
BUT I WANT TO.

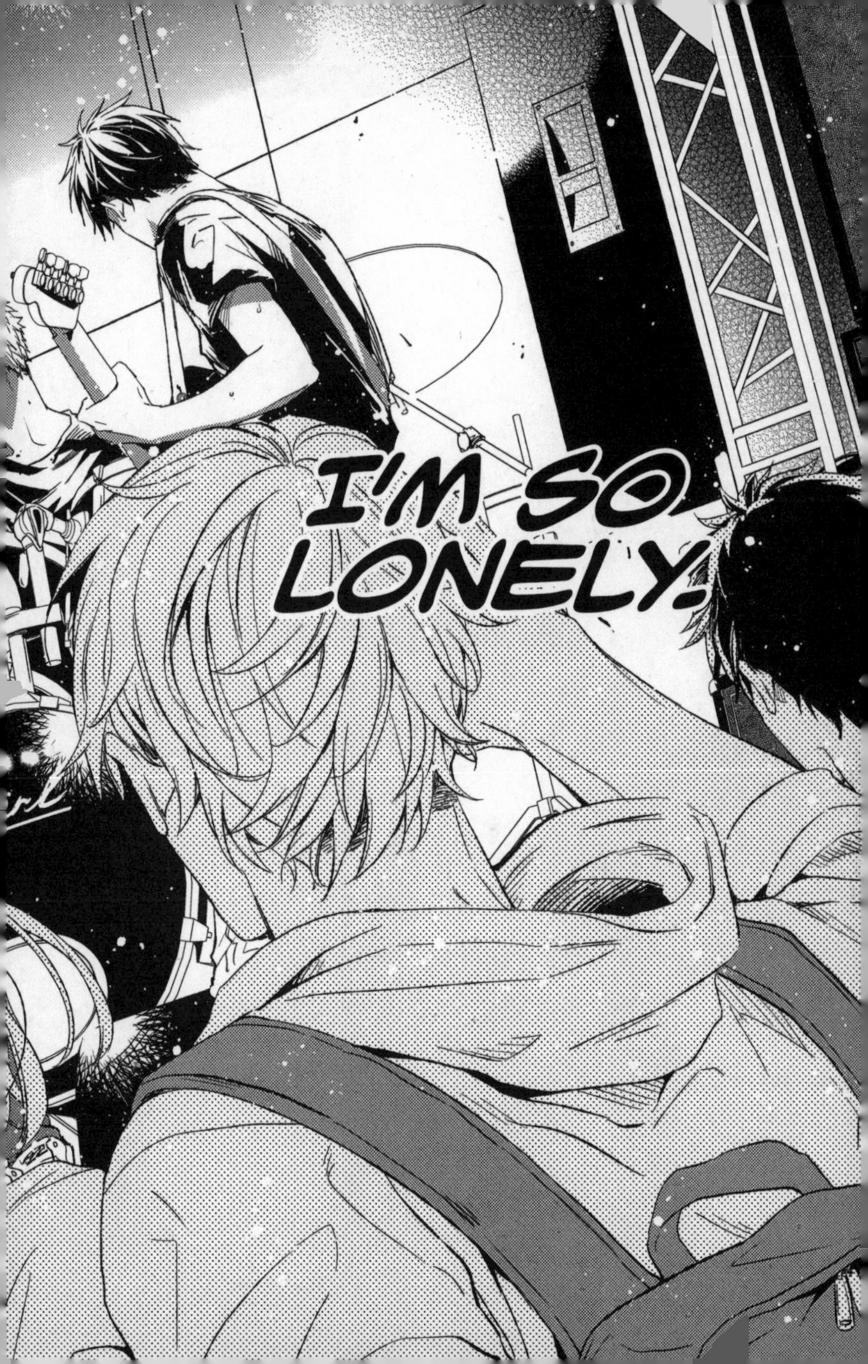
I'M SO LONELY.

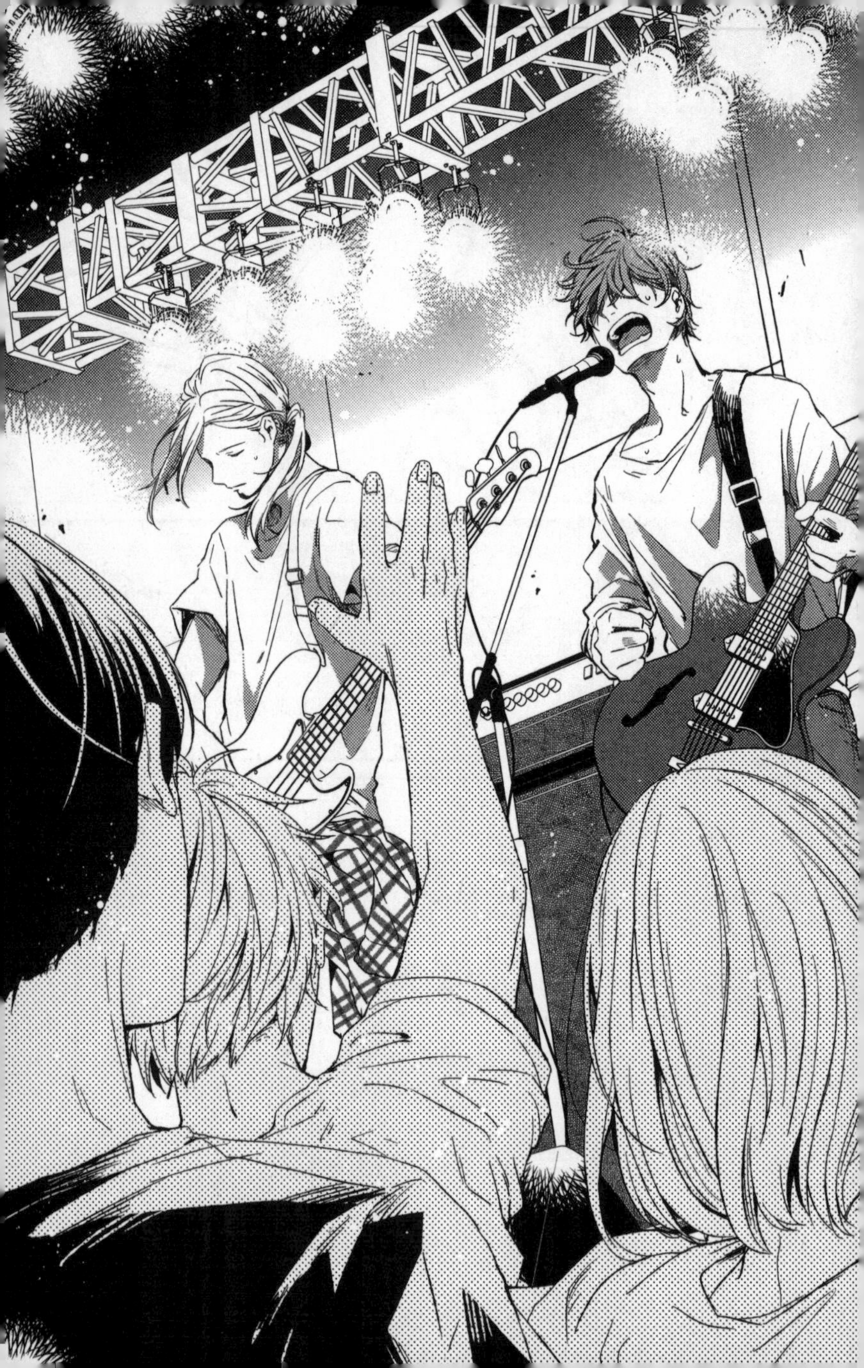

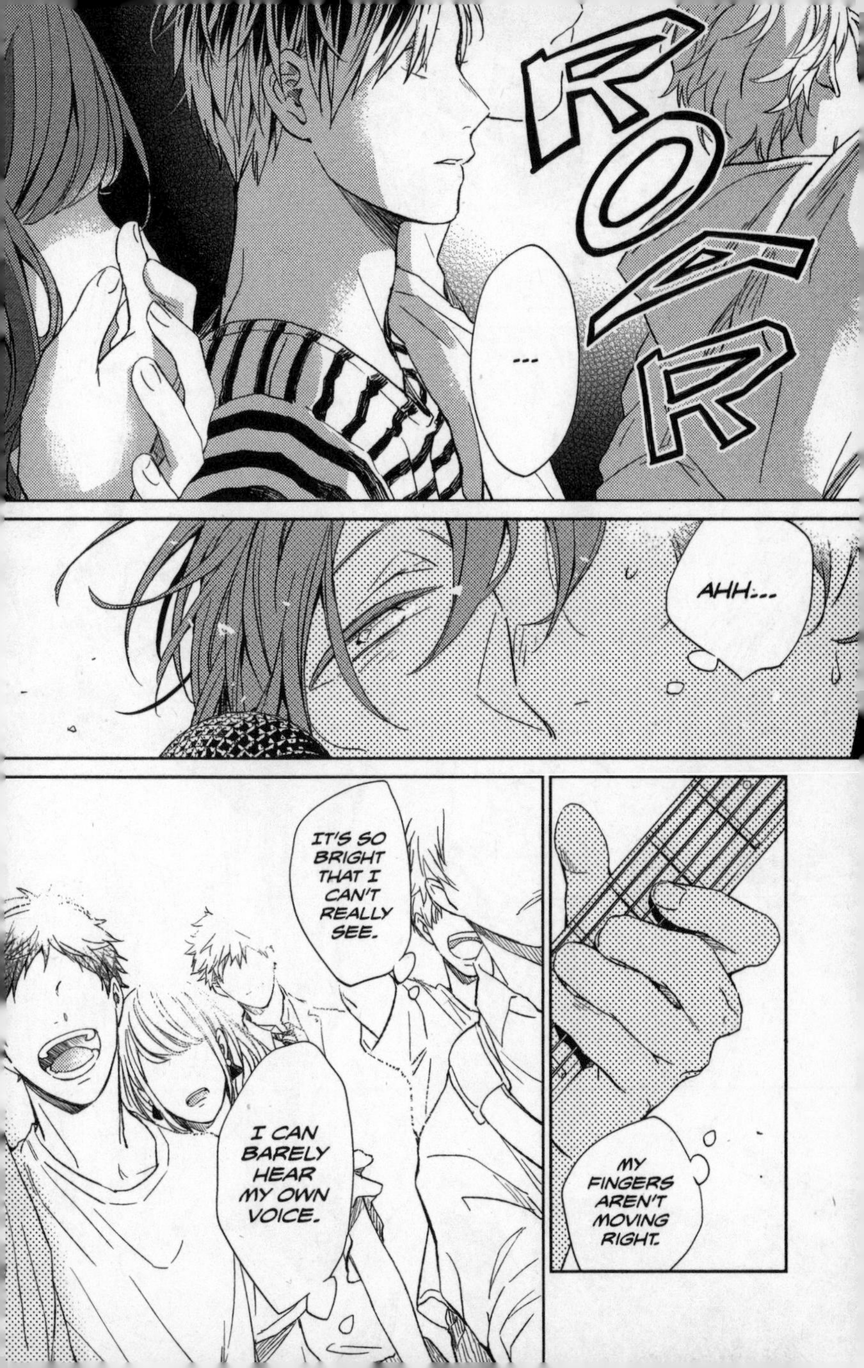
ROAR
...
AHH...
MY FINGERS AREN'T MOVING RIGHT.
IT'S SO BRIGHT THAT I CAN'T REALLY SEE.
I CAN BARELY HEAR MY OWN VOICE.

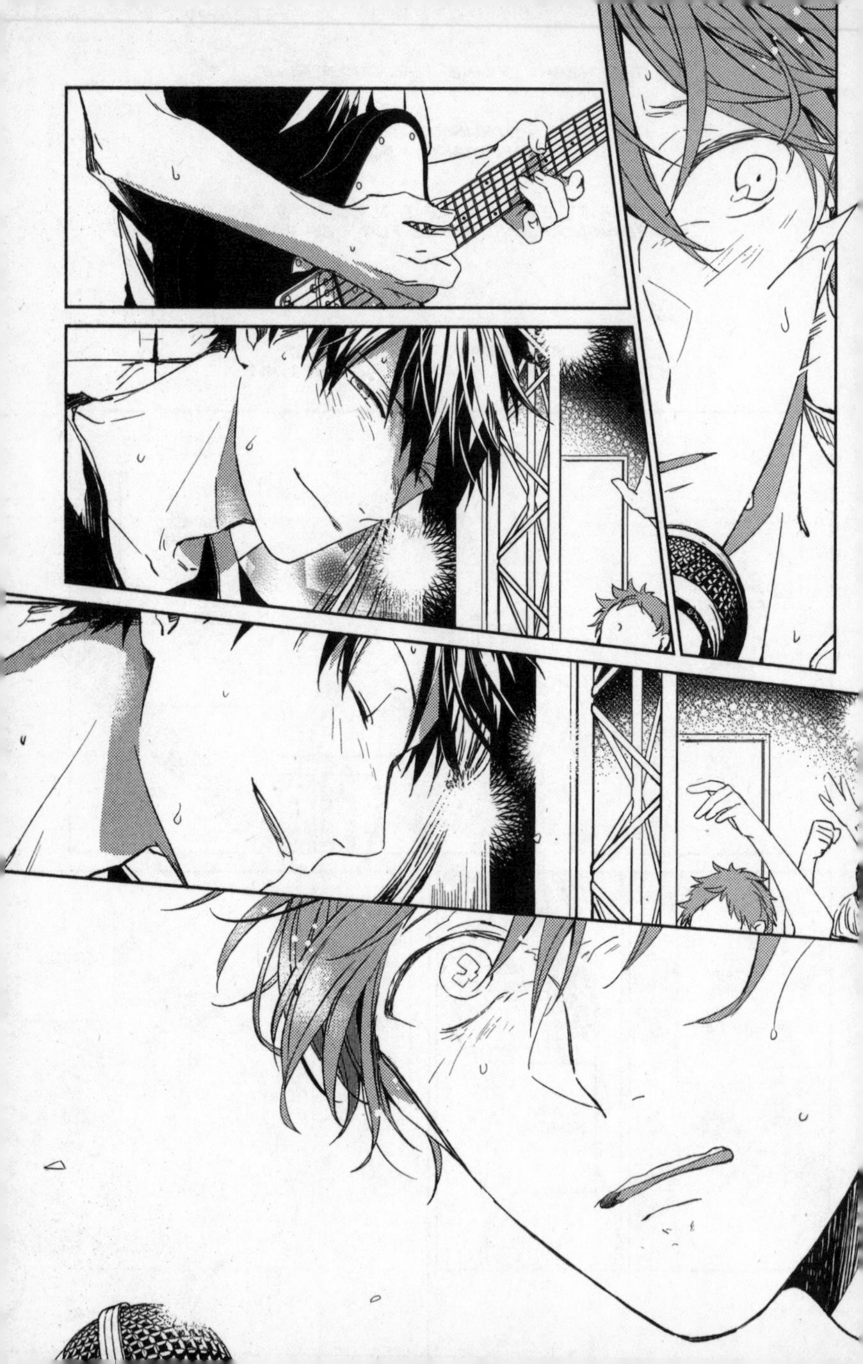

THE HEART IS LIKE A GUITAR STRING.

IF IT'S STRUNG TOO LOOSE,
IT WON'T MAKE A SOUND.

BUT IF IT'S STRUNG TIGHT, ALMOST TO THE
BREAKING POINT, TO THE POINT OF PAIN...

THEN...

IT CAN CREATE A SOUND THAT
CRASHES OVER YOU LIKE A GIANT WAVE.

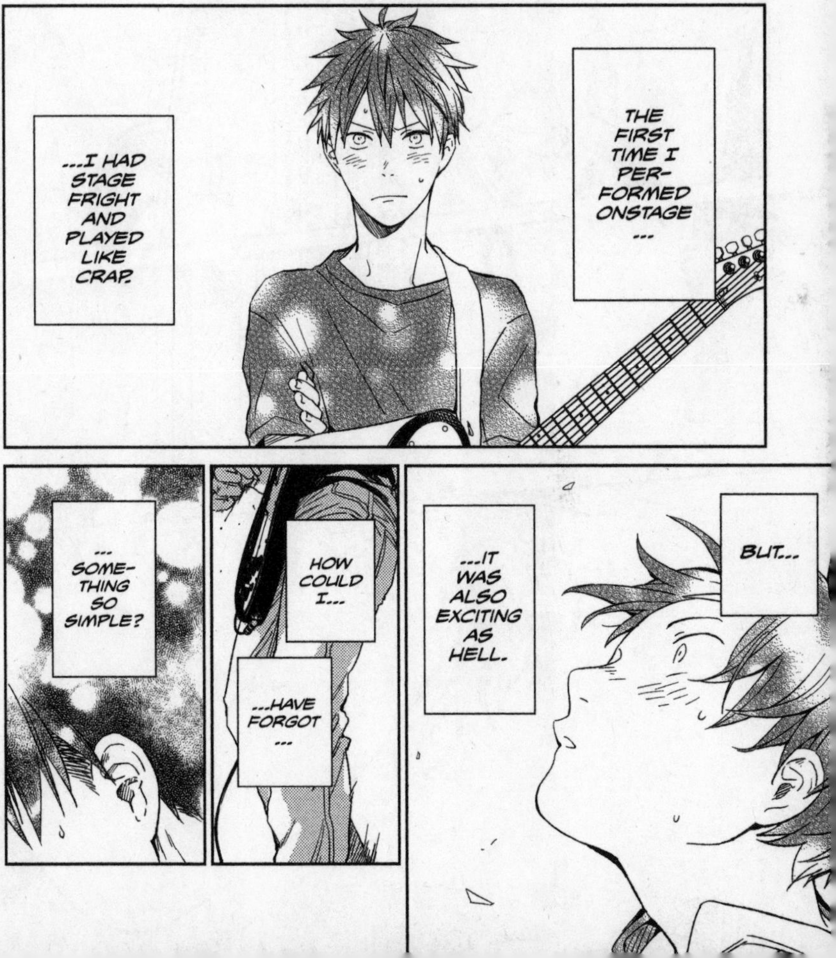
THE FIRST TIME I PER-FORMED ONSTAGE...
...I HAD STAGE FRIGHT AND PLAYED LIKE CRAP.
BUT...
...IT WAS ALSO EXCITING AS HELL.
HOW COULD I...
...HAVE FORGOT...
...SOME-THING SO SIMPLE?

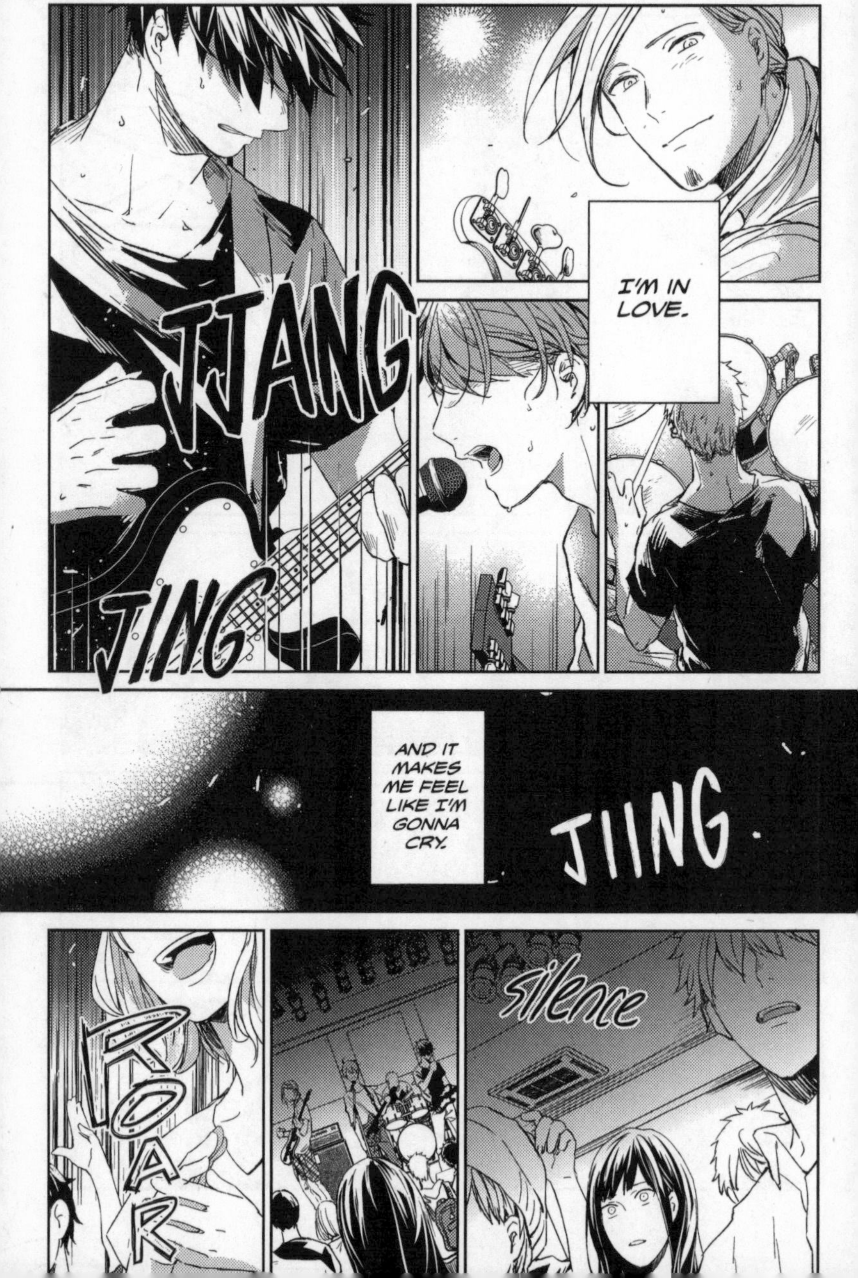
I'M IN LOVE.
JJANG
JING
AND IT MAKES ME FEEL LIKE I'M GONNA CRY.
JIING
silence
ROAR

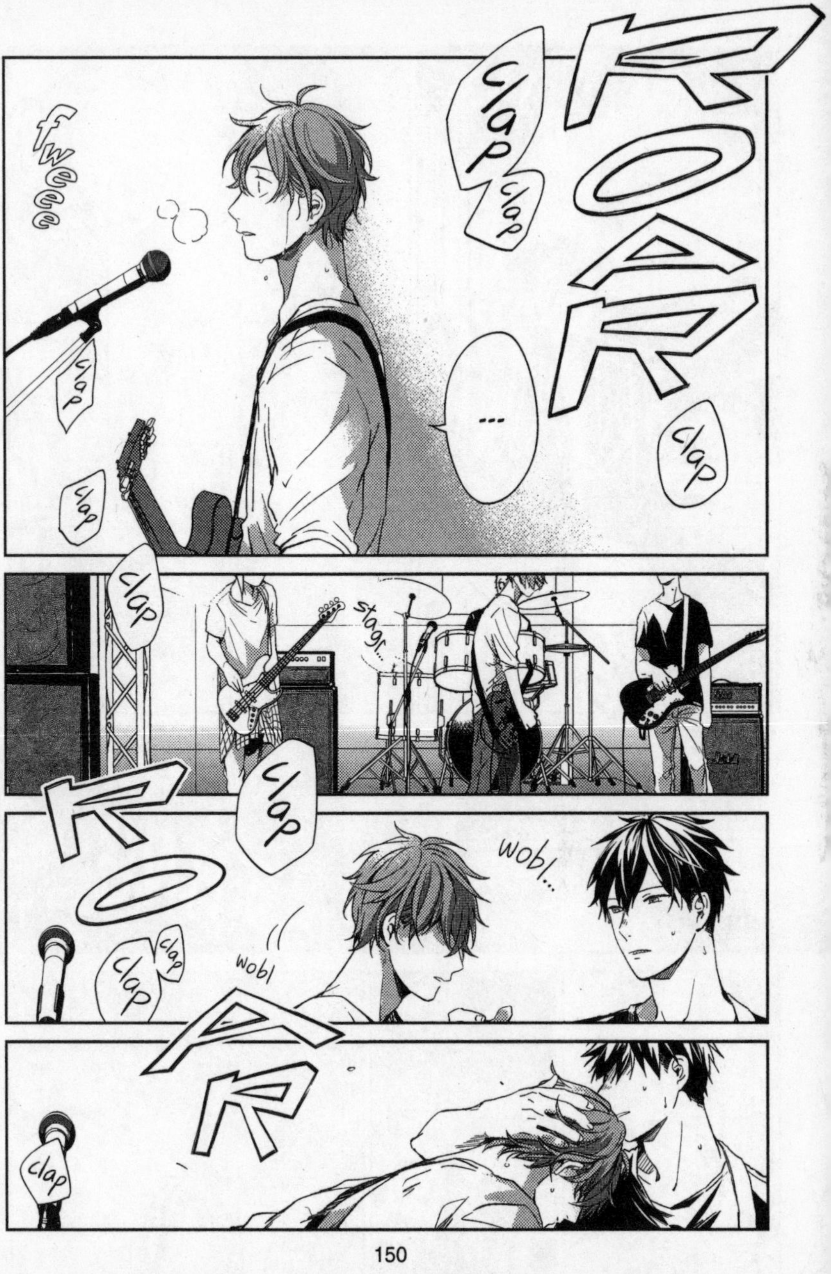
ROAR
clap clap
clap clap
...
clap
clap
clap
fweeee
clap
stagr...
wobl...
clap
wobl
clap
clap
ROAR
clap

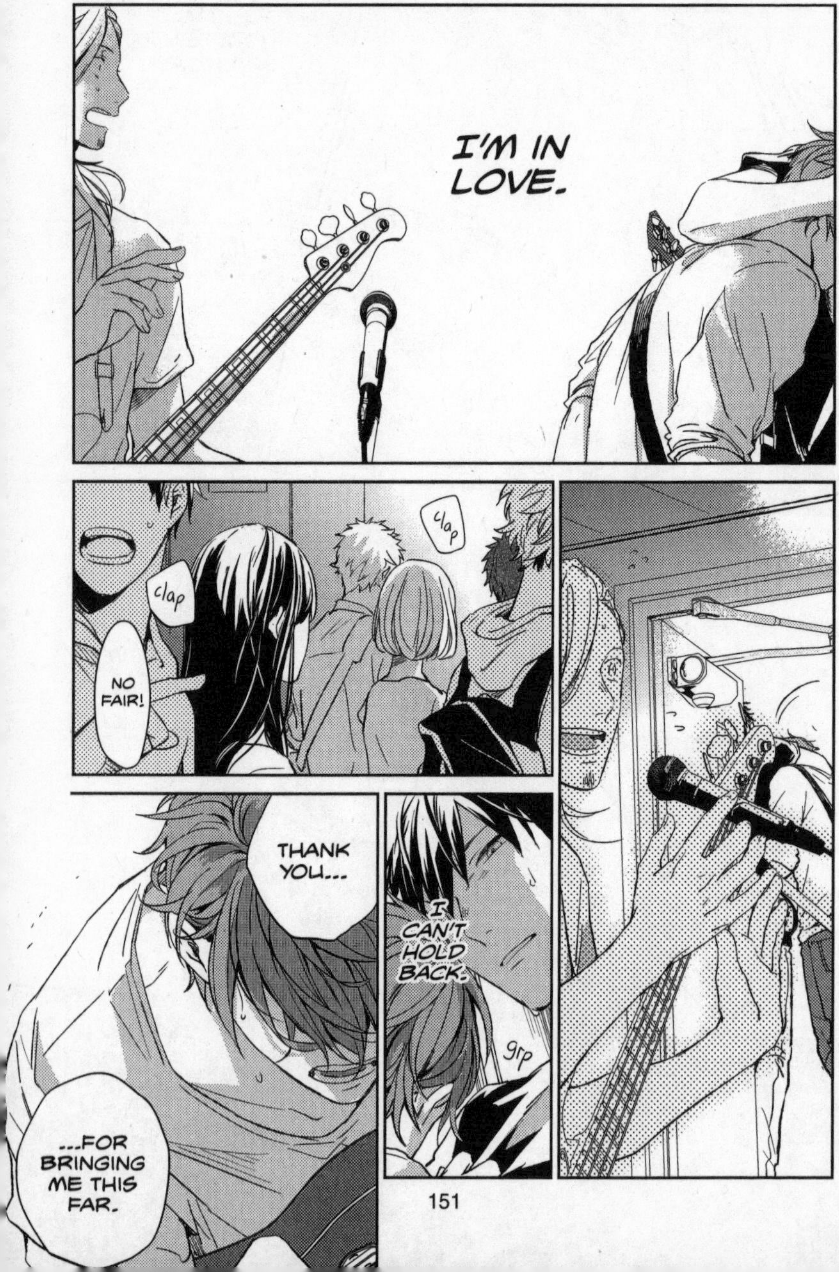
I'M IN LOVE.
clap
clap
NO FAIR!
I CAN'T HOLD BACK.
grp
THANK YOU...
...FOR BRINGING ME THIS FAR.

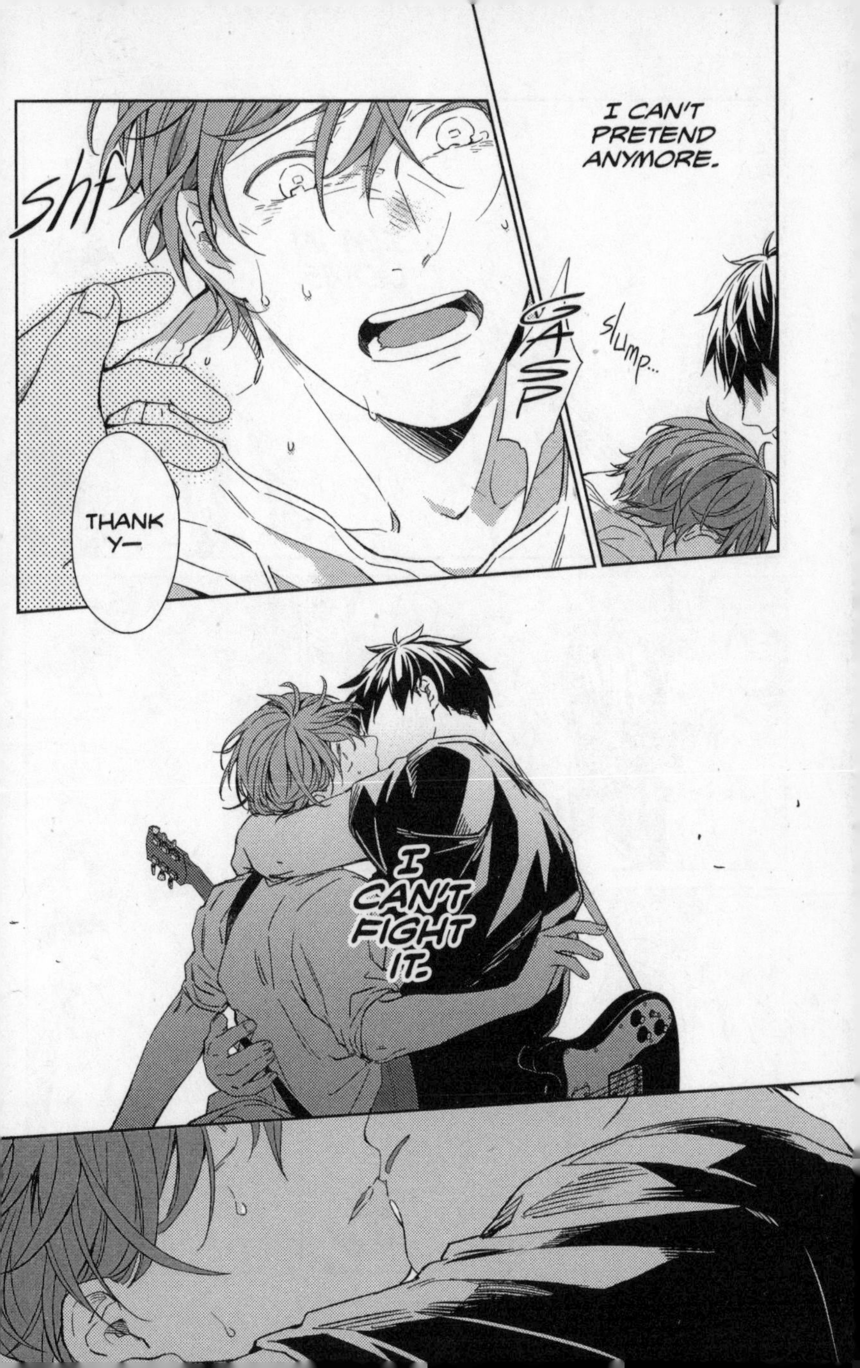
I CAN'T PRETEND ANYMORE.
slump...
GASP
shf
THANK Y—
I CAN'T FIGHT IT.

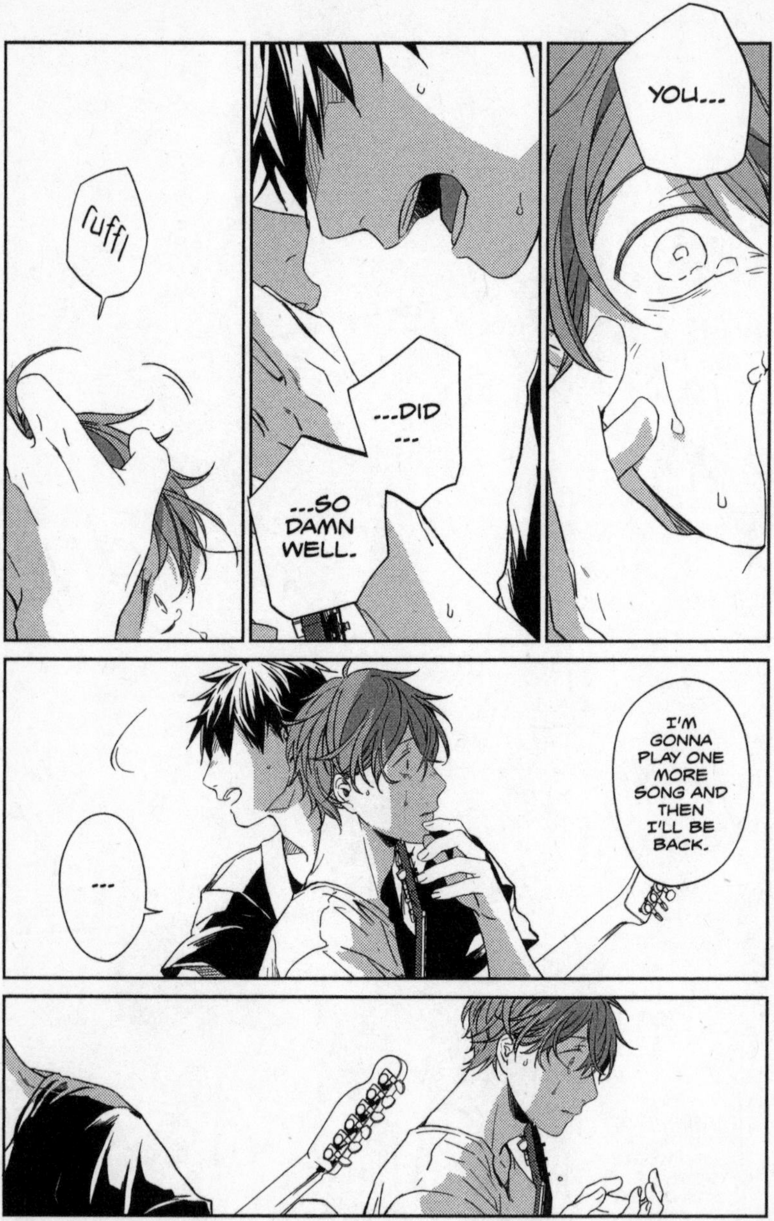
YOU...
...DID ...
...SO DAMN WELL.
ruffl
I'M GONNA PLAY ONE MORE SONG AND THEN I'LL BE BACK.
...

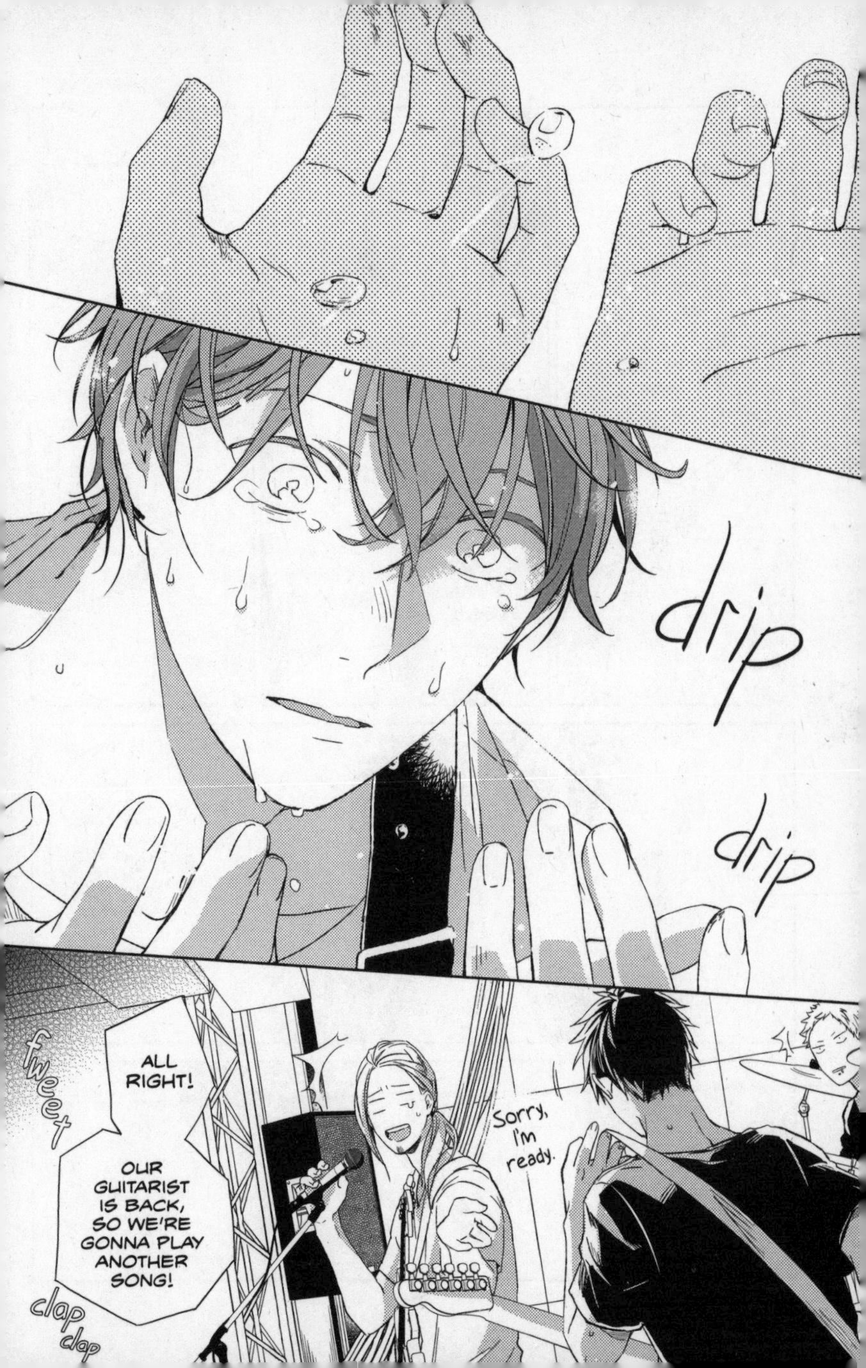
drip
drip
Sorry, I'm ready.
ALL RIGHT!
OUR GUITARIST IS BACK, SO WE'RE GONNA PLAY ANOTHER SONG!
fweet
clap clap

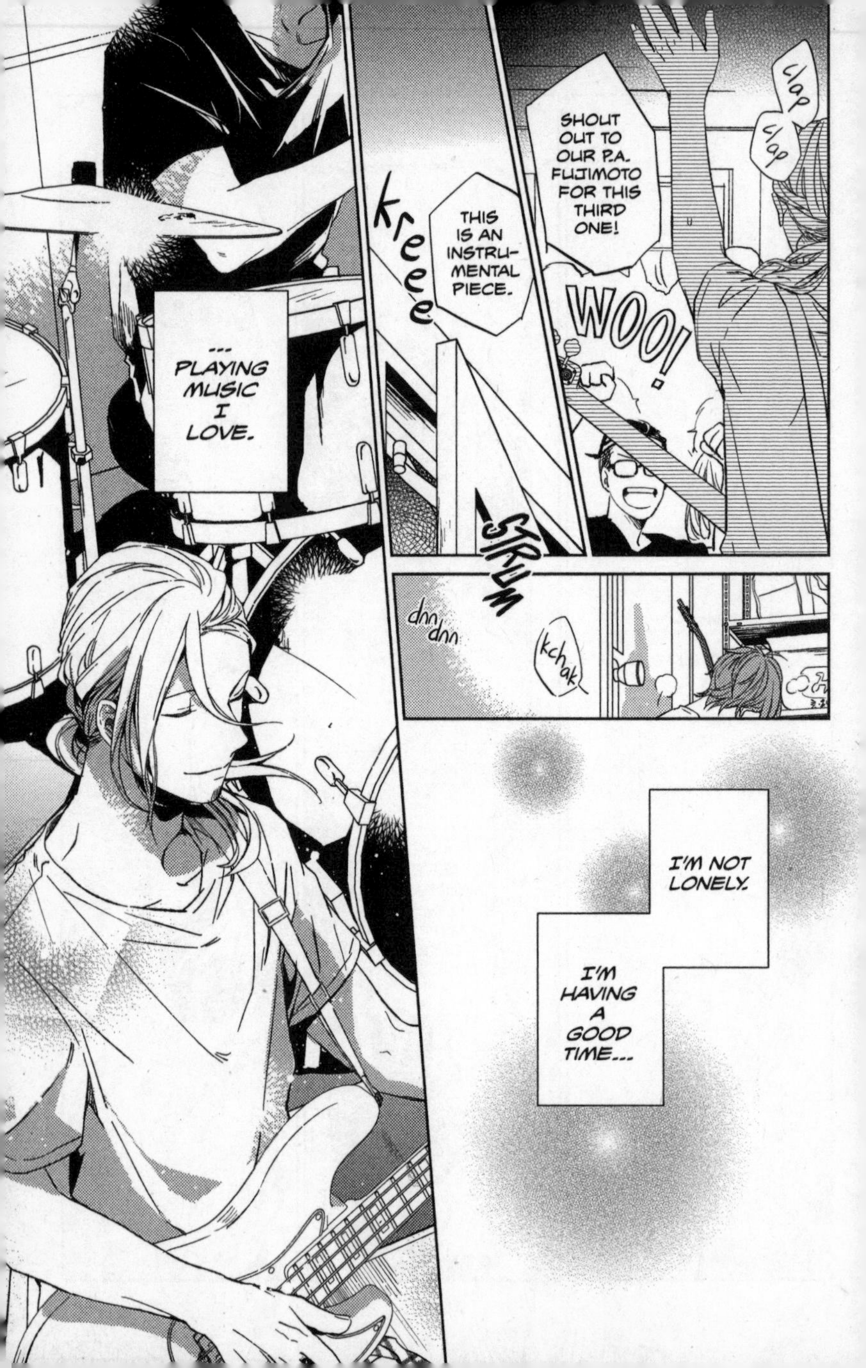
clap
clap
SHOUT OUT TO OUR P.A. FUJIMOTO FOR THIS THIRD ONE!
WOO!
THIS IS AN INSTRU-MENTAL PIECE.
kreee
STRUM
dnn dnn
kchak
I'M NOT LONELY.
I'M HAVING A GOOD TIME...
...PLAYING MUSIC I LOVE.

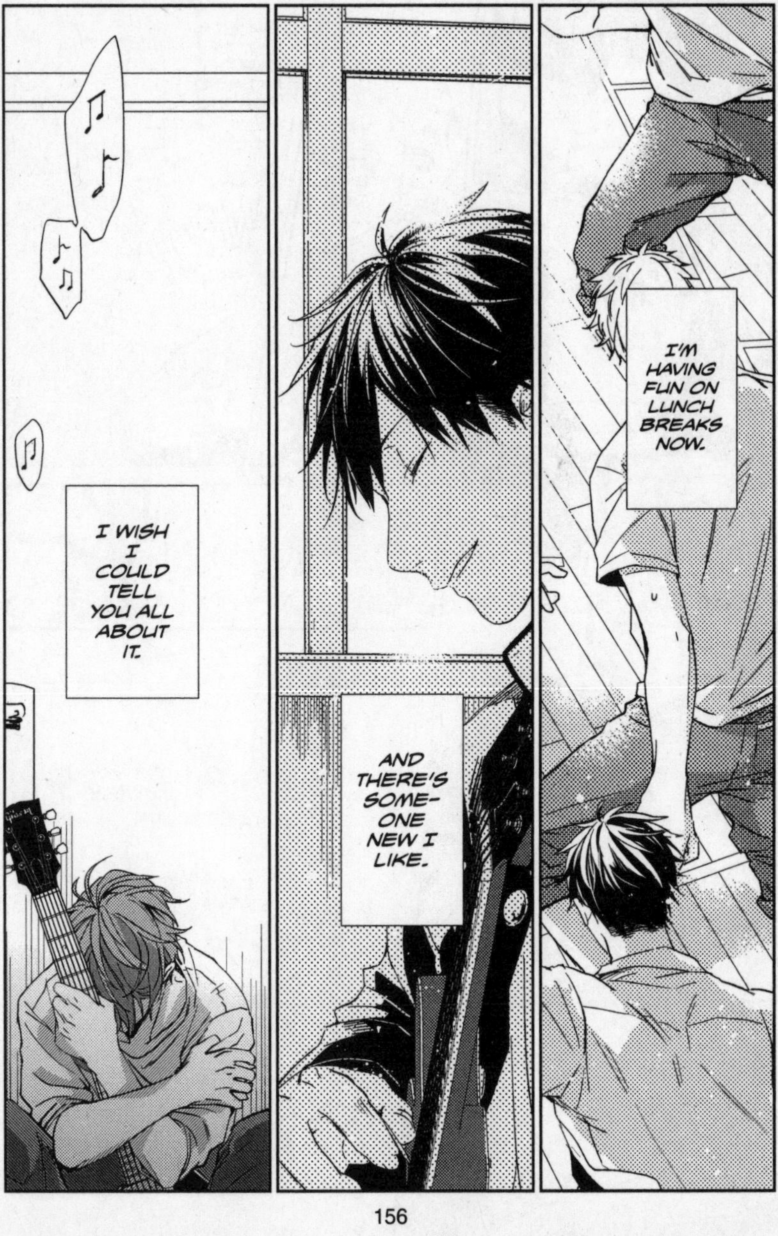
I'M HAVING FUN ON LUNCH BREAKS NOW.
AND THERE'S SOME-ONE NEW I LIKE.
I WISH I COULD TELL YOU ALL ABOUT IT.

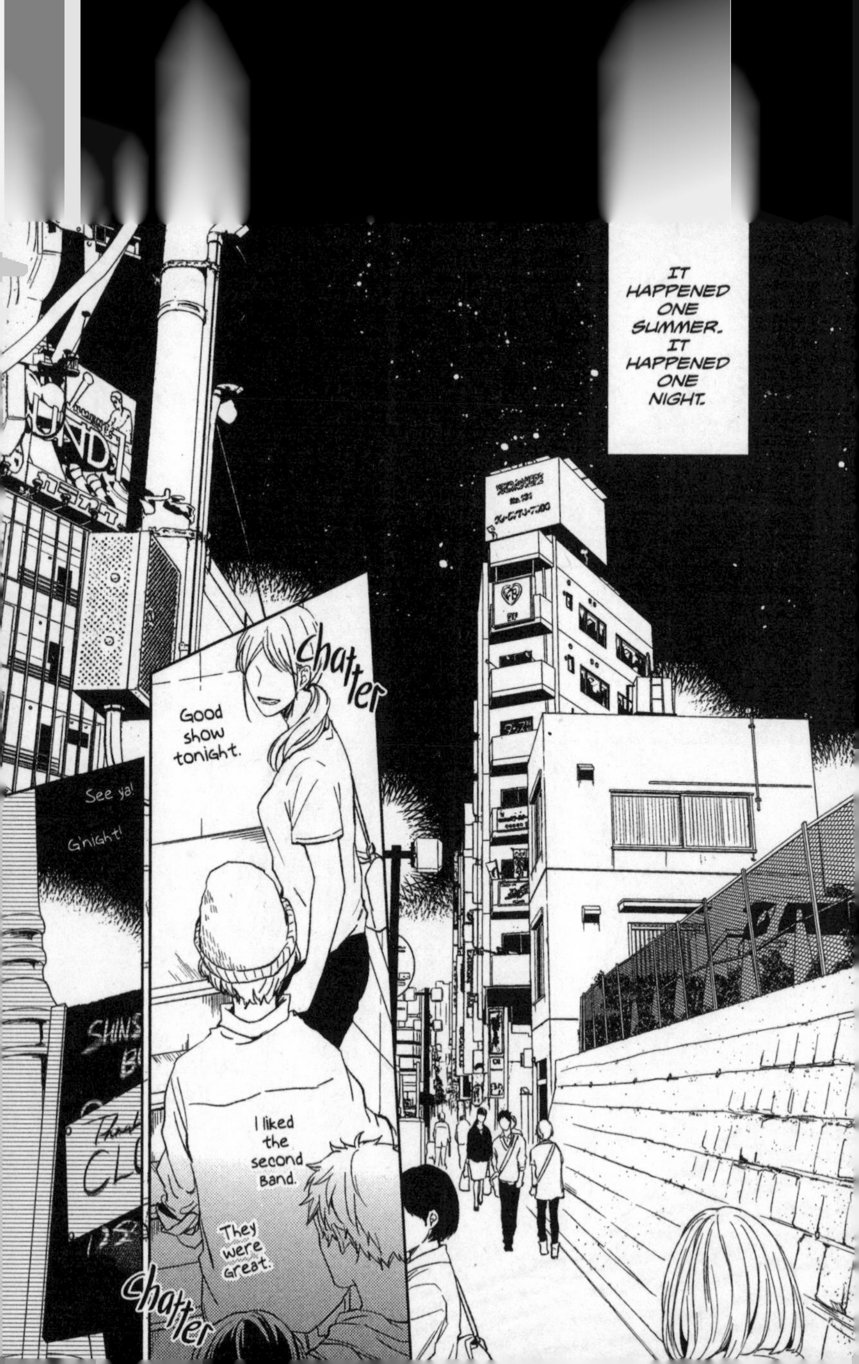
IT HAPPENED ONE SUMMER. IT HAPPENED ONE NIGHT.
chatter
Good show tonight.
I liked the second band.
They were great.
chatter
See ya!
G'night!

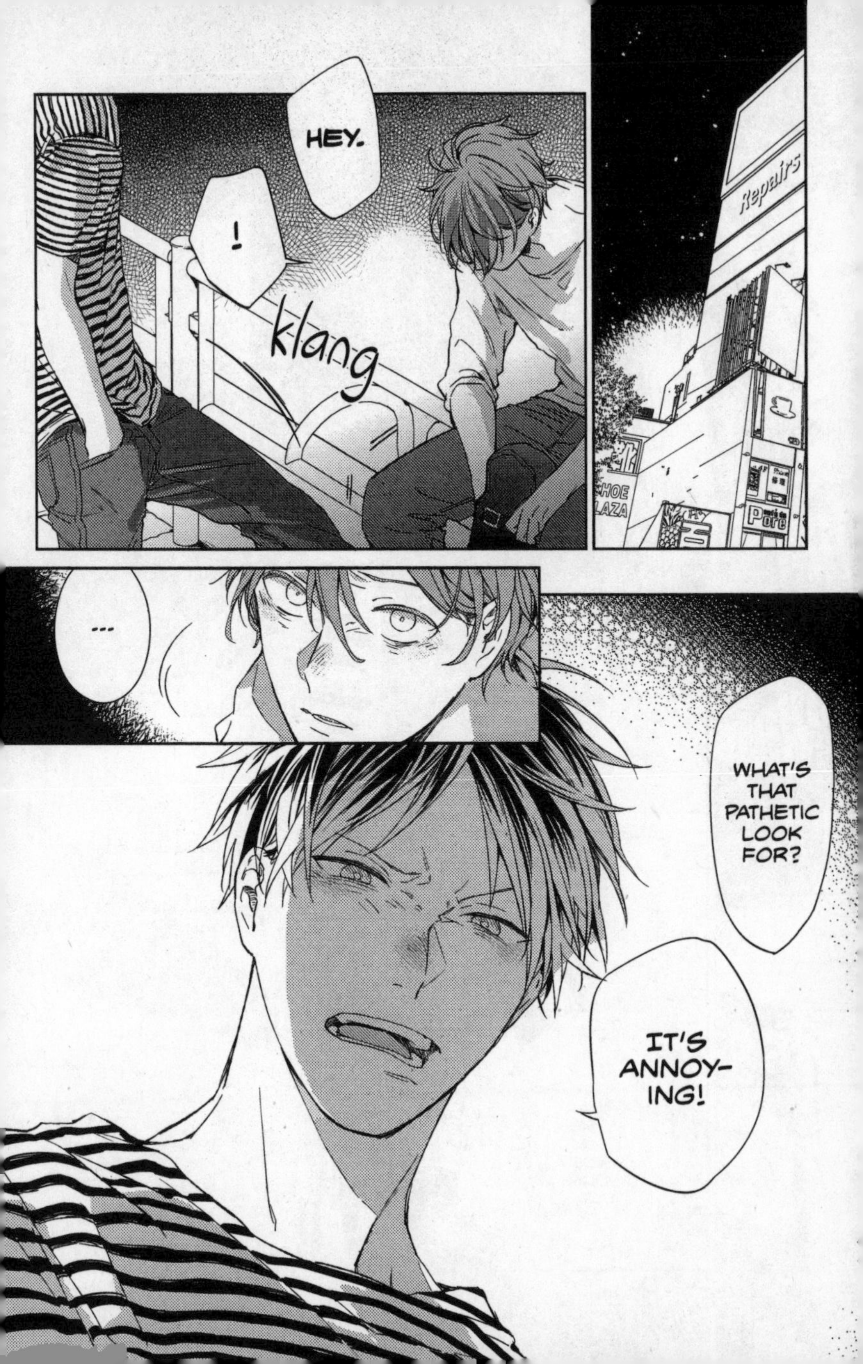
Repairs
HOE
LAZA
HEY.
!
klang
...
WHAT'S THAT PATHETIC LOOK FOR?
IT'S ANNOY-ING!

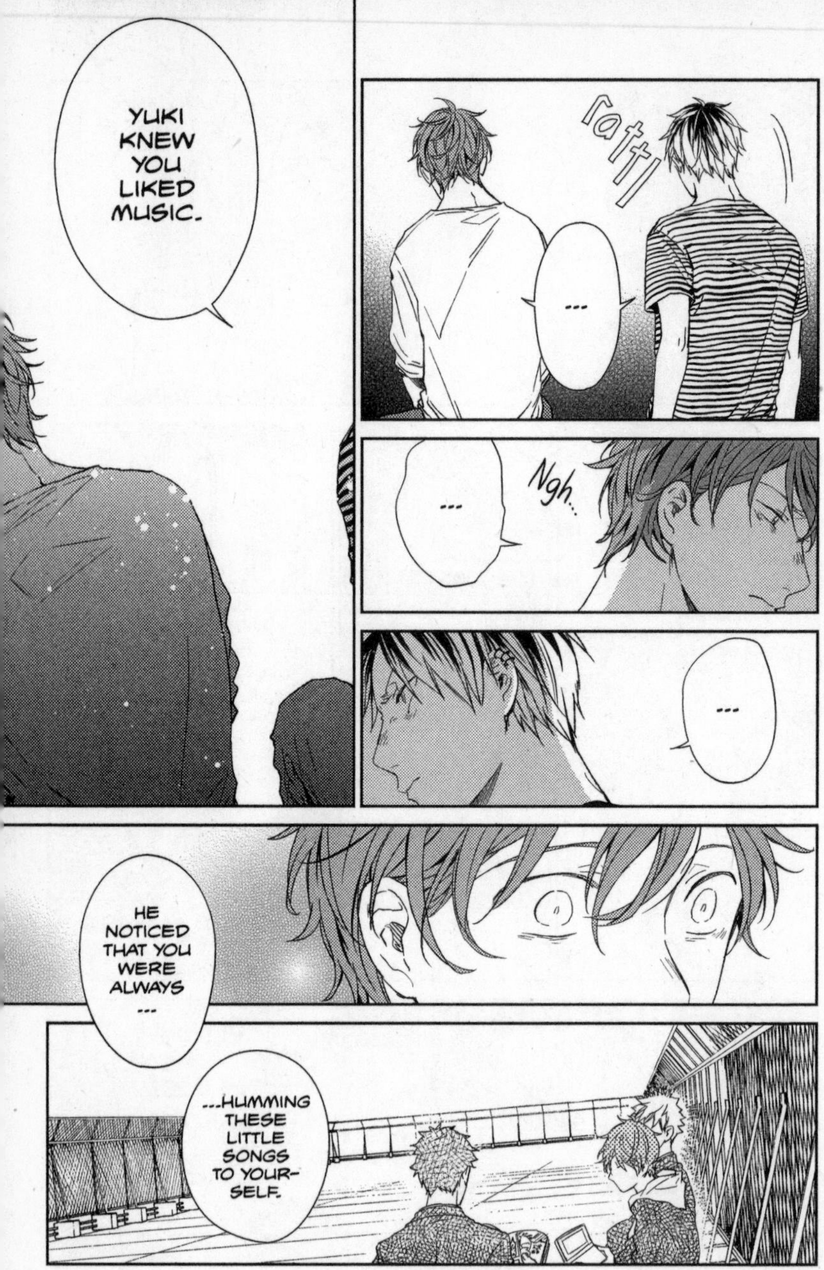
rattl
...
Ngh...
...
...
YUKI KNEW YOU LIKED MUSIC.
HE NOTICED THAT YOU WERE ALWAYS...
...HUMMING THESE LITTLE SONGS TO YOUR-SELF.

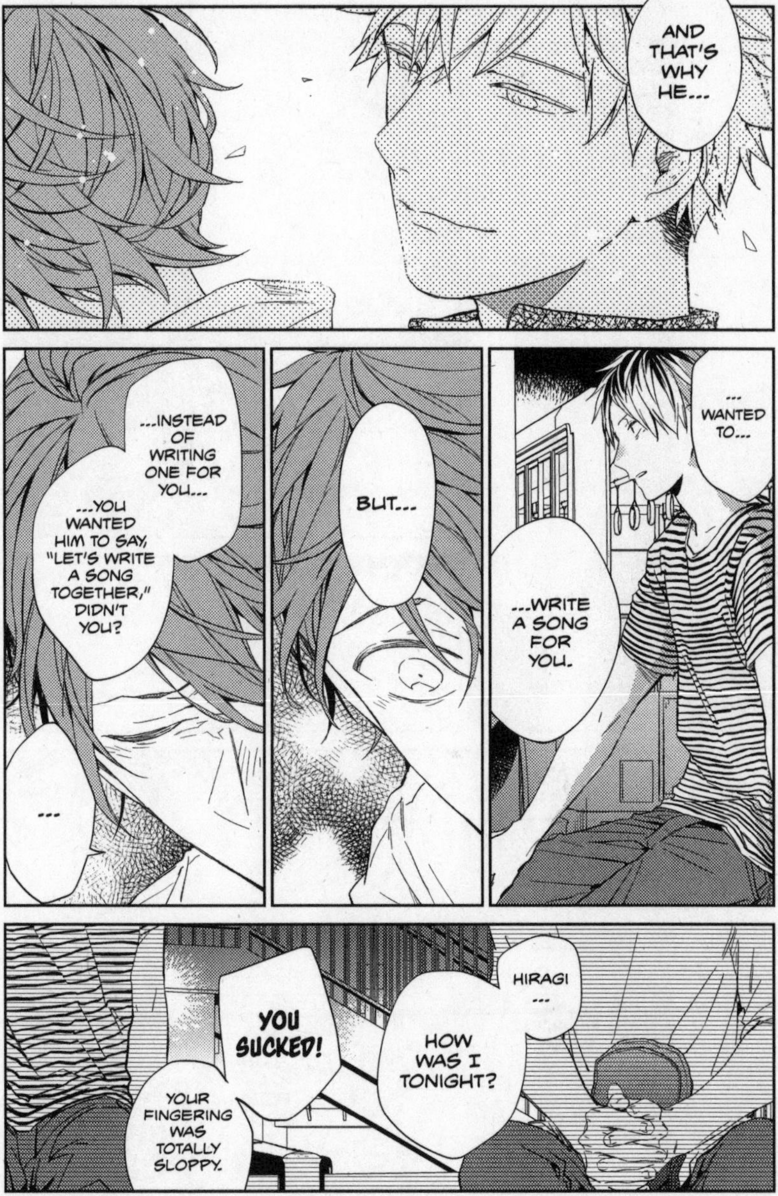
AND THAT'S WHY HE...
...WANTED TO...
...WRITE A SONG FOR YOU.
BUT...
...INSTEAD OF WRITING ONE FOR YOU...
...YOU WANTED HIM TO SAY, "LET'S WRITE A SONG TOGETHER," DIDN'T YOU?
...
HIRAGI...
HOW WAS I TONIGHT?
YOU SUCKED!
YOUR FINGERING WAS TOTALLY SLOPPY.

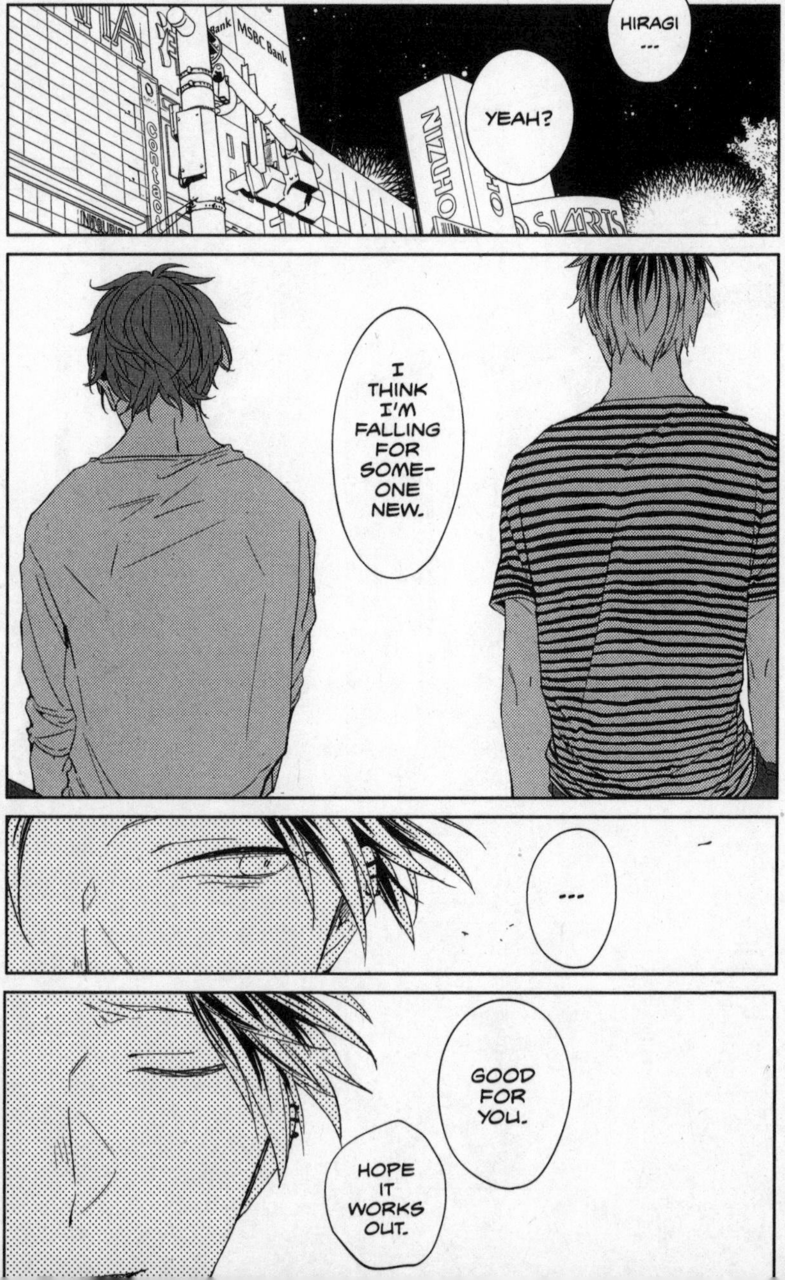

HIRAGI...
YEAH?
I THINK I'M FALLING FOR SOMEONE NEW.
...
GOOD FOR YOU.
HOPE IT WORKS OUT.

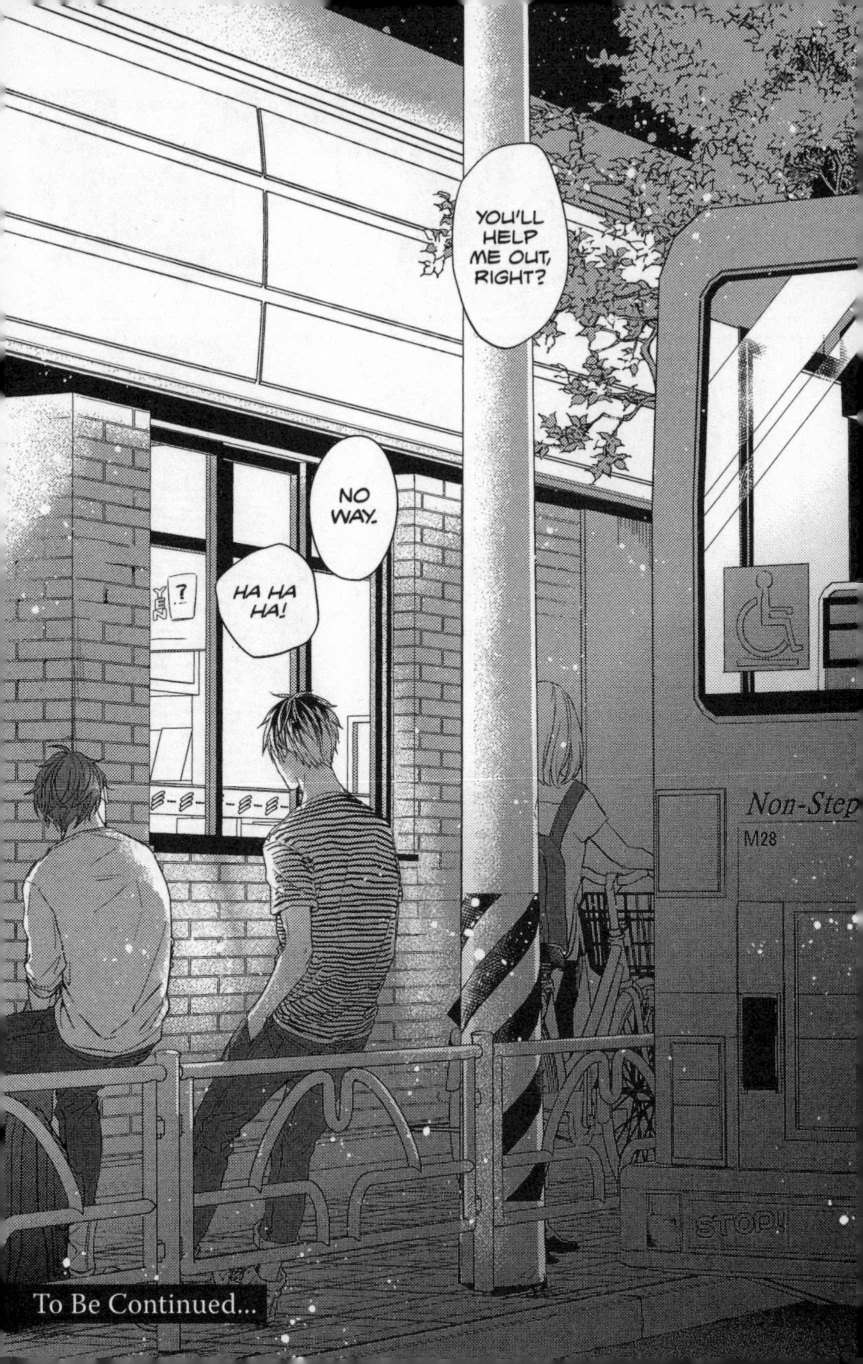
YOU'LL HELP ME OUT, RIGHT?
NO WAY.
HA HA HA!
YEN
?
Non-Step
M28
STOP!
To Be Continued...

given

by Natsuki Kizu

Backgrounds

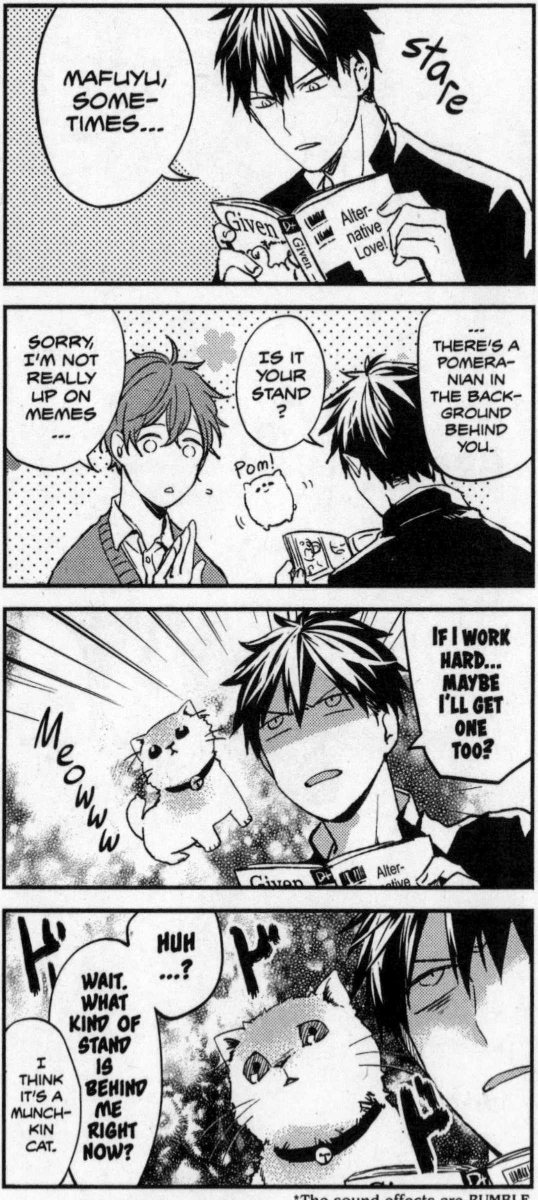
MAFUYU, SOMETIMES...
stare
Given
Alter-native Love!
...THERE'S A POMERANIAN IN THE BACKGROUND BEHIND YOU.
IS IT YOUR STAND?
SORRY, I'M NOT REALLY UP ON MEMES...
Pom!
IF I WORK HARD... MAYBE I'LL GET ONE TOO?
Meowwww
Given
Alter-
ド
ド
HUH...?
WAIT. WHAT KIND OF STAND IS BEHIND ME RIGHT NOW?
I THINK IT'S A MUNCHKIN CAT.

*The sound effects are RUMBLE.

You Know How a Dog Looks Proud When It Catches a Bug?

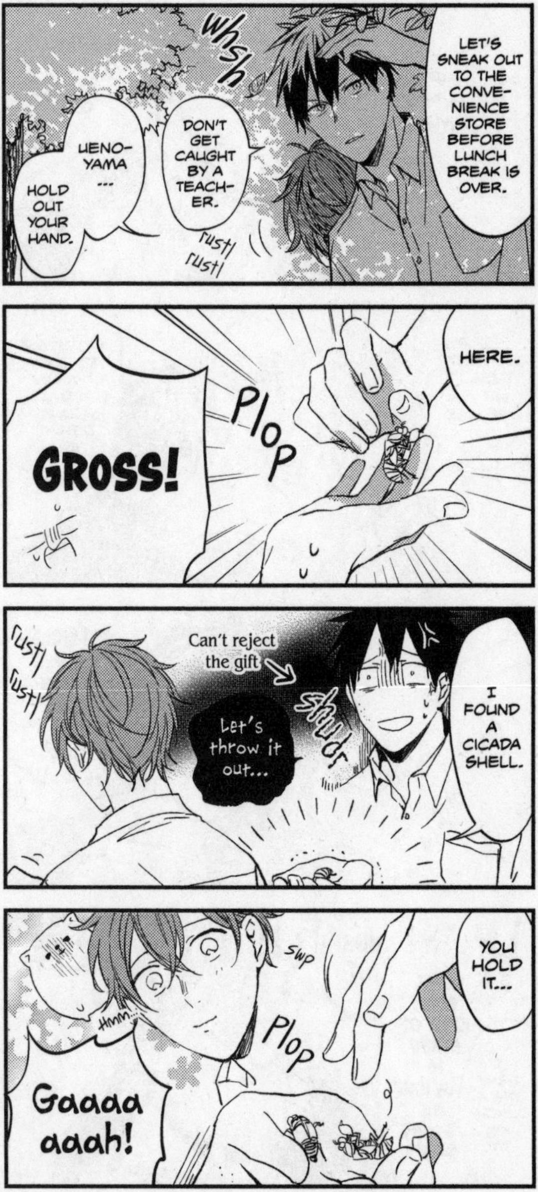
LET'S SNEAK OUT TO THE CONVE-NIENCE STORE BEFORE LUNCH BREAK IS OVER.
whsh
DON'T GET CAUGHT BY A TEACH-ER.
UENO-YAMA ...
HOLD OUT YOUR HAND.
rustl rustl
HERE.
Plop
GROSS!
I FOUND A CICADA SHELL.
shudr
Can't reject the gift
Let's throw it out...
rustl rustl
YOU HOLD IT...
swp
Plop
Hmm...
Gaaaa aaah!

A Precious Source of Protein

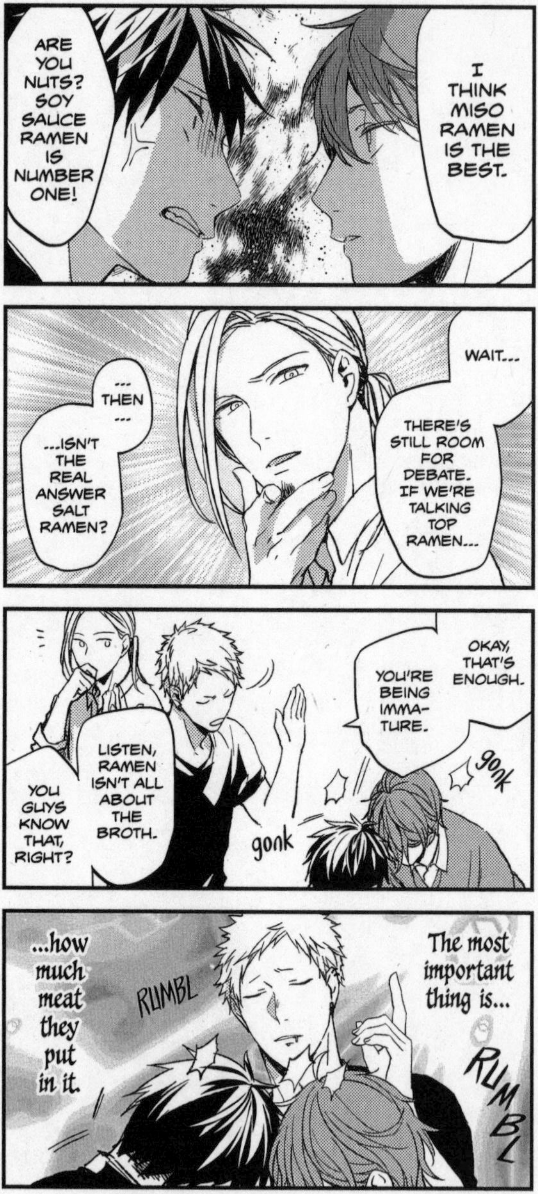
I THINK MISO RAMEN IS THE BEST.
ARE YOU NUTS? SOY SAUCE RAMEN IS NUMBER ONE!
WAIT...
THERE'S STILL ROOM FOR DEBATE. IF WE'RE TALKING TOP RAMEN...
...THEN...
...ISN'T THE REAL ANSWER SALT RAMEN?
OKAY, THAT'S ENOUGH.
YOU'RE BEING IMMA-TURE.
gonk
gonk
LISTEN, RAMEN ISN'T ALL ABOUT THE BROTH.
YOU GUYS KNOW THAT, RIGHT?
The most important thing is...
RUMBL
RUMBL
...how much meat they put in it.

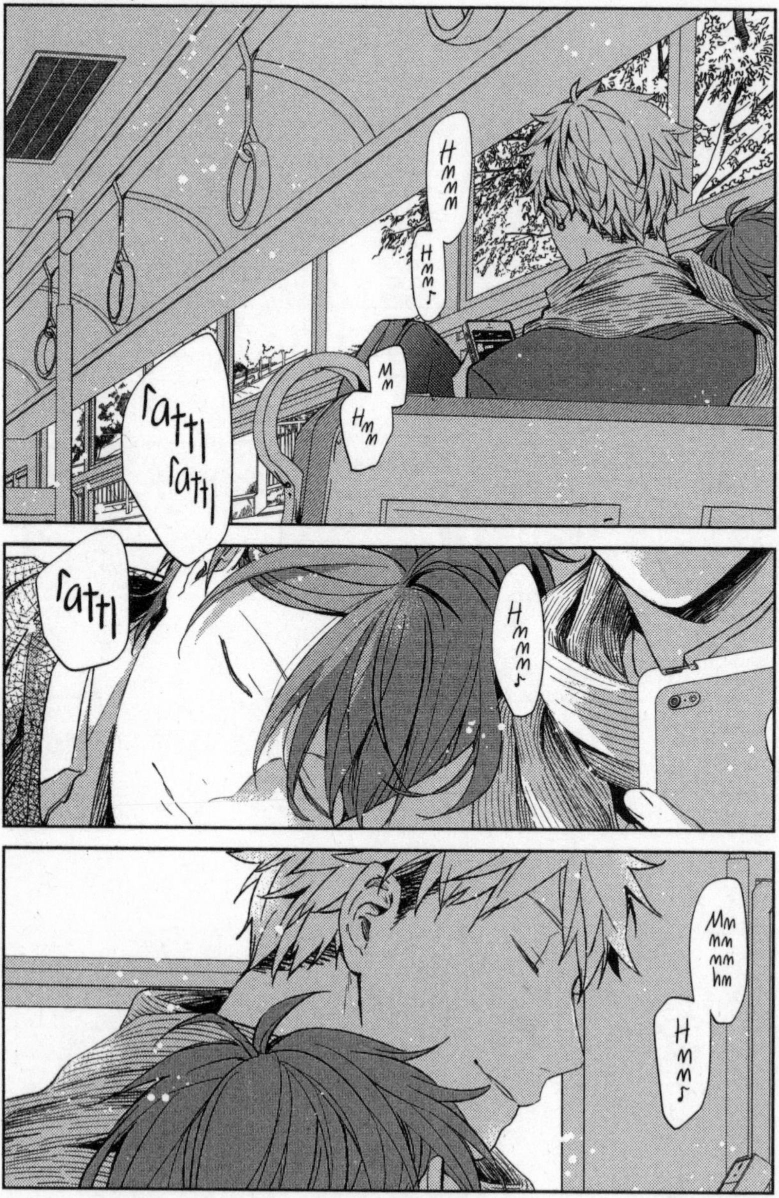
Hmmm
Hmm♪
Mm Hm
rattl rattl
Hmmm♪
rattl
Mm mm mm hm
Hmm♪

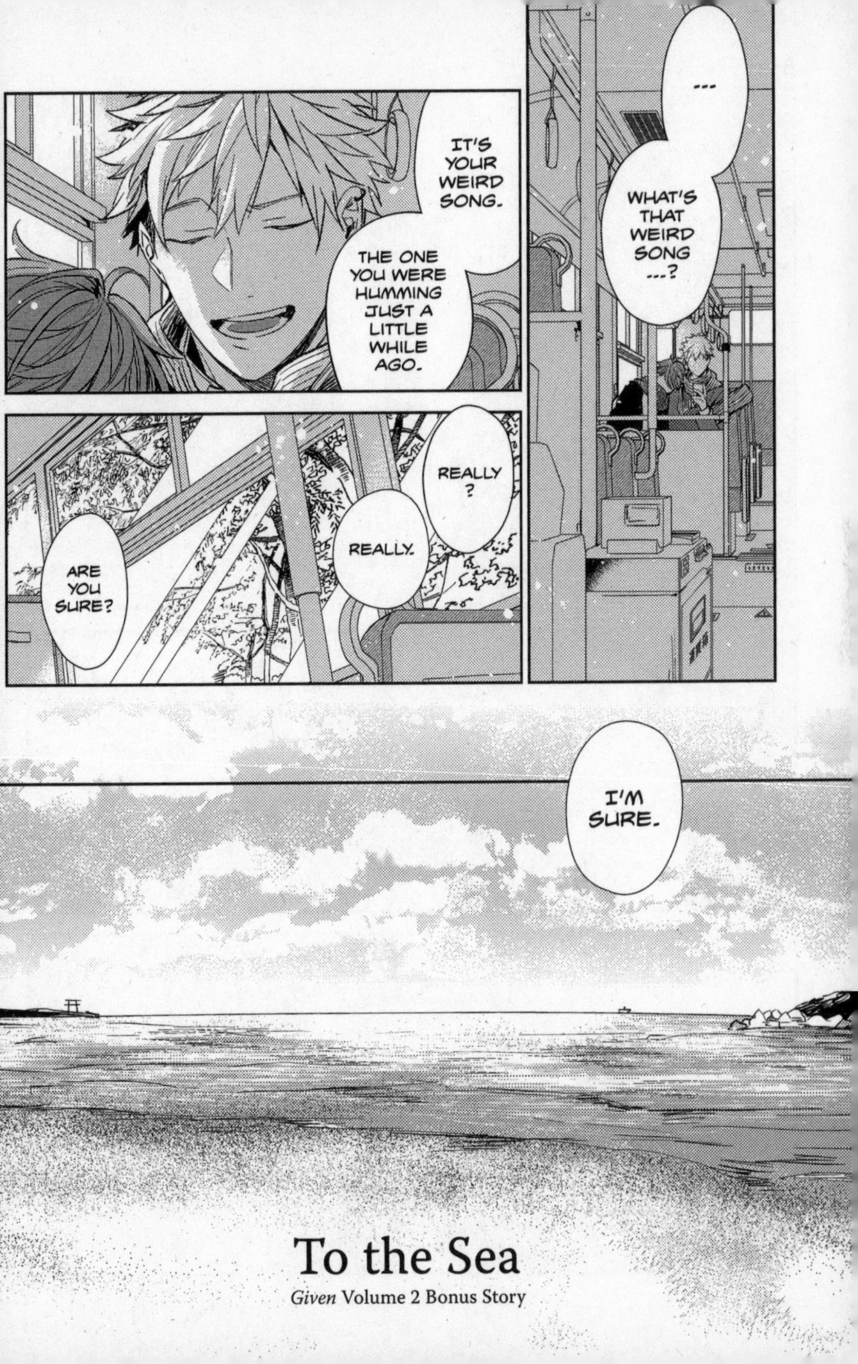
...
WHAT'S THAT WEIRD SONG...?
IT'S YOUR WEIRD SONG.
THE ONE YOU WERE HUMMING JUST A LITTLE WHILE AGO.
REALLY?
REALLY.
ARE YOU SURE?
I'M SURE.

To the Sea

Given Volume 2 Bonus Story

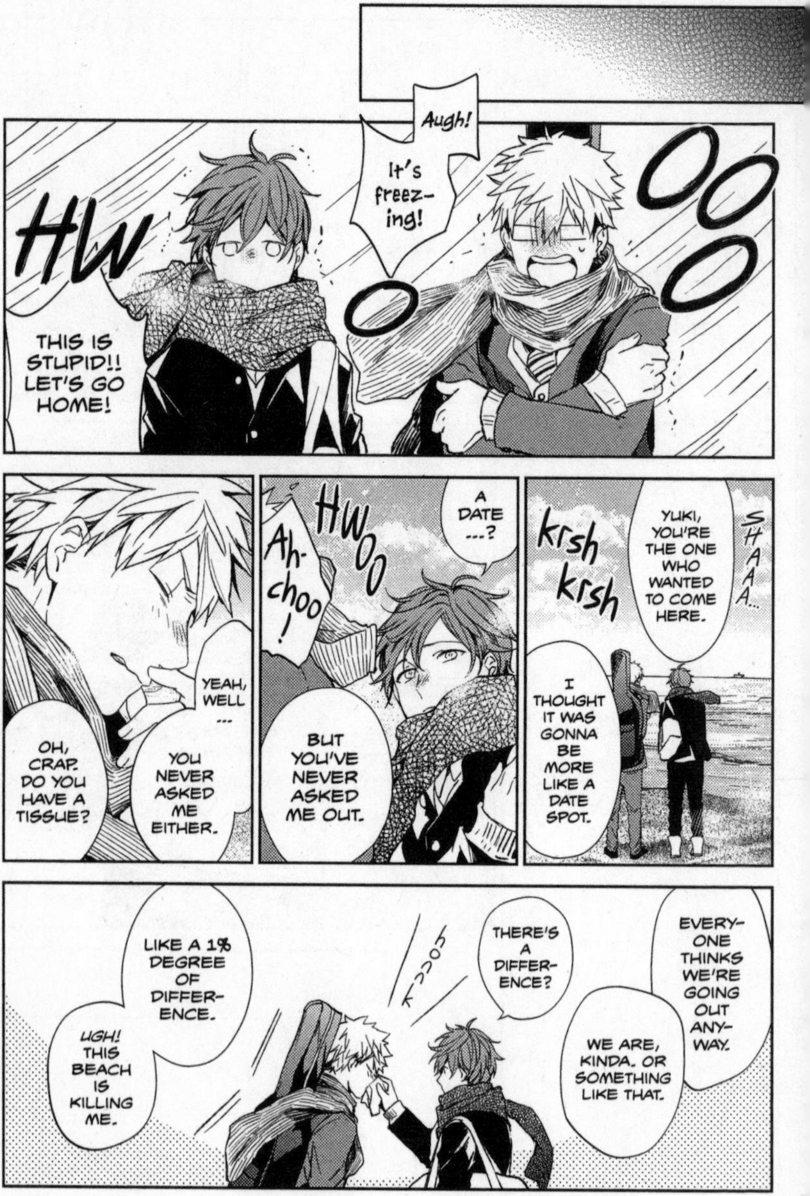
Augh!
It's freezing!
OOOO
HW
THIS IS STUPID!! LET'S GO HOME!
SHAAA...
YUKI, YOU'RE THE ONE WHO WANTED TO COME HERE.
krsh krsh
I THOUGHT IT WAS GONNA BE MORE LIKE A DATE SPOT.
A DATE...?
HWOO
Ah-choo!
BUT YOU'VE NEVER ASKED ME OUT.
YEAH, WELL...
YOU NEVER ASKED ME EITHER.
OH, CRAP. DO YOU HAVE A TISSUE?
EVERYONE THINKS WE'RE GOING OUT ANYWAY.
WE ARE, KINDA. OR SOMETHING LIKE THAT.
THERE'S A DIFFERENCE?
LIKE A 1% DEGREE OF DIFFERENCE.
UGH! THIS BEACH IS KILLING ME.

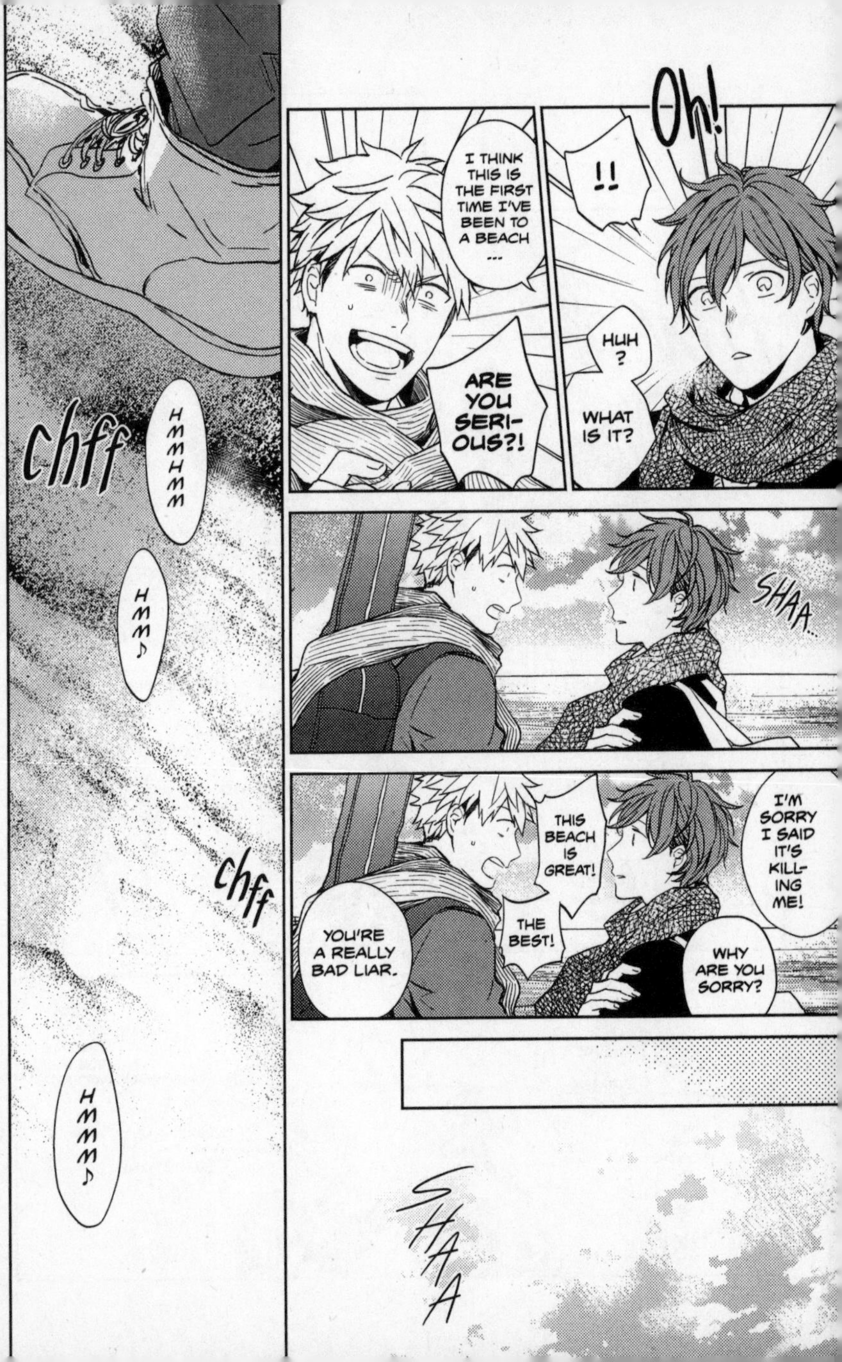
Oh!
!!
HUH?
WHAT IS IT?
I THINK THIS IS THE FIRST TIME I'VE BEEN TO A BEACH ...
ARE YOU SERI-OUS?!
SHAA...
I'M SORRY I SAID IT'S KILL-ING ME!
WHY ARE YOU SORRY?
THIS BEACH IS GREAT!
THE BEST!
YOU'RE A REALLY BAD LIAR.
SHAA
HMMHMM
chff
HMM♪
chff
HMMM♪

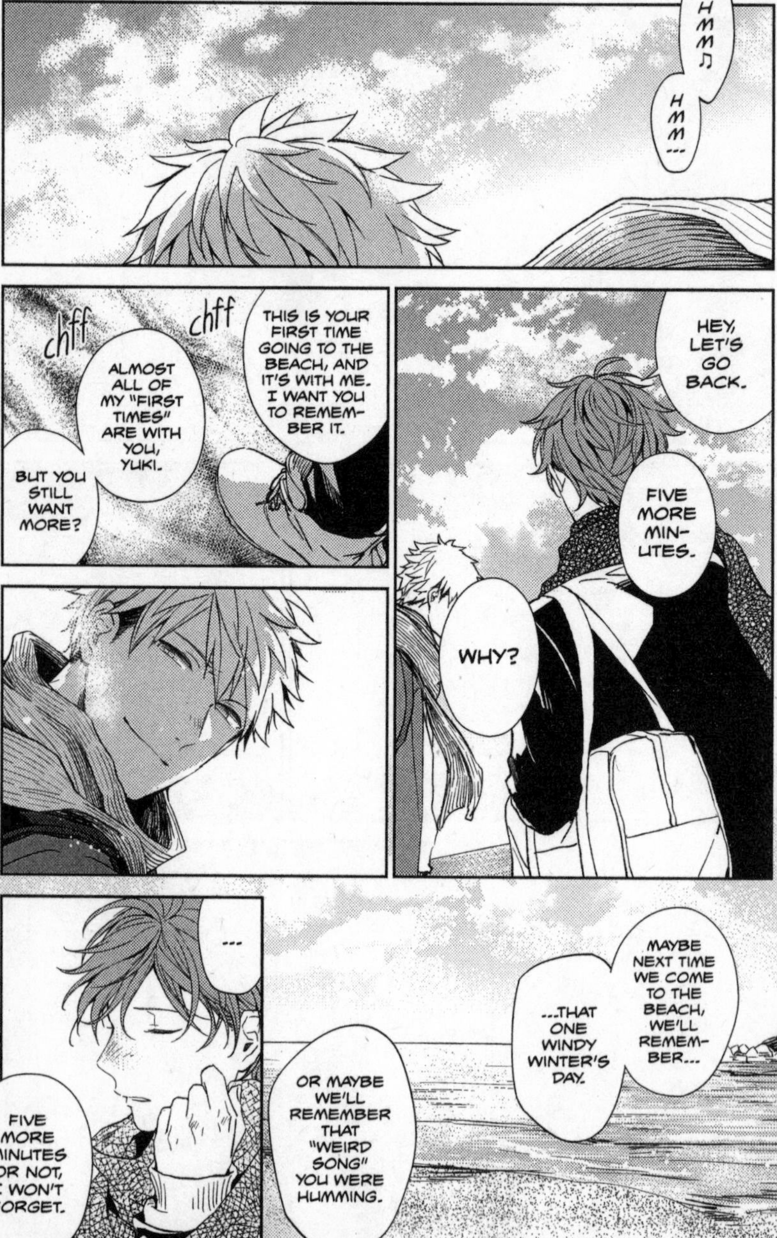
HHMM♫
HMM...
HEY, LET'S GO BACK.
FIVE MORE MIN-UTES.
WHY?
THIS IS YOUR FIRST TIME GOING TO THE BEACH, AND IT'S WITH ME. I WANT YOU TO REMEM-BER IT.
chff
chff
ALMOST ALL OF MY "FIRST TIMES" ARE WITH YOU, YUKI.
BUT YOU STILL WANT MORE?
MAYBE NEXT TIME WE COME TO THE BEACH, WE'LL REMEM-BER...
...THAT ONE WINDY WINTER'S DAY.
OR MAYBE WE'LL REMEMBER THAT "WEIRD SONG" YOU WERE HUMMING.
...
FIVE MORE MINUTES OR NOT, I WON'T FORGET.

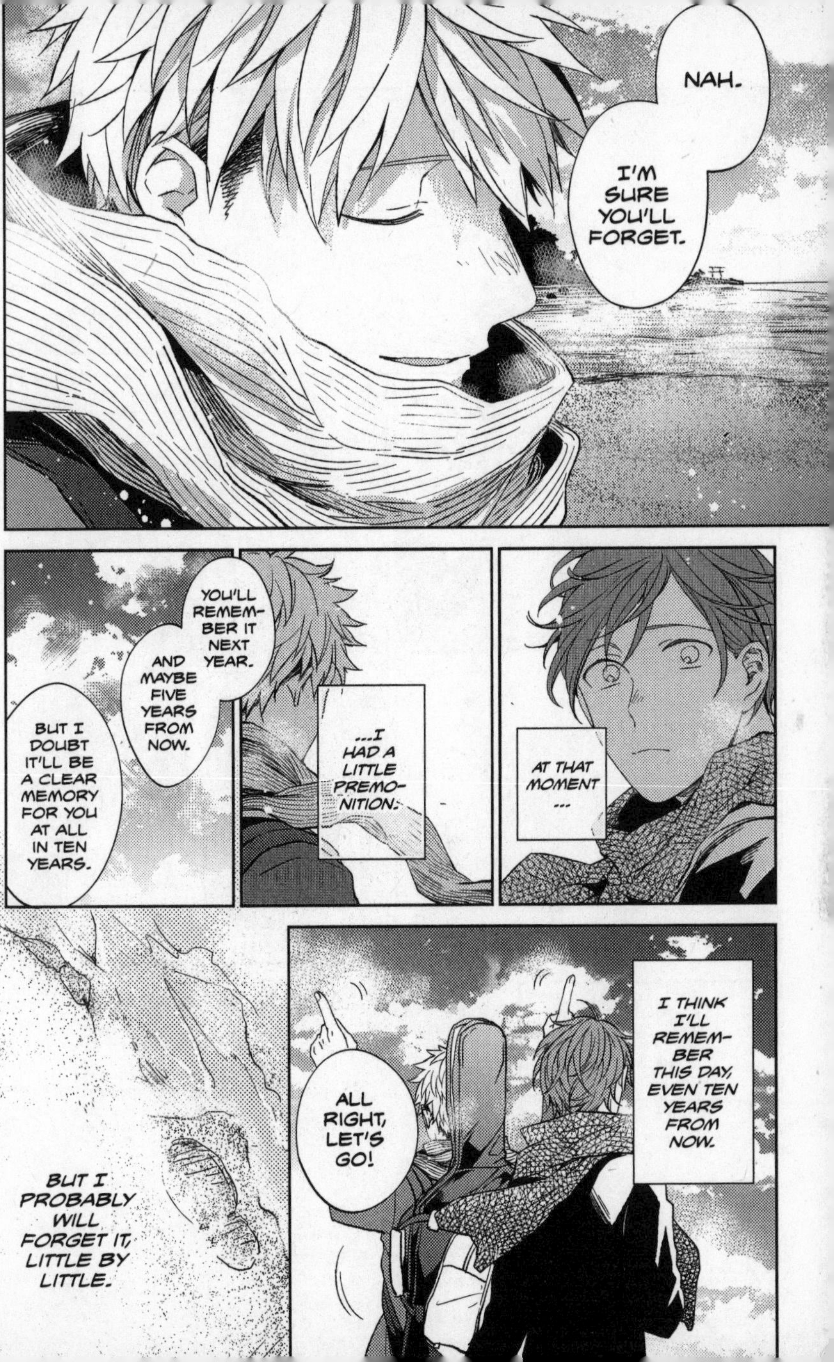
NAH.
I'M SURE YOU'LL FORGET.
AT THAT MOMENT ...
...I HAD A LITTLE PREMONITION.
YOU'LL REMEMBER IT NEXT YEAR.
AND MAYBE FIVE YEARS FROM NOW.
BUT I DOUBT IT'LL BE A CLEAR MEMORY FOR YOU AT ALL IN TEN YEARS.
I THINK I'LL REMEMBER THIS DAY, EVEN TEN YEARS FROM NOW.
ALL RIGHT, LET'S GO!
BUT I PROBABLY WILL FORGET IT, LITTLE BY LITTLE.

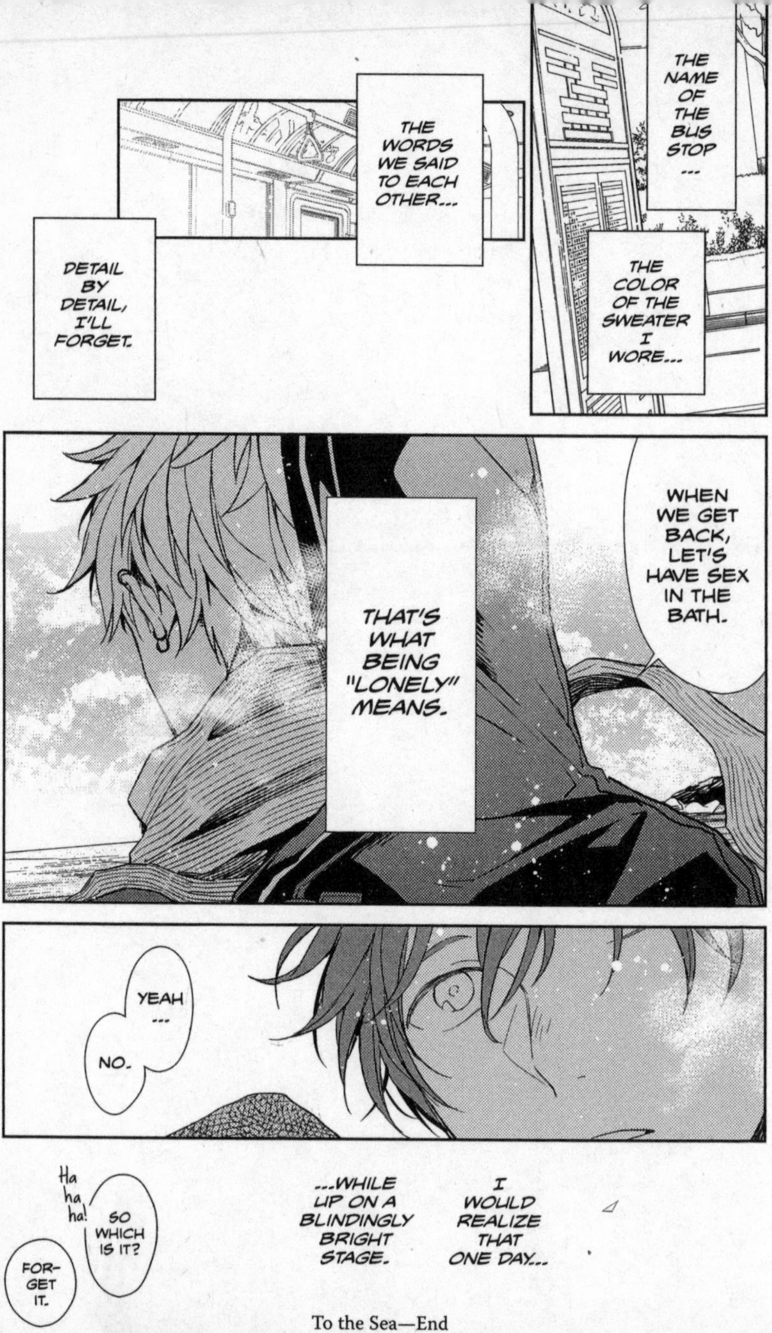
THE NAME OF THE BUS STOP...
THE COLOR OF THE SWEATER I WORE...
THE WORDS WE SAID TO EACH OTHER...
DETAIL BY DETAIL, I'LL FORGET.
WHEN WE GET BACK, LET'S HAVE SEX IN THE BATH.
THAT'S WHAT BEING "LONELY" MEANS.
YEAH...
NO.
I WOULD REALIZE THAT ONE DAY...
...WHILE UP ON A BLINDINGLY BRIGHT STAGE.
Ha ha ha!
SO WHICH IS IT?
FORGET IT.

To the Sea—End

given

by Natsuki Kizu

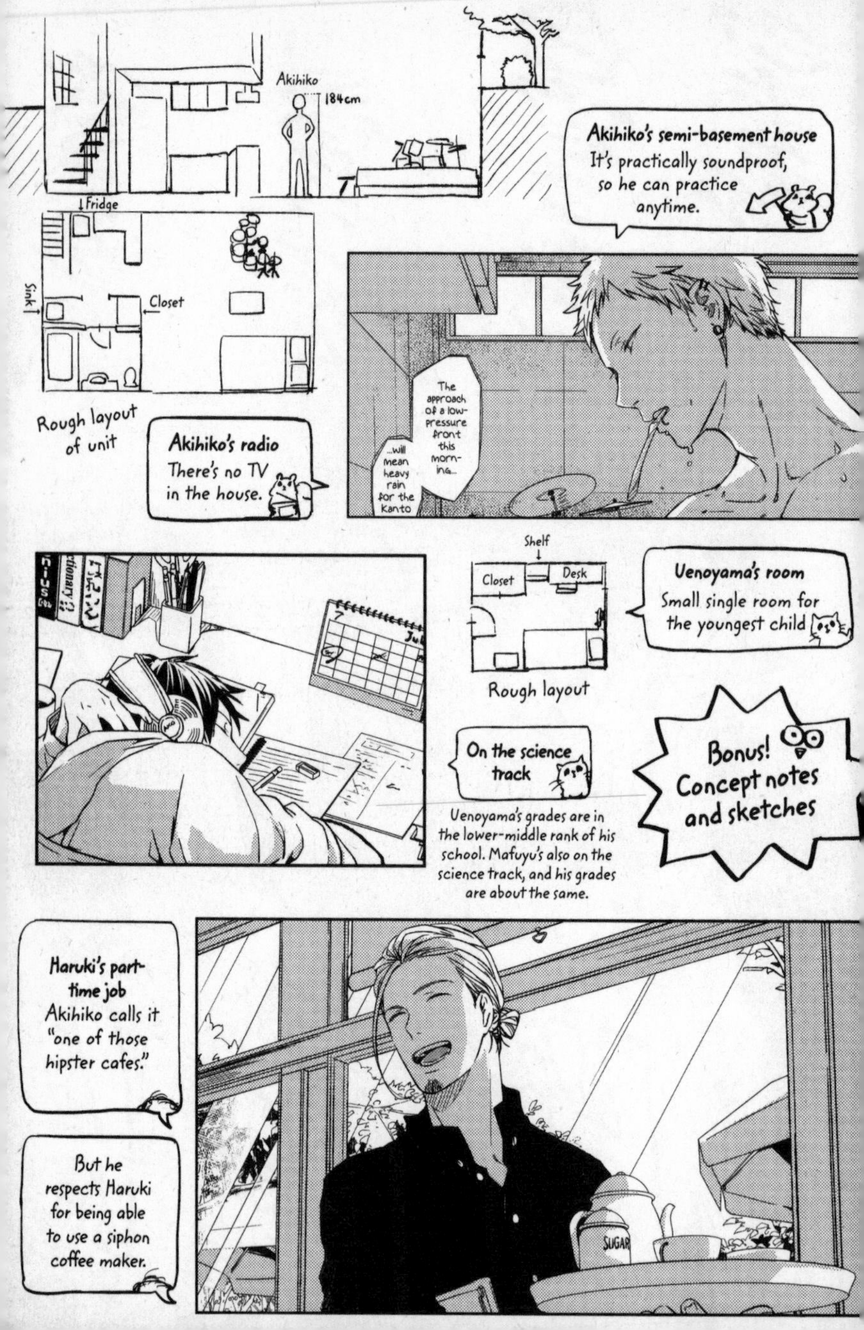

Akihiko's semi-basement house
It's practically soundproof, so he can practice anytime.
Akihiko
184cm
↓Fridge
Sink
Closet
Rough layout of unit
The approach of a low-pressure front this morning...
...will mean heavy rain for the Kanto
Akihiko's radio
There's no TV in the house.
Uenoyama's room
Small single room for the youngest child
Shelf
Closet
Desk
Rough layout
Bonus! Concept notes and sketches
On the science track
Uenoyama's grades are in the lower-middle rank of his school. Mafuyu's also on the science track, and his grades are about the same.
SUGAR
Haruki's part-time job
Akihiko calls it "one of those hipster cafes."
But he respects Haruki for being able to use a siphon coffee maker.

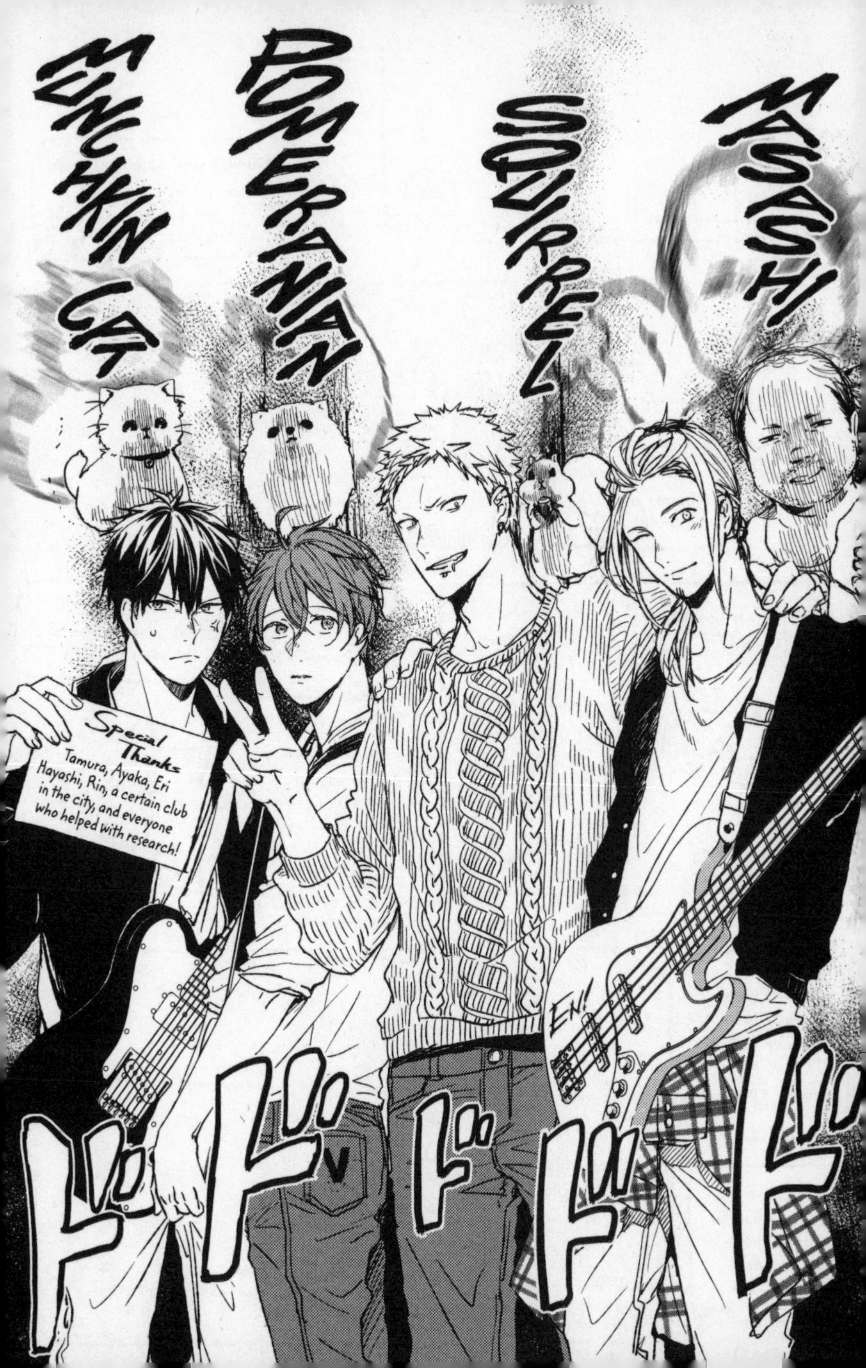
MASASHI
SQUIRREL
POMERANIAN
MUNCHKIN CAT
En!
Special Thanks
Tamura, Ayaka, Eri
Hayashi, Rin, a certain club
in the city, and everyone
who helped with research!
ドドドドド

About the Author

Natsuki Kizu made her professional debut in 2013 with *Yukimura Sensei and Kei-kun*, followed by the short story collection *Links* and her breakout series, *Given*, which has been adapted into drama CDs and an animated TV series. To find out more about her works, you can follow her on Twitter at **@kizu_ntk**.

Given

Volume 2

SuBLime Manga Edition

Story and Art by **Natsuki Kizu**

Translation—**Sheldon Drzka**
Touch-Up Art and Lettering—**Sabrina Heep**
Cover and Graphic Design—**Jimmy Presler**
Editor—**Beryl Becker**

Originally published in Japan in 2016 by Shinshokan Co., Ltd.

新書館 SHINSHOKAN

Printed in the U.S.A.

Published by SuBLime Manga
P.O. Box 77010
San Francisco, CA 94107

10 9 8 7 6 5 4 3 2 1
First printing, May 2020

T+ **PARENTAL ADVISORY**
GIVEN is rated T+ for Older Teen and is recommended for ages 16 and up. This volume contains suggestive themes.

SUBLIME
www.SuBLimeManga.com

For more information

on all our products, along with the most up-to-date news on releases, series announcements, and contests, please visit us at:

 SuBLimeManga.com

 twitter.com/**SuBLimeManga**

 facebook.com/**SuBLimeManga**

 instagram.com/**SuBLimeManga**

 SuBLimeManga.tumblr.com

Finder

DELUXE EDITION

PAIN AND PLEASURE COLLIDE when a sophisticated underworld boss crosses paths with a naive photographer hell-bent on bringing him down!

STORY AND ART BY AYANO YAMANE

This deluxe edition includes never-before-released material as well as a double-sided color insert and special cover treatment!

Photographer Akihito Takaba takes on a risky assignment trying to document the illegal activities of the Japanese underworld. When he captures its leader—the handsome, enigmatic Ryuichi Asami—in the cross-hairs of his viewfinder, Takaba's world is changed forever.

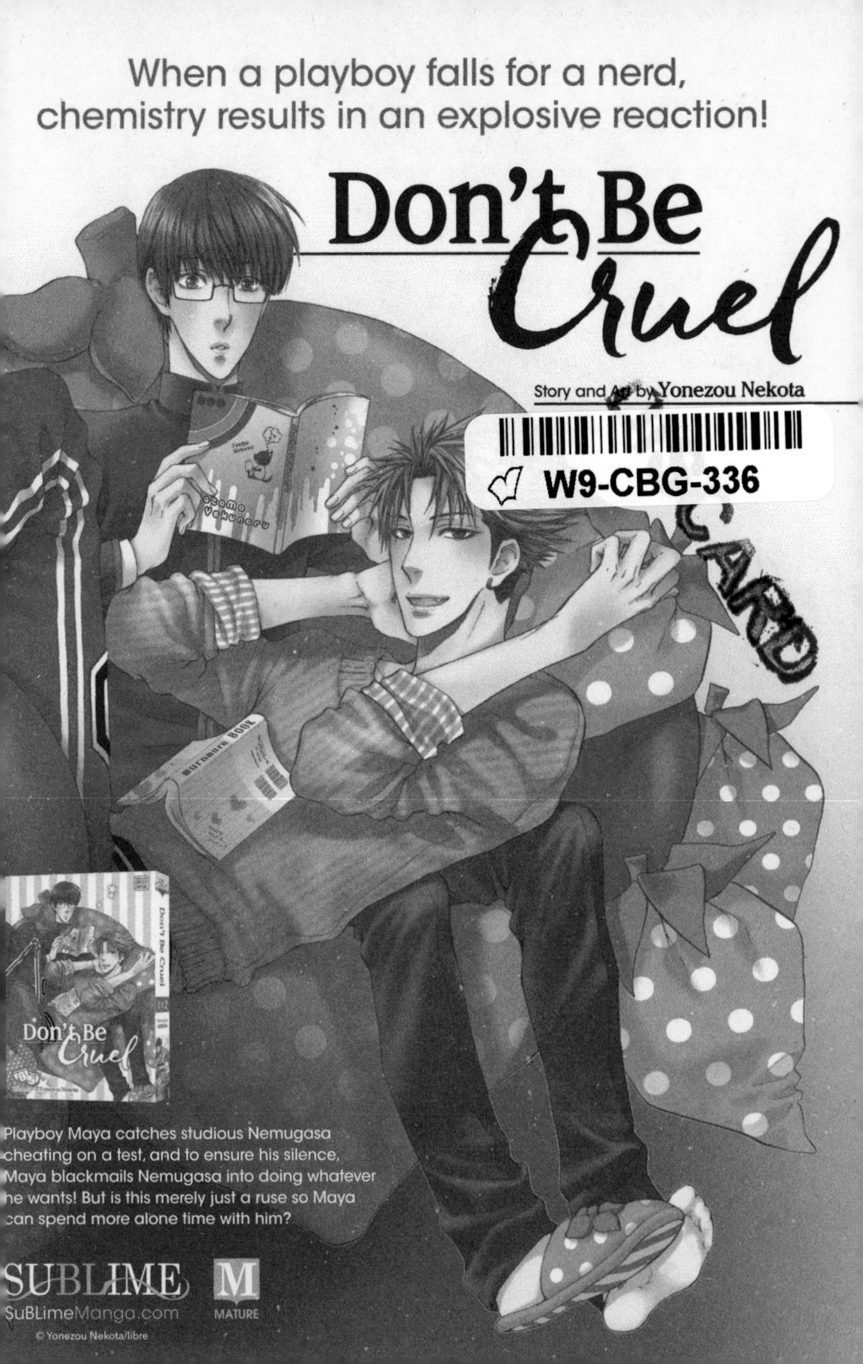
When a playboy falls for a nerd,
chemistry results in an explosive reaction!
Don't Be Cruel
Story and Art by Yonezou Nekota
Don't Be Cruel
Playboy Maya catches studious Nemugasa cheating on a test, and to ensure his silence, Maya blackmails Nemugasa into doing whatever he wants! But is this merely just a ruse so Maya can spend more alone time with him?
SUBLIME
SuBLimeManga.com
M
MATURE
© Yonezou Nekota/libre